T0255906

Lecture Notes in Computer Science   10734

Commenced Publication in 1973
Founding and Former Series Editors:
Gerhard Goos, Juris Hartmanis, and Jan van Leeuwen

Editorial Board

David Hutchison
  Lancaster University, Lancaster, UK
Takeo Kanade
  Carnegie Mellon University, Pittsburgh, PA, USA
Josef Kittler
  University of Surrey, Guildford, UK
Jon M. Kleinberg
  Cornell University, Ithaca, NY, USA
Friedemann Mattern
  ETH Zurich, Zurich, Switzerland
John C. Mitchell
  Stanford University, Stanford, CA, USA
Moni Naor
  Weizmann Institute of Science, Rehovot, Israel
C. Pandu Rangan
  Indian Institute of Technology, Madras, India
Bernhard Steffen
  TU Dortmund University, Dortmund, Germany
Demetri Terzopoulos
  University of California, Los Angeles, CA, USA
Doug Tygar
  University of California, Berkeley, CA, USA
Gerhard Weikum
  Max Planck Institute for Informatics, Saarbrücken, Germany

More information about this series at http://www.springer.com/series/7411

Ben Glocker · Jianhua Yao
Tomaž Vrtovec · Alejandro Frangi
Guoyan Zheng (Eds.)

Computational Methods and Clinical Applications in Musculoskeletal Imaging

5th International Workshop, MSKI 2017
Held in Conjunction with MICCAI 2017
Quebec City, QC, Canada, September 10, 2017
Revised Selected Papers

 Springer

Editors
Ben Glocker
Imperial College London
London
UK

Alejandro Frangi
University of Sheffield
Sheffield
UK

Jianhua Yao
National Institutes of Health
Bethesda, MD
USA

Guoyan Zheng
University of Bern
Bern
Switzerland

Tomaž Vrtovec
University of Ljubljana
Ljubljana
Slovenia

ISSN 0302-9743   ISSN 1611-3349 (electronic)
Lecture Notes in Computer Science
ISBN 978-3-319-74112-3   ISBN 978-3-319-74113-0 (eBook)
https://doi.org/10.1007/978-3-319-74113-0

Library of Congress Control Number: 2017963767

LNCS Sublibrary: SL5 – Computer Communication Networks and Telecommunications

© Springer International Publishing AG 2018
This work is subject to copyright. All rights are reserved by the Publisher, whether the whole or part of the material is concerned, specifically the rights of translation, reprinting, reuse of illustrations, recitation, broadcasting, reproduction on microfilms or in any other physical way, and transmission or information storage and retrieval, electronic adaptation, computer software, or by similar or dissimilar methodology now known or hereafter developed.
The use of general descriptive names, registered names, trademarks, service marks, etc. in this publication does not imply, even in the absence of a specific statement, that such names are exempt from the relevant protective laws and regulations and therefore free for general use.
The publisher, the authors and the editors are safe to assume that the advice and information in this book are believed to be true and accurate at the date of publication. Neither the publisher nor the authors or the editors give a warranty, express or implied, with respect to the material contained herein or for any errors or omissions that may have been made. The publisher remains neutral with regard to jurisdictional claims in published maps and institutional affiliations.

Printed on acid-free paper

This Springer imprint is published by Springer Nature
The registered company is Springer International Publishing AG
The registered company address is: Gewerbestrasse 11, 6330 Cham, Switzerland

Preface

The musculoskeletal system consists of the skeleton, muscles, cartilage, ligaments, joints, and other connective tissue that supports and binds tissues and organs together, and provides form, support, protection, stability, and movement to the body. Specific subsystems like the spine provide both a vital central axis for the musculoskeletal system and a flexible protective shell surrounding the most important neural pathway in the body, the spinal cord. The musculoskeletal system is involved in various disease processes associated with aging and degeneration of bones and joints, such as osteoporosis and osteoarthritis. Osteoporosis is a condition where bones become brittle and fragile from loss of tissue due to hormonal changes, or deficiency in calcium or vitamin D. Osteoporosis leads to an increased bone fracture risk, which is further exacerbated in the elderly due to the loss of muscular strength and frailty. Osteoarthritis, or degenerative arthritis, is caused by inflammation and the eventual loss of cartilage in the joints, which wears down with time. These are just a few relevant examples of the conditions associated to the musculoskeletal system, not to mention therapeutic procedures in orthopedic surgery, and the related medical implants and devices where imaging plays a crucial role in the planning, guidance, and monitoring phases. As a specialty of diagnostic radiology, musculoskeletal imaging involves the acquisition, analysis, and interpretation of medical images of bones, joints, and associated soft tissues for injury and disease diagnosis and treatment. Given the increasing volume of multimodal imaging examinations associated with musculoskeletal diseases and the complexity of their assessment, there is a pressing need for advanced computational methods that support the diagnosis, therapy planning, and interventional guidance, with several related challenges in both methodology and clinical applications.

The goal of the workshop series on Computational Methods and Clinical Applications in Musculoskeletal Imaging is to bring together clinicians, researchers, and industrial vendors in musculoskeletal imaging for reviewing the state-of-the-art techniques, sharing the novel and emerging analysis and visualization techniques, and discussing the clinical challenges and open problems in this field. Topics of interest include all major aspects of musculoskeletal imaging, for example: clinical applications of musculoskeletal computational imaging; computer-aided detection and diagnosis of conditions of the bones, muscles, and joints; image-guided musculoskeletal surgery and interventions; image-based assessment and monitoring of surgical and pharmacological treatment; segmentation, registration, detection, localization, and visualization of the musculoskeletal anatomy; statistical and geometrical modeling of the musculoskeletal shape and appearance; image-based microstructural characterization of musculoskeletal tissue; novel techniques for musculoskeletal imaging.

The 5th Workshop on Computational Methods and Clinical Applications in Musculoskeletal Imaging, MICCAI-MSKI2017[1], was a full-day satellite event of the 20th International Conference on Medical Image Computing and Computer-Assisted Intervention, MICCAI 2017[2], held during September 10–14, 2017, in Québec City, Canada. The workshop was a continuation of the former Workshop on Computational Methods and Clinical Applications for Spine Imaging, CSI, which was after four successful consecutive editions at MICCAI 2013, 2014, 2015, and 2016 opened up to a wider community by broadening the scope from spine to musculoskeletal imaging, therefore recognizing the progress made in spine imaging and the emerging needs in imaging of other bones, joints, and muscles of the musculoskeletal system. We received several high-quality submissions addressing many of the above-mentioned issues. All papers underwent a double-blind review, with each paper being reviewed by three members of the review committee. We finally accepted 13 papers collected into soft-copy electronic proceedings distributed at the workshop and during the conference.

MICCAI-MSKI2017 was held on September 10, 2017, with the program consisting of four oral sessions: Spine Imaging, Musculoskeletal Imaging, Anatomy Localization and Rendering, and Bone Density Estimation. To gain deeper insight into the field of musculoskeletal imaging and stimulating further ideas, two invited talks were held during the workshop. In his morning talk entitled "Musculoskeletal Imaging: An Overview," Dr. Cristian Lorenz from Philips Research Hamburg, Germany, overviewed musculoskeletal imaging by covering the most important areas from fetal and postnatal screening to poly-trauma, cancer, and interventional imaging, while providing discussion over the corresponding clinical context and imaging modalities. In the afternoon, Dr. Punam K. Saha from the University of Iowa, USA, gave a talk entitled "Topologic and Geometric Approaches for In Vivo Quantitative Assessment of Trabecular Bone Micro-Architecture," in which he focused on osteoporosis and related imaging, and presented the results of several human studies on this topic. The members of the Organizing Committee selected one outstanding contribution for the MICCAI-MSKI2017 Best Paper Award, which was given to the paper entitled "Reconstruction of 3D Muscle Fiber Structure Using High Resolution Cryosectioned Volume" by Otake et al. After the workshop, the authors were invited to revise and resubmit their papers by considering the comments of the reviewers and the eventual feedback from the workshop itself, to be considered for the publication in Springer's *Lecture Notes in Computer Science* (LNCS) series. All authors responded to the call, and after reviewing the resubmitted papers, the members of the Organizing Committee agreed that the revisions were of adequate quality, thus the papers now appear, in the chronological order of the initial submission, in these LNCS proceedings.

Finally, we would like to thank everyone who contributed to this workshop: the authors for their contributions, the members of the Program and Review Committee for their review work, promotion of the workshop, and general support, the invited

---

[1] http://mski2017.wordpress.com.

[2] http://www.miccai2017.org.

speakers for sharing their expertise and knowledge, and the MICCAI Society for the opportunity to exchange research ideas and build the community during the premier conference in medical imaging.

December 2017

Ben Glocker
Jianhua Yao
Tomaž Vrtovec
Alejandro F. Frangi
Guoyan Zheng

Organization

Program Chairs

Ben Glocker   Imperial College London, UK
Jianhua Yao   National Institutes of Health, USA
Tomaž Vrtovec   University of Ljubljana, Slovenia
Alejandro F. Frangi   The University of Sheffield, UK
Guoyan Zheng   University of Bern, Switzerland

Program Committee

Ulas Bagci   University of Central Florida, USA
Paul A. Bromiley   The University of Manchester, UK
Weidong Cai   The University of Sydney, Australia
Yunliang Cai   Amazon and Worcester Polytechnic Institute, USA
Ananda S. Chowdhury   Jadavpur University, India
Daniel Forsberg   Sectra and Linköping University, Sweden
Huiguang He   The Chinese Academy of Sciences, China
Bulat Ibragimov   Stanford University School of Medicine, USA
Jianfei Liu   National Institutes of Health, USA
Cristian Lorenz   Philips Research, Germany
Simon Pezold   University of Basel, Switzerland
Greg Slabaugh   City University of London, UK
Darko Štern   LBI CFI, Austria
Sovira Tan   National Institutes of Health, USA
Tamas Ungi   Queen's University, Canada
Yiqiang Zhan   Siemens Healthcare, USA

Proceedings Editors

Ben Glocker   Imperial College London, UK
Jianhua Yao   National Institutes of Health, USA
Tomaž Vrtovec   University of Ljubljana, Slovenia
Alejandro F. Frangi   The University of Sheffield, UK
Guoyan Zheng   University of Bern, Switzerland

Contents

Localization of Bone Surfaces from Ultrasound Data Using Local Phase
Information and Signal Transmission Maps   1
   Ilker Hacihaliloglu

Shape-Aware Deep Convolutional Neural Network
for Vertebrae Segmentation 12
   S. M. Masudur Rahman Al Arif, Karen Knapp,
   and Greg Slabaugh

Automated Characterization of Body Composition and Frailty
with Clinically Acquired CT. 25
   Peijun Hu, Yuankai Huo, Dexing Kong, J. Jeffrey Carr,
   Richard G. Abramson, Katherine G. Hartley, and Bennett A. Landman

Unfolded Cylindrical Projection for Rib Fracture Diagnosis 36
   Catalina Tobon-Gomez, Tyler Stroud, John Cameron, Dave Elcock,
   Andrew Murray, Daniel Wyeth, Chris Conway, Steven Reynolds,
   Pedro Augusto Gondim Teixeira, Alain Blum, and Costas Plakas

3D Cobb Angle Measurements from Scoliotic Mesh Models
with Varying Face-Vertex Density. 48
   Uroš Petković, Robert Korez, Stefan Parent, Samuel Kadoury,
   and Tomaž Vrtovec

Automatic Localization of the Lumbar Vertebral Landmarks in CT Images
with Context Features 59
   Dimitrios Damopoulos, Ben Glocker, and Guoyan Zheng

Joint Multimodal Segmentation of Clinical CT and MR
from Hip Arthroplasty Patients 72
   Marta Bianca Maria Ranzini, Michael Ebner, M. Jorge Cardoso,
   Anastasia Fotiadou, Tom Vercauteren, Johann Henckel, Alister Hart,
   Sébastien Ourselin, and Marc Modat

Reconstruction of 3D Muscle Fiber Structure Using High Resolution
Cryosectioned Volume. 85
   Yoshito Otake, Kohei Miyamoto, Axel Ollivier, Futoshi Yokota,
   Norio Fukuda, Lauren J. O'Donnell, Carl-Fredrik Westin,
   Masaki Takao, Nobuhiko Sugano, Beom Sun Chung, Jin Seo Park,
   and Yoshinobu Sato

Segmentation of Pathological Spines in CT Images Using a Two-Way CNN
and a Collision-Based Model   95
   Robert Korez, Boštjan Likar, Franjo Pernuš, and Tomaž Vrtovec

Attention-Driven Deep Learning for Pathological Spine Segmentation   108
   *Anjany Sekuboyina, Jan Kukačka, Jan S. Kirschke, Bjoern H. Menze,
and Alexander Valentinitsch*

Automatic Full Femur Segmentation from Computed Tomography Datasets
Using an Atlas-Based Approach   120
   *Bryce A. Besler, Andrew S. Michalski, Nils D. Forkert,
and Steven K. Boyd*

Classification of Osteoporotic Vertebral Fractures Using Shape
and Appearance Modelling   133
   *Paul A. Bromiley, Eleni P. Kariki, Judith E. Adams,
and Timothy F. Cootes*

DSMS-FCN: A Deeply Supervised Multi-scale Fully Convolutional
Network for Automatic Segmentation of Intervertebral Disc
in 3D MR Images   148
   Guodong Zeng and Guoyan Zheng

Author Index   161

Localization of Bone Surfaces from Ultrasound Data Using Local Phase Information and Signal Transmission Maps

Ilker Hacihaliloglu[1,2](✉)

[1] Department of Biomedical Engineering, Rutgers University, Piscataway, USA
`ilker.hac@soe.rutgers.edu`
[2] Department of Radiology, Rutgers Robert Wood Johnson Medical School,
New Brunswick, USA

Abstract. Low signal-to-noise ratio, imaging artifacts and bone boundaries appearing several millimeters in thickness have hampered the success of ultrasound (US) guided computer assisted orthopedic surgery procedures. In this paper we propose a robust and accurate bone localization method. The proposed approach is based on the enhancement of bone surfaces using the combination of three different local image phase features. The extracted local phase image features are used as an input to an L_1 norm-based contextual regularization method for the enhancement of bone shadow regions. During the final stage the enhanced bone features and shadow region information is combined into a dynamic programming solution for the localization of the bone surface data. Qualitative and quantitative validation was performed on 150 in vivo US scans obtained from seven subjects by scanning femur, knee, distal radius and vertebrae bones. Validation against expert segmentation achieved a mean surface localization error of 0.26 mm a 67% improvement over state of the art.

Keywords: Ultrasound · Bone segmentation · Orthopedics
Local phase · Signal transmission

1 Introduction

In order to decrease the total amount of radiation exposure, caused by intra-operative fluoroscopy, and provide real-time three-dimensional (3D) guidance, ultrasound (US) has been incorporated as an alternative imaging modality into various computer assisted orthopedic surgery (CAOS) procedures [1]. Nevertheless, due to the continuing challenges faced during the extraction of relevant anatomical information from US data, most of the proposed US-based CAOS guidance systems have not succeeded in clinical settings. Ultrasound images typically contain significant speckle and imaging artifacts, which do not correspond to any specific anatomy, complicating image interpretation and automatic processing. Furthermore, orientation of the US transducer with respect

© Springer International Publishing AG 2018
B. Glocker et al. (Eds.): MSKI 2017, LNCS 10734, pp. 1–11, 2018.
https://doi.org/10.1007/978-3-319-74113-0_1

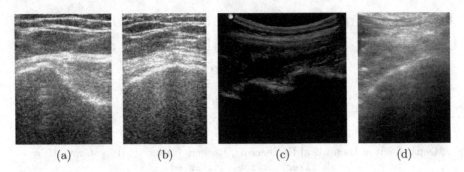

(a)   (b)   (c)   (d)

Fig. 1. Bone surface response appearance in ultrasound. (a), (b) High intensity soft tissue interfaces above the bone surface with similar intensity profile as the bone surfaces and reverberation artifacts inside the shadow region. (c) Separate low intensity spine bone surfaces. (d) Low intensity bone surface obtained due to non-optimal orientation of the US transducer.

to the imaged anatomy and the elevational beam width strongly influence bone surface response profile and corresponding bone boundaries appear several millimeters in thickness. In order to overcome some of these challenges bone segmentation or enhancement methods have been proposed by various groups.

The previously proposed image-based segmentation or enhancement methods can be classified into three groups: (i) methods using image intensity/gradient information [2,3], (ii) methods based on local phase image features [4,5], and (iii) hybrid approaches which combine the strengths of intensity and phase-based methods [6–8]. Intensity-based approaches are not robust to low contrast bone responses and high intensity soft tissue interfaces (Fig. 1). One of the distinct features in bone US data is the shadow region. A large transition in acoustic impedance between the tissue and the bone causes most of the acoustic signal to be reflected back creating a low intensity region extending from the bone boundary to the bottom of the image. Incorporating this information into their framework improved the accuracy and robustness of the proposed intensity- and phase-based methods [3,6–8]. In [6], the percentage of overlapping surfaces between the manual segmented and automatic method was 62.5%. The hybrid approach proposed in [7] integrated machine learning into their framework. The method was validated on 35 US scans obtained from a single subject achieving an accuracy score of 86% for 1 mm tolerance with 0.59 mm localization error for this tolerance. The computation time for the proposed method was 2 min. In [8], computed tomography (CT) derived bone surfaces were registered to US derived bone surfaces. The reported average surface fit error for the in vivo pelvis data was close to 0.5 mm.

Although previously reported results provided promising outcomes, acquisition of high quality US data in clinical settings continues to be and ongoing challenge in US-based CAOS procedures effecting the accuracy and robustness of the segmentation methods. In this work, we propose a bone localization method which is accurate and robust to different US imaging artifacts. Local phase-based

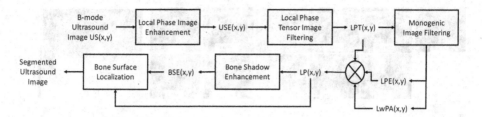

Fig. 2. Flowchart of the proposed bone localization method.

image features are utilized to enhance the bone surface response profile and suppress the soft tissue interfaces and imaging artifacts. The enhanced images are used as an input to an L_1 norm-based contextual regularization method which emphasizes uncertainty in the shadow regions. The enhanced bone response and shadow region images are incorporated into a dynamic programming solution for localizing the bone surfaces. Qualitative and quantitative validation results on scans collected from seven volunteers are presented. The proposed method is also compared against previously developed intensity-based [3] and phase-based [9] methods.

2 Methods

The flowchart of the proposed method is provided in Fig. 2 and is based on our previous experience where local phase image features are used for bone enhancement and/or segmentation.

2.1 Enhancement of Bone Surface Response

Bone surface response profile in US is highly affected by the orientation of the beam with respect to the imaged bone boundary and the 3D anatomy of the imaged surface. If the US beam is perfectly aligned and the attenuation from soft tissue interface is low the bone response profile appears as a dominant ridge edge along the scanline direction. However, while imaging complex shape bone surfaces, such as spine, or if the attenuation from soft tissue interface is large the bone response profile can be dominated by different edge profiles. The first step in our framework involves the enhancement of the low intensity bone surfaces by constructing a local phase enhancement metric, similar to [9], as:

$$USE(x,y) = \frac{\sum_r \sum_s \lfloor [e_{rs}(x,y) - o_{rs}(x,y)] - T_r \rfloor}{\sum_r \sum_s \sqrt{e_{rs}^2(x,y) - o_{rs}^2(x,y)} + \epsilon}. \tag{1}$$

Here $o(x,y)$ and $e(x,y)$ represent the even and odd symmetric filter response and are obtained by filtering the B-mode US image, $US(x,y)$, in the frequency domain using Log-Gabor filter [10]. Since the first step in the proposed framework is to provide an initial general ultrasound enhancement, in this new metric we are

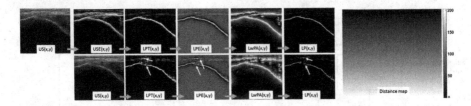

Fig. 3. Local phase image bone features. Top row shows the extracted local phase image features where the enhanced $USE(x, y)$ image was used to extract $LPT(x, y), LPE(x, y), LwPA(x, y)$, and $LP(x, y)$ image features. Bottom row shows the extracted local phase image features where the B-mode $US(x, y)$ image was used to extract $LPT(x, y), LPE(x, y), LwPA(x, y)$, and $LP(x, y)$ image features. Red arrows point to bone surfaces and soft tissue interfaces where the improvement was achieved. Distance map is shown on the far right. (Color figure online)

not using the absolute response values of the even and odd filter responses which was done previously for enhancement of bone interfaces [9]. Filter orientations and scale are represented with r and s respectively. ϵ is a small constant included to avoid division by zero. T_r is a noise dependent threshold calculated as a specified number of standard deviations above the mean of the local energy distribution because of noise [11]. The standard deviation and mean of the local energy is calculated for each orientation separately using the response of the smallest scale filter [10].

Figure 3 shows that $USE(x, y)$ results in the enhancement of low intensity bone surfaces and soft tissue interfaces. Hacihaliloglu et al. [12] recently proposed a tensor-based feature descriptor, called local phase tensor $(LPT(x, y))$, for the enhancement of bone features while suppressing high intensity soft tissue interfaces. The second step in the bone enhancement framework is to calculate the $LPT(x, y)$ image. $LPT(x, y)$ is obtained using even and odd filter responses which are defined as:

$$T_{even} = [\boldsymbol{H}(US_{DB}(x,y))][\boldsymbol{H}(US_{DB}(x,y))]^T,$$
$$T_{odd} = -0.5 \times ([\nabla US_{DB}(x,y)][\nabla\nabla^2 US_{DB}(x,y)]^T$$
$$+ [\nabla\nabla^2 US_{DB}(x,y)][\nabla US_{DB}(x,y)]^T). \quad (2)$$

Here T_{even} represents symmetric features and T_{odd} represents the asymmetric features. $\boldsymbol{H}$, ∇ and ∇^2 denote the Hessian, Gradient and Laplacian operations, respectively. $US_{DB}(x, y)$ is obtained by masking the band-pass filtered $USE(x, y)$ image with a distance map which improves the enhancement of bone surfaces located deeper in the image while masking out of soft tissue interfaces close to the transducer. Band-pass filtering was performed using a Log-Gabor filter [12]. The final $LPT(x, y)$ image is obtained using $LPT(x, y) = \sqrt{T_{even}^2 + T_{odd}^2} \times cos(\varphi)$. The instantaneous phase obtained from the symmetric (T_{even}) and asymmetric (T_{odd}) features responses is represented with φ [12]. Investigating the obtained $LPT(x, y)$ image (Fig. 1) we can see that the descriptor enhances soft tissue interfaces close the to bone surface as well. In order to provide an enhancement with less soft tissue interfaces and more compact bone representation, local phase energy $(LPE(x,y))$ and local weighted mean phase angle $(LwPA(x,y))$ image features are extracted using monogenic signal theory where the monogenic signal image $(US_M(\text{x,y}))$ is formed by combining the bandpass filtered $LPT(x,y)$ image $(LPT_B(x,y))$ with the Riesz filtered components as:

$$
\begin{aligned}
US_M(x,y) &= \left[US_{M1}(x,y),\ US_{M2}(x,y),\ US_{M3}(x,y),\right] \\
&= \left[LPT_B(x,y),\ LPT_B(x,y)xh_1(x,y),\ LPT_B(x,y)xh_2(x,y),\right].
\end{aligned}
\tag{3}
$$

Here h_1 and h_2 represent the vector valued odd filter (Riesz filter) [13]. For band-pass filtering α-scale space derivative quadrature filters (ASSD) are used which are shown to produce produce improved edge detection results on simulated US images [14]. The $LPE(x,y)$ image is obtained by averaging the phase sum of the response vectors over many scales using:

$$
LPE(x,y) = \sum_{sc} |US_{M1}(x,y)| - \sqrt{US_{M2}^2(x,y) + US_{M3}^2(x,y)}.
\tag{4}
$$

In the above equation sc represents the number of scales. $LPE(x,y)$ encodes the underlying shape of the bone boundary by accumulating the local energy of the image along several filter responses. $LwPA(x,y)$ is calculated using:

$$
LwPA(x,y) = \arctan\left(\frac{\sum_{sc} US_{M1}(x,y)}{\sqrt{\sum_{sc} US_{M1}^2(x,y) + \sum_{sc} US_{M2}^2(x,y)}}\right)
\tag{5}
$$

during the calculation of the $LwPA(x,y)$ feature map noise compensation is not performed and the $LwPA(x,y)$ image preserves all the structural details of the US image such as the soft tissue interfaces and bone surface. The final improved local phase bone image $(LP(x,y))$ is obtained using: $LP(x,y) = LPT(x,y) \times LPE(x,y) \times LwPA(x,y)$. Figure 3 shows the obtained local phase feature images $(LPT(x,y), LPE(x,y), LwPA(x,y))$. One common property of the extracted local phase image feature images is that the enhanced bone surfaces are well localized in all of the three images while soft tissue interfaces are not. Therefore, the combination of these three phase feature images results in the suppression of soft tissue interfaces while keeping the bone surfaces more compact and localized. In Fig. 3 (bottom row) we also show the bone enhancement results obtained if we used $US(x,y)$ image as an input to the tensor-based phase descriptor. Red arrows point to the enhanced soft tissue artifacts and missing bone boundaries since. These are the locations in the B-mode US image $(US(x,y))$ where the bone response is weaker compared to the soft tissue interfaces above the bone surface. The obtained $LP(x,y)$ image is used in the next section for the enhancement of bone shadow region.

2.2 Enhancement of Shadow Region

Automatic identification of shadow regions is important since it can be used as an additional feature to improve the robustness and accuracy of the segmentation

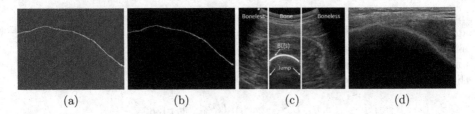

(a)   (b)   (c)   (d)

Fig. 4. (a) Enhanced bone shadow image $BSE(x,y)$. (b) Bone probability image obtained by masking $LP(x,y)$ with $BSE(x,y)$. (c) Bone localization presented as curve $BL(s)$. The curve $BL(s)$ is overlaid on the actual bone surface for better representation. (d) Localized bone surface is overlaid on the B-mode ultrasound image of in vivo knee. (Color figure online)

or registration methods. The bone shadow enhancement is based on the modification of previously proposed US confidence map (CM) approach [15]. However, instead of using the US image intensity information we use $LP(x,y)$ image features. We achieve this by modeling the interaction of the US signal within the tissue using scattering and attenuation information. The model, denoted as US signal transmission map ($USA(x,y)$), maximizes the visibility of high intensity features inside a local region and satisfies the constraint that the mean intensity of the local region is less than the echogenicity of the tissue confining the bone. The scattering and attenuation effects in the tissue are combined as: $CM_{LP}(x,y) = USA(x,y)BSE(x,y) + (1 - USA(x,y))\rho$. Here $CM_{LP}(x,y)$ represents CM image obtained from $LP(x,y)$ using [15], ρ is a constant value representative of echogenicity in the tissue surrounding the bone, and $BSE(x,y)$ is the enhanced bone shadow image which we are trying to calculate. In order to calculate $BSE(x,y)$, $USA(x,y)$ is estimated first by minimizing the following objective function [16]:

$$\frac{\lambda}{2}\left\|USA(x,y) - CM_{LP}(x,y)\right\|_2^2 + \sum_{j \in \chi}\left\|W_j \circ (D_j * USA(x,y))\right\|_1. \qquad (6)$$

Here $\circ$ represents element-wise multiplication, χ is an index set, and $*$ is convolution operator. D_j is calculated using a bank of high order differential filters [17]. The filter bank results in the enhancement of bone features in the local region while attenuating the image noise. W_j is a weighting matrix calculated using: $W_j(x,y) = exp(-|D_j(x,y) * CM_{LP}(x,y)|^2)$. In (6), the first part measures the dependence of $USA(x,y)$ on $CM_{LP}(x,y)$ and the second part models the contextual constraints of $USA(x,y)$. These two terms are balanced using a regularization parameter λ [16]. After estimating $USA(x,y)$, $BSE(x,y)$ image is obtained using: $BSE(x,y) = [(CM_{LP}(x,y) - \rho)/[max(USA(x,y), \epsilon)]^\delta] + \rho$. δ is related to tissue attenuation coefficient (η), ρ is a constant value representative of echogenicity in the tissue surrounding the bone, and ϵ is a small constant used to avoid division by zero [16]. Figure 4 shows the enhanced bone shadow image $BSE(x,y)$ where the soft tissue interface above the bone surface is represented with uniform intensity and the shadow region is represented with low intensity values corresponding to a low probability value that the signal reaching back to the transducer imaging array (high intensity denoted with dark red and low intensity with blue color coding). Investigating the $BSE(x,y)$ image we can see that the transition from soft tissue interface to bone shadow region is represented with a sharp intensity change clearly differentiating the two interfaces. The enhanced bone shadow region image ($BSE(x,y)$) and local phase bone image ($LP(x,y)$) are used during the bone surface localization which is explained in the next section.

2.3   Bone Surface Localization

The localization of the bone feature within a column s, denoted as $BL(s)$, is achieved by minimizing a cost function composed of two energy functions denoted as internal energy ($E_{int}(x,y)$) and external energy ($E_{ext}(x,y)$). $E_{int}(x,y)$ is obtained by masking the $LP(x,y)$ image with the $BSE(x,y)$ image which provides a bone probability map (Fig. 4(b)). The external energy ($E_{ext}(x,y)$) is constructed by dividing the US image into three regions denotes as bone region, boneless region and the jump region (the region between the first two regions) (Fig. 4(c)). $E_{ext}(x,y)$ is constructed using these three regions as [3]:

$$E_{ext}(i,j) = \begin{cases} \nu||\frac{dBL}{ds}||^2 + \xi||\frac{d^2BL}{ds^2}||^2 + \varsigma; & \text{Bone region,} \\ JumpCost; & \text{Jump region,} \\ \nu D_1^2 + \xi D_2^2; & \text{Boneless region.} \end{cases} \quad (7)$$

Here ν and ξ are the weights of the smoothness (the first derivative of $BL(s)$) and the curvature (the second derivative of $BL(s)$), and ς is small negative scalar ensuring larger connected bone regions to stay connected. Bone connectivity is further maintained with the $JumpCost$ constant which penalizes frequent jumps between bone and boneless regions. As there is no bone information present in the boneless region, first and second order derivatives are assigned constant values D_1 and D_2. Dynamic programming optimization is used to solve:

$$BLmin(i,j) = E_{int}(i,j) + \min_k \left[BLmin(k,j-1) + E_{ext}(k,j) \right]. \quad (8)$$

$BLmin(i,j)$ represents the minimum cost of moving from first column to the pixel in ith row and jth column. Row index is represented with k. The index of the pixel k, j with its minima is stored in $Indexmin(i,j) = \text{argmin}_k[BLmin(k,j-1) + E_{ext}(k,j)]$. Dynamic programming provides a fast optimization of the cost function. The final optimized bone localization if obtained by tracing back from the last column of the US image using:

$$BL_{opt}(s) = \begin{cases} NR+1 & s = NC; \\ Indexmin[s+1, BL_{opt}(s+1)]; & s = 1,\ldots,(NC-1). \end{cases} \quad (9)$$

BL_{opt} is the optimized segmentation path where the energy cost function is minimized. The number of rows and columns are indicated with NR and NC of the B-mode US image. NR and NC also indicate the last row and last column in the US image. The final localized bone surfaces is shown in Fig. 4.

2.4 Data Acquisition and Experiments

After obtaining the institutional review board (IRB) approval a total of 150 different US images, from seven healthy subjects, were collected using Sonix-Touch US machine (Analogic Corporation, Peabody, MA, USA). Depending on the anatomical region of interest two different transducers were used (C5-2 curvilinear, L14-5 linear transducer). Depth settings and image resolutions varied between 3–8 cm and 0.12–0.19 mm respectively. All the proposed image enhancement and localization methods were implemented using MATLAB 2014a software package and run on a 2.3 GHz Intel(R) Core^{TM} i5 CPU, 16 GB RAM windows PC. The localized bone surfaces were compared to manual localization results obtained from an expert user. The quality of the localization was evaluated by computing average Euclidean distance (AED) between the two surfaces. We also compare the localization results against the methods proposed in [3,9]. For bone shadow enhancement, $\lambda = 2$ and ρ, the constant related to tissue echogenicity, was chosen as 90% of the maximum intensity value of $CM_{LP}(x,y)$. $LPT(x,y)$ images were calculated using the filter parameter values defined in [12]. The $CM(x,y)$ and $CM_{LP}(x,y)$ images were obtained using the constant values as: $\eta = 2$, $\beta = 90$, $\gamma = 0.03$. For bone surface localization the constant values were chosen as: $\nu = 50$, $\xi = 100$, $JumpCost = 0.8$, $\varsigma = 0.15$, $D_1 = D_2 = 1$. These values were determined empirically and kept constant during qualitative and quantitative analysis.

3 Results

Investigating the qualitative results we can see that the surfaces localized with the proposed method have a good alignment with the expert manual localization (Fig. 5). The combination of enhanced local phase bone features and shadow region information provides a robust estimate even if (i) the shadow region had intensity variations (Fig. 5; femur and spine), (ii) disconnected bone surfaces (Fig. 5; spine), (iii) low intensity bone boundary (Fig. 5; radius, spine and femur), and (iv) high intensity soft tissue interfaces (Fig. 5; femur, spine and radius). The overall AED error for the proposed method was 0.26 mm (SD: 0.22). The overall AED error for [9] and [3] were 0.78 mm (SD: 0.68) and 4.5 mm (SD: 4.39) respectively. The maximum AED was 1.36 mm for the proposed method, and 19.08 mm for [3], and 4.2 mm for [9] (Table 1). Table 1 also shows the 95% confidence level calculated for the localization results obtained for all the three methods compared. We can see that the the proposed method outperforms [3,9]. The average computation time was 9.4 s.

4 Discussion and Conclusion

We have presented a method for accurate, robust and fully automatic localization of bone surfaces in two-dimensional US data based on enhanced local phase bone and shadow region information. The method was validated on 150

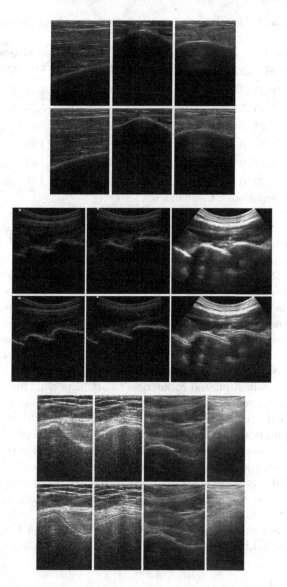

Fig. 5. Qualitative results. First, third and fifth rows represent the B-mode ultrasound image of in vivo radius, spine and femur respectively. Second, fourth and sixth rows present the localization result. Green represents manual expert segmentation and red is obtained using the proposed algorithm. (Color figure online)

in vivo US data, obtained from seven volunteers, and achieved an overall AED error of 0.26 mm. We achieved a 67% improvement in terms of surface localization over state of the art methods and 94% improvement compared to intensity-based localization methods. Although we have not directly compared our method to machine learning-based approaches [7] our reported localization results have

Table 1. Comparative results of the proposed approach.

	Proposed			Phase symmetry [9]			Dynamic programming [3]		
	Mean	SD	95% CL	Mean	SD	95% CL	Mean	SD	95% CL
Femur	0.32	0.25	0.64	0.74	0.50	1.43	7.60	4.27	15.42
Radius	0.44	0.26	0.81	1.08	0.88	2.93	6.97	5.73	16.00
Tibia	0.22	0.24	0.56	0.68	0.42	1.58	6.69	0.41	11.20
Knee	0.19	0.16	0.42	0.83	0.88	2.5	3.29	4.23	11.96
Spine	0.34	0.17	0.53	0.73	0.65	1.95	1.77	1.61	5.25
Overall	0.26	0.22	0.63	0.78	0.68	2.21	4.50	4.39	13.79

(SD - standard deviation, CL - confidence level)

54% improved accuracy. However, the proposed shadow enhancement method and local phase features extracted in the proposed work can also be incorporated into existing machine learning approaches as additional features which could results in the improvement of the localization results reported for these methods. The specific contributions include: (1) the use of α-scale filters for extraction of bone phase features, (2) calculation of a new bone probability map for improved bone surface localization, and (3) combination of enhanced bone shadow features with three different image phase features for bone localization. Previously, it was shown that by optimizing the filter parameter selection, using information derived from the collected data, improvements can be achieved in terms of surface localization and robustness to artifacts [9]. Therefore, the filter parameter selection process should be automated. Another limitation of the proposed method is the achieved mean computation time which was around 9.4 s. This is a large computational cost considering that any intra-operative procedure performed requires real time feedback. Future work will involve (i) improvement of the computation speed, (ii) validation on more in vivo scans, and (iii) optimization of the filter parameters. Finally, we would like to mention that although there were no failed cases for the proposed method a more extensive validation is required in order to fully address clinical challenges that can be faced during the application of the method. Specifically, volunteers with high body mass index will require a special investigation which we will be performing as part of our future work.

References

1. Tonetti, J., Carrat, L., Blendea, S., Merloz, P., Troccaz, J., Lavallée, S., Chirossel, J.P.: Clinical results of percutaneous pelvic surgery. Computer assisted surgery using ultrasound compared to standard fluoroscopy. Comput. Aided Surg. **6**(4), 204–211 (2001)
2. Baka, N., Leenstra, S., van Walsum, T.: Machine learning based bone segmentation in ultrasound. In: Yao, J., Vrtovec, T., Zheng, G., Frangi, A., Glocker, B., Li, S. (eds.) CSI 2016. LNCS, vol. 10182, pp. 16–25. Springer, Cham (2016). https://doi.org/10.1007/978-3-319-55050-3_2

3. Foroughi, P., Boctor, E., Swartz, M., Taylor, R., Fichtinger, G.: P6d-2 ultrasound bone segmentation using dynamic programming. In: Proceedings of the 2007 IEEE Ultrasonics Symposium, pp. 2523–2526. IEEE (2007)
4. Anas, E.M.A., et al.: Bone enhancement in ultrasound based on 3D local spectrum variation for percutaneous scaphoid fracture fixation. In: Ourselin, S., Joskowicz, L., Sabuncu, M.R., Unal, G., Wells, W. (eds.) MICCAI 2016. LNCS, vol. 9900, pp. 465–473. Springer, Cham (2016). https://doi.org/10.1007/978-3-319-46720-7_54
5. Hacihaliloglu, I., Guy, P., Hodgson, A., Abugharbieh, R.: Automatic extraction of bone surfaces from 3D ultrasound images in orthopaedic trauma cases. Int. J. Comput. Assist. Radiol. Surg. **10**(8), 1279–1287 (2015)
6. Jia, R., Mellon, S., Hansjee, S., Monk, A., Murray, D., Noble, J.: Automatic bone segmentation in ultrasound images using local phase features and dynamic programming. In: Proceedings of the 13th IEEE International Symposium on Biomedical Imaging, ISBI 2016, pp. 1005–1008. IEEE (2016)
7. Ozdemir, F., Ozkan, E., Goksel, O.: Graphical modeling of ultrasound propagation in tissue for automatic bone segmentation. In: Ourselin, S., Joskowicz, L., Sabuncu, M.R., Unal, G., Wells, W. (eds.) MICCAI 2016. LNCS, vol. 9901, pp. 256–264. Springer, Cham (2016). https://doi.org/10.1007/978-3-319-46723-8_30
8. Quader, N., Hodgson, A., Abugharbieh, R.: Confidence weighted local phase features for robust bone surface segmentation in ultrasound. In: Linguraru, M.G., Oyarzun Laura, C., Shekhar, R., Wesarg, S., González Ballester, M.Á., Drechsler, K., Sato, Y., Erdt, M. (eds.) CLIP 2014. LNCS, vol. 8680, pp. 76–83. Springer, Cham (2014). https://doi.org/10.1007/978-3-319-13909-8_10
9. Hacihaliloglu, I., Abugharbieh, R., Hodgson, A., Rohling, R.: Automatic adaptive parameterization in local phase feature-based bone segmentation in ultrasound. Ultrasound Med. Biol. **37**(10), 1689–1703 (2011)
10. Hacihaliloglu, I., Abugharbieh, R., Hodgson, A., Rohling, R.: Bone surface localization in ultrasound using image phase-based features. Ultrasound Med. Biol. **35**(9), 1475–1487 (2009)
11. Kovesi, P.: Image features from phase congruency. Videre: J. Comput. Vis. Res. **1**(3), 1–26 (1999)
12. Hacihaliloglu, I., Rasoulian, A., Rohling, R., Abolmaesumi, P.: Local phase tensor features for 3D ultrasound to statistical shape+pose spine model registration. IEEE Trans. Med. Imaging **33**(11), 2167–2179 (2014)
13. Felsberg, M., Sommer, G.: The monogenic signal. IEEE Trans. Signal Process. **49**(12), 3136–3144 (2001)
14. Belaid, A., Boukerroui, D.: α scale spaces filters for phase based edge detection in ultrasound images. In: Proceedings of the 11th IEEE International Symposium on Biomedical Imaging, ISBI 2014, pp. 1247–1250. IEEE (2014)
15. Karamalis, A., Wein, W., Klein, T., Navab, N.: Ultrasound confidence maps using random walks. Med. Image Anal. **16**(6), 1101–1112 (2012)
16. Hacihaliloglu, I.: Enhancement of bone shadow region using local phase-based ultrasound transmission maps. Int. J. Comput. Assist. Radiol. Surg. **12**(6), 951–960 (2017)
17. Meng, G., Wang, Y., Duan, J., Xiang, S., Pan, C.: Efficient image dehazing with boundary constraint and contextual regularization. In: Proceedings of the IEEE International Conference on Computer Vision, ICCV 2013, pp. 617–624. IEEE (2013)

Shape-Aware Deep Convolutional Neural Network for Vertebrae Segmentation

S. M. Masudur Rahman Al Arif[1]([✉]), Karen Knapp[2], and Greg Slabaugh[1]

[1] City, University of London, London, UK
s.al-arif@city.ac.uk
[2] University of Exeter, Exeter, UK

Abstract. Shape is an important characteristic of an object, and a fundamental topic in computer vision. In image segmentation, shape has been widely used in segmentation methods, like the active shape model, to constrain a segmentation result to a class of learned shapes. However, to date, shape has been underutilized in deep segmentation networks. This paper addresses this gap by introducing a shape-aware term in the segmentation loss function. A deep convolutional network has been adapted in a novel cervical vertebrae segmentation framework and compared with traditional active shape model-based methods. The proposed framework has been trained on an augmented dataset of 26370 vertebrae and tested on 792 vertebrae collected from a total of 296 real-life emergency room lateral cervical X-ray images. The proposed framework achieved an average error of 1.11 pixels, signifying a 36% improvement over the traditional methods. The introduction of the novel shape-aware term in the loss function significantly improved the performance by further 12%, achieving an average error of only 0.99 pixel.

Keywords: Convolutional neural networks · Vertebrae
Segmentation · Shape-aware · X-rays

1 Introduction

Deep learning has revolutionized the field of image classification [1–4], segmentation [5–7] and many other aspects of computer vision. Segmenting an anatomical body part in medical images is a challenging problem in the field. Although, training a deep network requires huge amount of data, which is usually not available for medical images, recent techniques using data augmentation have shown promising results for segmentation problem on medical images [8,9]. Shape characteristics have long been used for image segmentation problems, especially in medical images [10–13]. Medical image modalities, e.g. X-ray, dual-energy X-ray absorptiometry, magnetic resonance imaging, often produce noisy captures of anatomical body parts, where segmentation must rely on the shape information to produce reliable results. However, combining shape information in a deep segmentation network is not straightforward. In this paper, we try to

© Springer International Publishing AG 2018
B. Glocker et al. (Eds.): MSKI 2017, LNCS 10734, pp. 12–24, 2018.
https://doi.org/10.1007/978-3-319-74113-0_2

solve the problem by introducing a novel shape-aware term in the segmentation loss function. To test its capability of shape preservation, we adapted the novel shape-aware deep segmentation network in a semi-automatic cervical vertebrae segmentation framework.

Segmenting the vertebrae correctly is a crucial part for further analysis in an injury detection system. Previous work in vertebrae segmentation has largely been dominated by statistical shape model (SSM)-based approaches [14–22]. These methods record statistical information about the shape and/or the appearance of the vertebrae based on a training set. Then the mean shape is initialized either manually or semi-automatically near the actual vertebra. The model then tries to converge to the actual vertebral boundary based on a search procedure. Recent work [19–22] utilizes random forest-based machine learning models in order to achieve shape convergence. In contrast to these methods, we propose a novel deep convolutional neural network-based method for vertebrae segmentation. Instead of predicting the shape of a vertebra, our framework predicts the segmentation mask of a vertebral patch. In order to preserve the vertebral shape, a novel shape-aware loss term has been proposed. From a training set of 124 X-ray images containing 586 cervical vertebrae, 26370 vertebra patch-segmentation mask pairs have been generated through data augmentation for training the deep network. The trained framework has been tested on dataset of 172 images containing 792 vertebrae. An average pixel-level accuracy of 97.01%, Dice similarity coefficient 0.9438 and shape error of 0.99 pixel have been achieved.

The key contributions of this work are two fold. First, the introduction of a novel shape-aware term in the loss function of a deep segmentation network which learns to preserve the shape of the target object and significantly improved the segmentation accuracy. Second, the application and adaptation of deep segmentation networks to achieve vertebrae segmentation in real life medical images which outperformed the traditional SSM-based methods by 35%.

2   Data

A total of 296 lateral cervical spine X-ray images were collected from Royal Devon and Exeter Hospital in association with the University of Exeter, UK. The age of the patients varied from 17 to 96. Different radiographic systems (Philips, Agfa, Kodak, GE) were used to produce the scans. Image resolution

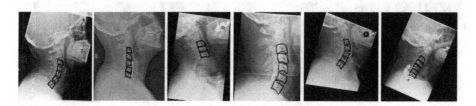

Fig. 1. X-ray images and manual annotations: center (+) and vertebral boundary ( ). (Color figure online)

varied from 0.1 to 0.194 mm per pixel. The images include examples of vertebrae with fractures, degenerative changes and bone implants. The data is anonymized and standard research protocols have been followed. The size, shape, orientation of spine, image intensity, contrast, noise level all varied greatly in the dataset. For this work, five vertebrae C3–C7 are considered. C1 and C2 have an ambiguous appearance due to their overlap in lateral cervical radiographs, and our clinical experts were not able to provide ground truth segmentations for these vertebral bodies. For this reason they are excluded in this study, similar to other cervical spine image analysis research [15,23]. Each vertebra from the images was manually annotated for the vertebral body boundaries and centers by an expert radiographer. A few examples with corresponding manual annotations are shown in Fig. 1.

The images were received in two sets. The first set of 124 images are used for training and the rest are kept for testing. The manually clicked center points and the vertebral boundary curves are used extract the vertebral image patch and corresponding segmentation masks. Different patch size and rotation angles are considered in order to augment the training data. After data augmentation, we ended up with 26370 vertebra training patches. All the patches were then resized to 64 × 64 pixel patches. The corresponding vertebral curves were converted to binary segmentation masks of the same size. A few training vertebra patches and corresponding overlaid segmentation masks are shown in Fig. 2. Similarly, vertebral patches were also collected from the test images. The orientation and scale for the test vertebrae were computed by the manually clicked center points only, shape information was not used. Our assumption is that the center points will be manually provided at test time, making the process semi-automatic. Some test vertebrae are shown in Fig. 3. Note the differences in intensity, texture, and contrast, coupled with the possibility of surgical implants, making for a challenging problem on real-world data.

3 Methodology

Several deep segmentation networks have achieved outstanding performance in natural images [5–7]. However, medical images have their own set of challenges to overcome. The UNet architecture have shown excellent capability of segmenting

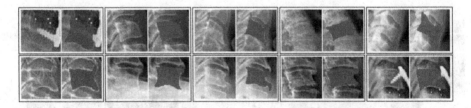

Fig. 2. Training vertebra patches and corresponding segmentation masks (blue). (Color figure online)

Fig. 3. Examples of test vertebra patches.

different target objects in different medical image modalities [8,9]. Following the literature, for our shape-aware vertebrae segmentation problem, we have chosen a modified version of the original UNet [8] deep segmentation network.

3.1 Network Architecture

The UNet architecture consists of a contracting path and an expanding path in the network. The contracting path reduces the spatial dimension of an input image to a smaller version and the expanding path expands spatial dimension and results in a segmentation map at the output. In the original architecture [8], the spatial dimension output segmentation map is smaller than that of the input images due to the use of convolution layers without padding. In our version, we want to keep the spatial dimension of the input image and the output segmentation map same. Our architecture has nine convolutional layers in the contracting path. Each convolutional layer is followed by a batch normalization and a rectified linear unit (ReLU) layer. Three 2×2 pooling layers, one each after two consecutive convolutional layers, reduce the input size of 64×64 to a smaller dimension of 8×8 at the end of the contracting path. This data is then forwarded through a mirrored expanding path of the network. The upsampling after every two convolution layer in the expanding path is achieved by a deconvolution layer with 2×2 kernel size. The network shares intermediate information from the contracting path to the expanding path by concatenation of data. After each upsampling, the data in the expanding path is concatenated by the corresponding data from the contracting path. This helps the network to recover some of the information lost during max-pooling operation. Our network takes a single channel vertebra patch of spatial dimension 64×64 and predicts a two channel probabilistic output for the prediction vertebra mask of the same size. Figure 4 details the network diagram. The number of filters in each convolutional/deconvolutional layer can be tracked from the intermediate data dimensions in Fig. 4. The total number of parameters in the network is 24,238,210.

3.2 Loss Function

Given a dataset of training image (x)-segmentation label (y) pairs, training a deep segmentation network means finding a set of parameters $\boldsymbol{W}$ that minimizes a loss function, L_t. The simplest form of the loss function for segmentation problem is the pixel-wise log loss:

$$\hat{\boldsymbol{W}} = \arg \min_{\boldsymbol{W}} \sum_{n=1}^{N} L_t \left(\{x^{(n)}, y^{(n)}\}; \boldsymbol{W} \right), \tag{1}$$

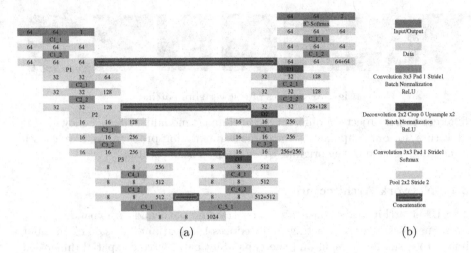

(a)   (b)

Fig. 4. UNet architecture. (a) Network diagram (b) Legends.

where N is the number of training examples and $\{x^{(n)}, y^{(n)}\}$ represents n-th example in the training set with corresponding manual segmentation. The pixel-wise segmentation loss per image can be defined as:

$$L_t(\{x, y\}; \boldsymbol{W}) = -\sum_{i \in \Omega_p} \sum_{j=1}^{M} y_i^j \log P(y_i^j = 1 | x_i; \boldsymbol{W}), \tag{2}$$

$$P(y_i^j = 1 | x_i; \boldsymbol{W}) = \frac{\exp(a_j(x_i))}{\sum_{k=1}^{M} \exp(a_k(x_i))}, \tag{3}$$

where $a_j(x_i)$ is the output of the penultimate activation layer of the network for the pixel x_i, Ω_p represents the pixel space, M is the total number of segmentation class labels and P are the corresponding class probabilities. However, this term does not constrain the predicted masks to conform to possible vertebral shapes. Since vertebral shapes are known from the provided manual segmentation curves, we add a novel shape-aware term in the loss function to force the network to learn to penalize predicted areas outside the curve.

3.3   Shape-Aware Term

For training the deep segmentation network, we introduce a novel shape-based term, L_s. This term forces the network to produce a prediction masks similar to the training vertebral shapes. This term can be defined as:

$$L_s(\{x, y\}; \boldsymbol{W}) = -\sum_{i \in \hat{\Omega}_p} \sum_{j=1}^{M} y_i^j E_i \log P(y_i^j = 1 | x_i; \boldsymbol{W}); \quad E_i = D(\hat{C}, C_{GT}), \tag{4}$$

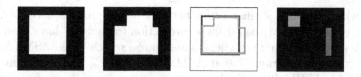

Fig. 5. Shape-aware loss: (a) Ground truth mask. (b) Predicted mask. (c) Ground truth shape, C_{GT} (green) and predicted shape, $\hat{C}$ (red). (d) Refined pixel space, $\hat{\Omega}_p$: false positive (purple) and false negative (red). (Color figure online)

where $\hat{C}$ is the curve surrounding the predicted regions and C_{GT} is ground truth curve. The function, $D(\cdot)$, computes the average point to curve Euclidean distance between the predicted shape, $\hat{C}$ and the ground truth shape, C_{GT}. $\hat{C}$ is generated by locating the boundary pixels of the predicted mask. The redefined pixel space, $\hat{\Omega}_p$, contains the set of pixels where the prediction mask does not match the ground truth mask. These terms can also be explained using the toy example shown in Fig. 5. Given a ground truth mask (Fig. 5(a)) and a prediction mask (Fig. 5(b)), E_i is computed by measuring the average distance between the ground truth (green) curve and prediction (red) curve (Fig. 5(c)). Figure 5(d) shows the redefined pixel space, $\hat{\Omega}_p$. This term adds additional penalty proportional to Euclidean distance between predicted and ground truth curve to the pixels that do not match the ground truth segmentation mask. In the case when the predicted mask is a cluster of small regions, especially during the first few epochs in training, E_i becomes very large because of the increase in the boundary perimeters from the disjoint predictions. Thus, this term also implicitly forces the network to learn to predict single connected prediction masks faster.

3.4 Updated Loss Function

Finally, the loss function of (1) can be extended as:

$$\hat{W} = \arg\min_{W} \sum_{n=1}^{N} \left(L_t \left(\{x^{(n)}, y^{(n)}\}; W \right) + L_s \left(\{x^{(n)}, y^{(n)}\}; W \right) \right). \quad (5)$$

The contribution of each term in the total loss can be controlled by introducing a weight parameter in (5). However, in our case, best performance was achieved when both terms contributed equally.

4   Experiments

We have two versions of the deep segmentation network: UNet and UNet-S, where "-S" signifies the use of updated shape-aware loss function of (5). The networks are trained for 30 epochs with batch size of 25 vertebra patches. To update the network parameters, RMSprop version of mini-batch gradient descent algorithm is used [24]. Each network took around 30 h to complete training in computer equipped with a NVIDIA Pascal Titan X GPU. In order to compare with the deep segmentation network-based prediction results, three active shape model (ASM)-based shape prediction frameworks have been implemented. A simple maximum gradient-based image search-based ASM (ASM-G) [14], a Mahalanobis distance-based ASM (ASM-M) [15] and a random forest based ASM (ASM-RF) [21]. The later two have been used in cervical vertebrae segmentation in different datasets.

4.1   Inference and Metrics

At test time, 792 vertebrae from 172 test images are extracted based on the manually clicked vertebral centers. These patches are forwarded through each of the networks to get the prediction masks. These prediction masks are compared with the ground truth segmentation mask to compute number pixels detected as true positive (TP), true negative (TN), false positive (FP) and false negative (FN). Based on these measures two metrics are computed for each set of test vertebra patch and prediction masks: pixel-wise accuracy (pA) and Dice similarity coefficients (DSC). For the ASM-based shape predictors, the predicted shape is converted to a prediction map to measure these metrics.

$$DSC = \frac{2TP}{2TP + FP + FN}, \tag{6}$$

$$pA = \frac{TP + TN}{TP + TN + FP + FN} \times 100\%. \tag{7}$$

These metrics are well suited to capture the number of correctly segmented pixels, but they fail to capture the differences in shape. In order to compare the shape of the predicted mask appropriately with the ground truth vertebral boundary, the predicted masks of the deep segmentation networks are converted into shapes by locating the boundary pixels. These shapes are then compared manually annotated vertebral boundary curves by measuring average point to curve Euclidean distance between them, similar to (4). A final metric, called fit failure [20], is also computed which measures the percentage of vertebrae having an average point to ground truth curve error of greater than 2 pixels.

5   Results

Table 1 reports the average median, mean and standard deviation metrics over the test dataset of 792 vertebrae for all the methods. The deep segmentation networks clearly outperform the ASM-based methods. Even the worst version of our framework, UNet achieves a 2.9% improvement in terms of pixel-wise accuracy and an increase of 0.055 for Dice similarity coefficient. Among the two version of deep networks, the use of novel loss function improves the performance by 0.31% in terms of pixel-wise accuracy. In terms of Dice similarity coefficient, the improvement is in the range of 0.006. Although, subtle, the improvements are statistically significant according to a paired t-test at a 5% significance level.

Table 1. Average quantitative metrics for mask prediction.

	Pixel-wise accuracy (%)				Dice similarity coefficient			
	Median	Mean	Std	p-value	Median	Mean	Std	p-value
ASM-RF	95.09	90.77	8.98		0.881	0.774	0.220	
ASM-M	95.09	93.48	4.92		0.900	0.877	0.073	
ASM-G	95.34	93.75	4.48		0.906	0.883	0.066	
UNet	97.71	96.69	3.04	$<10^{-12}$	0.952	0.938	0.048	$<10^{-12}$
UNet-S	**97.92**	**97.01**	**2.79**		**0.957**	**0.944**	**0.044**	

Corresponding p-values between the two versions of the network are reported in Table 1. Bold fonts indicates the best performing metrics. Interestingly, among the ASM-based methods, the simplest version, ASM-G, performs better than the alternatives. Recent methods [15,21], have failed to perform robustly on our challenging dataset of test vertebrae.

The average point to curve error for the methods are reported in Table 2. The deep segmentation framework, UNet, produced a 35% improvement over the ASM-based methods in terms of the mean values. The introduction of the novel loss term in the training further reduced the average error by 12% achieving the best error of 0.99 pixels. The most significant improvement can be seen in the fit failure which denotes the percentage of the test vertebrae having an average error of higher than 2 pixels. The novel shape-aware network, UNet-S, has achieved drop of around 37% from the ASM-RF method. The cumulative distribution of the point to curve error is also plotted in the performance curve of Fig. 6. It can be seen adaptation deep segmentation network provides a big improvement in area under the curve. The boxplots of the quantitative metrics are shown in Fig. 7. It can be seen that, even the worst outlier for shape-aware network, UNet-S, have a pixel-wise accuracy higher than 70%, signifying the regularizing capability of the novel term. Most of the outliers are caused by bone implants, fractured vertebrae or abnormal artifacts in the images. A few examples for qualitative assessment are shown in Fig. 8. Figure 8(a) shows an easy example where all the methods perform well. Examples with bone implants are shown

Table 2. Average quantitative metric for shape prediction.

	Average point to curve error (pixels)				Fit failure (%)
	Median	Mean	Std	p-value	
ASM-RF	1.82	2.59	1.85		43.43
ASM-M	1.54	1.88	1.05		32.70
ASM-G	1.38	1.73	0.99		26.89
UNet	0.77	1.11	1.29	0.0043	8.59
UNet-S	**0.78**	**0.99**	**0.67**		**6.06**

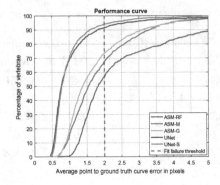

Fig. 6. Performance curve: cumulative distribution of point to curve errors.

in Fig. 8(b), (c). Figure 8(d), (e) shows vertebrae with abrupt contrast change. Vertebrae with fracture and osteoporosis are shown in Fig. 8(f), (g). Figure 8(g) also shows how UNet-S has been able capture the vertebral fracture pattern. Figure 8(h), (i) show vertebrae with image artefacts. A complete failure case is shown in Fig. 8(j). In all cases, the shape-aware network, UNet-S, has produced better segmentation results than its counterpart.

5.1   Analysis on Harder Cases

Although statistically significant, the difference in performance between the UNet and UNet-S is subtle over the whole dataset of test vertebrae. This is because majority of the vertebrae are healthy and shape-awareness does not improve the results by a big margin. To show the shape-awareness capability of UNet-S a selection 52 vertebrae with severe clinical conditions are chosen. The average metrics for this subset of test vertebrae between UNet and UNet-S is reported in Table 3. An improvement of 1.2% and 0.02 have been achieved in terms of pixel-wise accuracy and Dice similarity coefficient, respectively. The

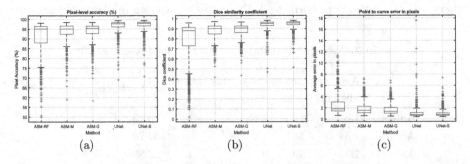

Fig. 7. Boxplots of quantitative metrics. (a) Pixel-level accuracy. (b) Dice similarity coefficients. (c) Point to manual segmentation curve error.

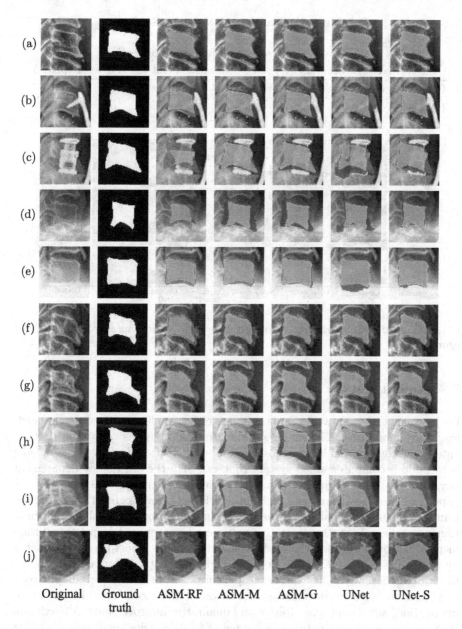

| (a) | (b) | (c) | (d) | (e) | (f) | (g) | (h) | (i) | (j) |

Original   Ground   ASM-RF   ASM-M   ASM-G   UNet   UNet-S
truth

Fig. 8. Qualitative segmentation results: true positive (green), false positive (blue) and false negative (red). (Color figure online)

difference over the whole dataset were only 0.31% and 0.006. The metric, point to curve error produces the most dramatic change. The novel shape-aware network, UNet-S, reduced the error by 22.9% for this subset of vertebrae with severe clinical conditions. Figure 9 shows a few example of these subset of images.

Table 3. Comparison of UNet and UNet-S.

	Average quantitative metrics		
	Pixel-wise accuracy (%)	Dice coefficient	Point to curve error (pixels)
UNet	94.01	0.91	1.61
UNet-S	95.21	0.93	1.24

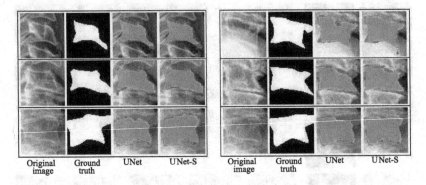

Original   Ground   UNet   UNet-S   Original   Ground   UNet   UNet-S
image   truth   image   truth

Fig. 9. Comparison of performance for vertebrae with severe clinical condition. (Color figure online)

6   Conclusion

Deep segmentation networks have shown exciting application in different medical image modalities. The shape of an anatomical object is very important for automated computer aided diagnosis and injury detection. Our overarching goal is to build a computer aided system that can help the emergency department physicians to detect injuries with better accuracy. Towards this goal, in this paper, we proposed a robust semi automatic vertebrae segmentation method using deep convolutional neural networks that incorporate the shape information in to achieve better segmentation accuracy. The proposed deep segmentation method has outperformed the traditional active shape model-based approaches by a significant margin. In order to incorporate shape information with the mask prediction capability of the deep neural networks, a novel shape-aware loss function has been formulated. Inclusion of this novel term in the training provided significant quantitative and qualitative improvements. A maximum average pixel-level segmentation accuracy of 97.01%, Dice coefficient of 0.9438 and point to ground truth curve error of less than 1 pixel has been achieved over a diverse dataset of 792 test vertebrae collected from real life medical emergency rooms. Currently, we are working on a fully automatic localization framework to locate the vertebral centers in arbitrary X-ray images. In the future, we will be using the segmented vertebral column to automatically determine various clinical conditions like misalignment of the vertebral body, osteoporosis, bone density abnormality and type and severity of different vertebral fractures.

Acknowledgements. We gratefully acknowledge the support of NVIDIA Corporation with the donation of the Titan X Pascal GPU used for this research.

References

1. Krizhevsky, A., Sutskever, I., Hinton, G.: ImageNet classification with deep convolutional neural networks. In: Pereira, F., et al. (eds.) Proceedings of the Neural Information Processing Systems - NIPS 2012, vol. 25, pp. 1097–1105 (2012)
2. Simonyan, K., Zisserman, A.: Very deep convolutional networks for large-scale image recognition (2014). arXiv:1409.1556
3. Szegedy, C., Liu, W., Jia, Y., Sermanet, P., Reed, S., Anguelov, D., Erhan, D., Vanhoucke, V., Rabinovich, A.: Going deeper with convolutions. In: Proceedings of the IEEE Conference on Computer Vision and Pattern Recognition - CVPR 2015, pp. 1–9. IEEE (2015)
4. He, K., Zhang, X., Ren, S., Sun, J.: Deep residual learning for image recognition. In: Proceedings of the IEEE Conference on Computer Vision and Pattern Recognition - CVPR 2016, pp. 770–778. IEEE (2016)
5. Shelhamer, E., Long, J., Darrell, T.: Fully convolutional networks for semantic segmentation. IEEE Trans. Pattern Anal. Mach. Intell. **39**(4), 640–651 (2017)
6. Zheng, S., Jayasumana, S., Romera-Paredes, B., Vineet, V., Su, Z., Du, D., Huang, C., Torr, P.: Conditional random fields as recurrent neural networks. In: Proceedings of the IEEE International Conference on Computer Vision - ICCV 2015, pp. 1529–1537. IEEE (2015)
7. Noh, H., Hong, S., Han, B.: Learning deconvolution network for semantic segmentation. In: Proceedings of the IEEE International Conference on Computer Vision - ICCV 2015, pp. 1520–1528. IEEE (2015)
8. Ronneberger, O., Fischer, P., Brox, T.: U-Net: Convolutional networks for biomedical image segmentation. In: Navab, N., Hornegger, J., Wells, W.M., Frangi, A.F. (eds.) MICCAI 2015. LNCS, vol. 9351, pp. 234–241. Springer, Cham (2015). https://doi.org/10.1007/978-3-319-24574-4_28
9. BenTaieb, A., Hamarneh, G.: Topology aware fully convolutional networks for histology gland segmentation. In: Ourselin, S., Joskowicz, L., Sabuncu, M.R., Unal, G., Wells, W. (eds.) MICCAI 2016. LNCS, vol. 9901, pp. 460–468. Springer, Cham (2016). https://doi.org/10.1007/978-3-319-46723-8_53
10. Yushkevich, P., Piven, J., Hazlett, H., Smith, R., Ho, S., Gee, J., Gerig, G.: User-guided 3D active contour segmentation of anatomical structures: significantly improved efficiency and reliability. Neuroimage **31**(3), 1116–1128 (2006)
11. Pluempitiwiriyawej, C., Moura, J., Wu, Y.J., Ho, C.: STACS: new active contour scheme for cardiac MR image segmentation. IEEE Trans. Med. Imaging **24**(5), 593–603 (2005)
12. Weese, J., Wächter-Stehle, I., Zagorchev, L., Peters, J.: Shape-Constrained deformable models and applications in medical imaging. In: Li, S., Tavares, J.M.R.S. (eds.) Shape Analysis in Medical Image Analysis. LNCVB, vol. 14, pp. 151–184. Springer, Cham (2014). https://doi.org/10.1007/978-3-319-03813-1_5
13. Farag, A.A., Shalaby, A., El Munim, H.A., Farag, A.: Variational shape representation for modeling, elastic registration and segmentation. In: Li, S., Tavares, J.M.R.S. (eds.) Shape Analysis in Medical Image Analysis. LNCVB, vol. 14, pp. 95–121. Springer, Cham (2014). https://doi.org/10.1007/978-3-319-03813-1_3
14. Cootes, T., Taylor, C., Cooper, D., Graham, J.: Active shape models - their training and application. Comput. Vis. Image Understand. **61**(1), 38–59 (1995)

15. Benjelloun, M., Mahmoudi, S., Lecron, F.: A framework of vertebra segmentation using the active shape model-based approach. Int. J. Biomed. Imaging **2011**, 621905 (2011)
16. Larhmam, M.A., Mahmoudi, S., Benjelloun, M.: Semi-automatic detection of cervical vertebrae in X-ray images using generalized hough transform. In: Proceedings of the 3rd IEEE International Conference on Image Processing Theory, Tools and Applications - IPTA 2012, pp. 396–401. IEEE (2012)
17. Roberts, M., Cootes, T., Adams, J.: Vertebral morphometry: semiautomatic determination of detailed shape from dual-energy X-ray absorptiometry images using active appearance models. Invest. Radiol. **41**(12), 849–859 (2006)
18. Roberts, M., Pacheco, E., Mohankumar, R., Cootes, T., Adams, J.: Detection of vertebral fractures in DXA VFA images using statistical models of appearance and a semi-automatic segmentation. Osteoporos. Int. **21**(12), 2037–2046 (2010)
19. Roberts, M.G., Cootes, T.F., Adams, J.E.: Automatic location of vertebrae on DXA images using random forest regression. In: Ayache, N., Delingette, H., Golland, P., Mori, K. (eds.) MICCAI 2012. LNCS, vol. 7512, pp. 361–368. Springer, Heidelberg (2012). https://doi.org/10.1007/978-3-642-33454-2_45
20. Bromiley, P., Adams, J., Cootes, T.: Localisation of vertebrae on DXA images using constrained local models with random forest regression voting. In: Yao, J., et al. (eds.) Recent Advances in Computational Methods and Clinical Applications for Spine Imaging. LNCVB, vol. 20, pp. 159–171. Springer, Cham (2015). https://doi.org/10.1007/978-3-319-14148-0_14
21. Al Arif, S.M.M.R., Gundry, M., Knapp, K., Slabaugh, G.: Improving an active shape model with random classification forest for segmentation of cervical vertebrae. In: Yao, J., Vrtovec, T., Zheng, G., Frangi, A., Glocker, B., Li, S. (eds.) CSI 2016. LNCS, vol. 10182, pp. 3–15. Springer, Cham (2016). https://doi.org/10.1007/978-3-319-55050-3_1
22. Bromiley, P.A., Kariki, E.P., Adams, J.E., Cootes, T.F.: Fully automatic localisation of vertebrae in CT images using random forest regression voting. In: Yao, J., Vrtovec, T., Zheng, G., Frangi, A., Glocker, B., Li, S. (eds.) CSI 2016. LNCS, vol. 10182, pp. 51–63. Springer, Cham (2016). https://doi.org/10.1007/978-3-319-55050-3_5
23. Mahmoudi, S., Lecron, F., Manneback, P., Benjelloun, M., Mahmoudi, S.: GPU-based segmentation of cervical vertebra in X-ray images. In: Proceedings of the IEEE International Conference on Cluster Computing Workshops and Posters - CLUSTER WORKSHOPS, pp. 1–8. IEEE (2010)
24. Ruder, S.: An overview of gradient descent optimization algorithms (2016). arXiv:1609.04747

Automated Characterization of Body Composition and Frailty with Clinically Acquired CT

Peijun Hu[1,2(✉)], Yuankai Huo[3], Dexing Kong[1], J. Jeffrey Carr[4],
Richard G. Abramson[4], Katherine G. Hartley[4], and Bennett A. Landman[2,3,4]

[1] School of Mathematical Sciences, Zhejiang University, Hangzhou, China
peijunhu.zju@gmail.com
[2] Computer Science, Vanderbilt University, Nashville, USA
[3] Electrical Engineering, Vanderbilt University, Nashville, USA
[4] Radiology and Radiological Sciences, Vanderbilt University, Nashville, USA

Abstract. Quantification of fat and muscle on clinically acquired computed tomography (CT) scans is critical for determination of body composition, a key component of health. Manual tracing has been regarded as the gold standard method of body segmentation; however, manual tracing is time-consuming. Many semi-automated/automated algorithms have been proposed to avoid the manual efforts. Previous efforts largely focused on segmenting two-dimensional cross-sectional images (e.g., at L3/T4 vertebra locations) rather than on the whole-body volume. In this paper, we propose a fully automated three-dimensional (3D) body composition estimation framework for segmenting the muscle and fat from abdominal CT scans. The 3D whole body segmentations are reconstructed from a slice-wise multi-atlas label fusion (MALF) based framework. First, we use a low-dimensional atlas representation to estimate each class for each axial slice. Second, the abdominal wall and psoas muscle are segmented by combining MALF with active shape models and deformable models. Third, skeletal muscle, visceral adipose tissue (VAT) and subcutaneous adipose tissue (SAT) are measured to assess the areas of muscle and fat tissue. The proposed method was compared to manual segmentation and demonstrated high accuracy. Then, we evaluated the approach on 40 CT scans comparing the new method to a prior atlas-based segmentation method and achieved 0.854, 0.740, 0.887 and 0.933 on Dice similarity index for the skeletal muscle, psoas muscle, VAT and SAT, respectively. Compared with the baseline, our method showed significantly ($p < 0.001$) higher accuracy on skeletal muscle, VAT and SAT estimation.

Keywords: Skeletal muscle · Psoas muscle · Visceral fat
Subcutaneous fat · Multi-atlas

© Springer International Publishing AG 2018
B. Glocker et al. (Eds.): MSKI 2017, LNCS 10734, pp. 25–35, 2018.
https://doi.org/10.1007/978-3-319-74113-0_3

1 Introduction

Body composition of fat and muscle mass is an important biomarker in cancer treatment. The quantitative measurement of body composition is related to the efficacy and toxicity of chemotherapy, post therapy functional status, surgical complication rates, length of hospital stay and overall survival [1]. In addition, body composition estimation will lead to a more reliable replacement of basic measures of healthy weight, such as body mass index. Manual delineation on computed tomography (CT) images has been regarded as the gold standard in body composition estimation [2]. However, manual tracing on muscle and fat regions are time-consuming and cannot be easily applied to large cohorts. Therefore, many automated or semi-automated methods have been proposed to perform the segmentation. The previous studies estimated the body composition of muscle and fat based on the two-dimensional (2D) axial slice at the 3rd lumbar vertebra (L3) position. However, single slice based estimation is a rough approximation of the whole-body composition, which is sensitive to the slice selection.

For fat segmentation, the Hounsfield unit (HU) intensity is typically used to distinguish muscle and fat on CT images when performing the manual segmentation (e.g., $[-29, 150]$ for muscle tissue and $[-190, -30]$ for fat tissue [3]). Importantly, the compartment in which adipose tissue resides relates to the clinical significance of that fat. For example, it is found that nonagenarian individuals with and without frailty syndrome presented marked differences in the pericardial and visceral adipose tissue [4]. Therefore, to generate a meaningful measurement, efforts are required to separate fat into visceral adipose tissue (VAT) and subcutaneous adipose tissue (SAT). The VAT is the adipose tissue included in intra-abdominal cavity, while SAT is the adipose tissue bounded by the inner abdominal wall musculature and the skin surface [4]. Muscle segmentation presents a greater challenge as the HU of muscle overlaps with other abdominal organs and tissues. Moreover, the variable shape and location of muscle make the segmentation even more difficult (Fig. 1).

Previous efforts were typically focused on segmenting either muscle or fat. For fat segmentation, Yao et al. [5] separated the subcutaneous and visceral fat by a single surface at the abdominal wall driven by active contour models (ACM). For muscle segmentation, shape models are typically used. For instance, Tsutomu et al. [6] incorporated a shape prior represented as logistic curves in higher-order graph cut models to segment psoas from CT images. Chung et al. [7] presented a muscle segmentation method in which a thresholded binary image was warped to a mean shape prior by a free deformation model. Popuri et al. [3] proposed a FEM-based registration model to perform template-based segmentation of skeletal muscle. Although these methods achieved high accuracy, they were based on 2D cross-sectional images taken at the 3rd lumbar vertebra (L3) or the 4th thoracic vertebra (T4) locations rather than on whole three-dimensional (3D) volumes. Zhang et al. [8] presented an atlas-based approach to segment the musculature on CT volumes using five pre-defined muscle atlas models, and then the initial segmentation was refined by an ACM. Xu et al. [9] proposed a

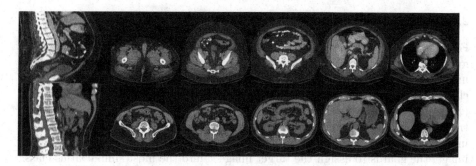

Fig. 1. Illustration of challenges in muscle and fat segmentation. The sagittally reconstructed images show differing fields of view while the axial images demonstrated the large intra-slice and inter-slice variations in muscle and fat cross-sectional area on CT images.

slice-wise method called augmented active shape model (AASM) that integrated multi-atlas label fusion (MALF) and level set into the active shape model (ASM) framework. To overcome the large intra-slice variations in the abdominal wall along the cranial-caudal direction, this method pre-classified slice-wise images to five exclusive classes using landmarks. However, for clinical data with large variations on fields of view (FOV), such landmarks are not typically available (Fig. 1).

In this study, we propose a fully automated framework to segment the skeletal muscle, psoas muscle, VAT and SAT from clinically acquired CT scans. Briefly, we first use a PCA-based low-dimensional representation to estimate the atlas class for the target image. Second, the abdominal wall is segmented using AASM under a slice-wise MALF framework. Here, the abdominal wall is characterized as an enclosed region bounded by the inner surface and outer surface [9]. Then, the psoas muscle is segmented using combination of MALF and a deformable model. Finally, the skeletal muscle, VAT and SAT are extracted using the generated abdominal wall mask and pre-defined HU ranges. The main novelty of our work lies in the application of MALF on the challenging problem of muscle and fat quantification. Considering different anatomies of target regions, an augmented active shape model and a deformable model are used to refine and regularize the initial results of MALF. The whole pipeline is fully automated, without the need of user interaction or parameter adjustment, which gives it potential to be applied in clinic.

2   Methods

The proposed pipeline is shown in Fig. 2. It integrates a slice-wise multi-atlas label fusion framework with an active shape model and a deformable model.

2.1   Atlas Class Estimation via PCA

Following [9], five atlas groups are pre-classified in the training slice images
for multi-atlas label fusion. Instead of detecting landmarks in testing CT volumes, we use a PCA-based low-dimensional representation to decide the atlas
class for each testing image. As in [9], three biomarkers, i.e., xiphoid process
(XP), pubic symphysis (PS) and umbilicus (UB) are manually labeled on each
training volume. According to the relative locations of these biomarkers, training axial slices are separated into five exclusive atlas groups. Given a test slice
image, the goal is to assign the target image x into the most similar atlas class.
Firstly, we align all training images to the same space. Specifically, one image
is randomly selected and others are registered to it using an affine transform.
Then, an average image is generated from all registered images and all images
are registered to the average image again. Secondly, for a training image j, we
reshape it into a vector, thus this image is represented as a high-dimensional
data point $a_j \in \mathbb{R}^D$ with its atlas class c_j, where D is the total number of
pixels and $c_j \in \{1, 2, 3, 4, 5\}$. We denote the aligned training data set as matrix
$\mathbf{A} = (a_{11}, \ldots, a_{1n1}, \ldots, a_{51}, \ldots, a_{5n5}) \in \mathbb{R}^{D \times N}$, where $N = \sum_{i=1}^{5} n_i$ is the total
number of training images. Thirdly, by using PCA dimension reduction, the high-
dimensional data points $\mathbf{A}$ are transformed into a low-dimensional representation
$\mathbf{Y} = (y_{11}, \ldots, y_{1n1}, \ldots, y_{51}, \ldots, y_{5n5}) \in \mathbb{R}^{d \times N}$, where $d \ll D$. The PCA is per-
formed by minimizing the cost function $\phi(\mathbf{Y}) = \sum_{i,j} \left(d_{ij}^2 - \|y_i - y_j\|^2 \right)$, where
d_{ij} represents the Euclidean distance between the high-dimensional points a_i
and a_j. Finally, the target image x is projected to the low-dimensional space
and k-nearest neighbors in Euclidean distance are selected to estimate its class
by majority voting.

2.2   Abdominal Wall and Psoas Segmentation

Prior Probability Map Learned from MALF. For each axial slice of the
test CT volume, all the training images in the estimated class are considered
as atlases to perform slice-wise multi-atlas label fusion with respect to regions
of interest, i.e., the abdominal wall and psoas muscle. Each atlas is non-rigidly
registered to the target image with NiftyReg package [10]. Atlas labels are then
warped to the target image and combined using the joint label fusion algorithm
[11], yielding prior probability maps for the abdominal wall and psoas muscle.

Abdominal Wall Segmentation. In abdominal wall segmentation, we use
AASM [9] to search the optimal shape iteratively. In the training stage, an
active shape model and a local appearance model are trained from each atlas
class. In testing, the trained ASM, local appearance model and the probability
map generated from MALF guide landmarks along current contour move to new
positions. The AASM is actually a combination of level set and ASM. Specifically,
firstly level set evolution is applied on the probability map to move the current
contour. Then, the zero-crossing points along the normal direction of the zero

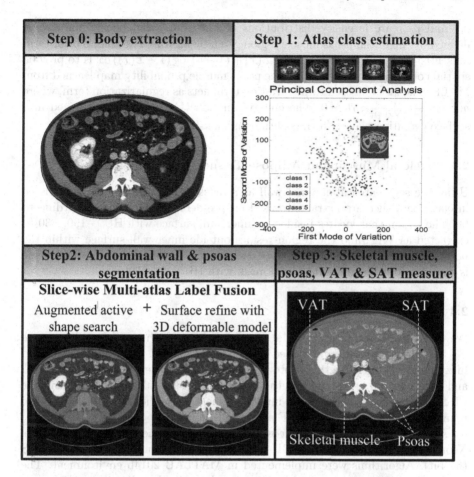

Fig. 2. Flowchart of the proposed segmentation framework.

level set are collected as landmarks. These landmarks are updated with the active shape search and active shape regularization. The new positions of landmarks are used as the initialization of level set evolution for the next iteration. This process goes iteratively until convergence.

Psoas Muscle Segmentation. For psoas muscle, we adopt a 3D deformable model that integrates intensity statistical information, a prior probability map, and a gradient map to refine the initial surface. Given a volume image $I: x \in \Omega \to \mathbb{R}$ defined on $\Omega \subset \mathbb{R}^3$, we denote the indicator function of psoas as $u(x) = \{0, 1\}, x \in \Omega$, which is obtained by minimizing the energy functional:

$$E(u) = \lambda_1 E_{data}(u) + \lambda_2 E_{prior}(u) + \int_{\Omega} g(x)|\nabla u| dx. \tag{1}$$

The first data term formulates the intensity statistics inside and outside the region, i.e., $E_{data}(u) = -\int_{\Omega} u \log p_{in}(I(x)) + (1 - u) \log p_{out}(I(x)) dx$, where

p_{in} and p_{out} are intensity distributions of foreground and background pixels defined by the initial psoas muscle region given by MALF. The second prior term presented as $E_{prior}(u) = -\int_\Omega u \log L(x) + (1 - u) \log (1 - L(x))\, dx$ is to provide spatial constraints, where $L(x)$ is the psoas muscle probability map learned from MALF. The last weighted total-variation term acts as regularization term, where $g(x) = \frac{1}{1+\beta|\nabla I(x)|^2}$, $\beta > 0$. The energy function (1) is globally optimized in a surface evolution way with the continuous max-flow algorithm [12,13].

2.3   Skeletal Muscle and Adipose Tissue Measurement

Using the segmented abdominal wall as a mask, skeletal muscle and fat tissue in each axial slice are extracted based on pre-defined HU ranges according to [3]. The region that locates inside the inner wall surface with HU $[-190, -30]$ is extracted as VAT, and the region resides outside inner wall surface within the body mask with HU $[-190, -30]$ is extract as SAT. The skeletal muscle tissue is segmented inside abdominal wall mask with HU $[-29, 150]$.

2.4   Baseline Method

We take the method of Zhang et al. [8] as baseline, which also focused on whole CT volume segmentation and used slice-wise algorithms. Following [8], we used fuzzy c-means and an active contour model (ACM) to segment VAT and SAT, and then used an atlas-based method to segment skeletal muscle. To avoid the effect of atlas model selection on muscle segmentation, the ACM was applied to refine the results from our MALF as re-implemented.

All experiments in this paper were run on a machine with 8 cores of Intel Xeon W3520 processors and 12 GB RAM available running Ubuntu 14.04.1 LTS (64 bit). Algorithms were implemented in MATLAB 2014b environment. The proposed segmentation method has been made available online in open-source[1].

3   Experiments and Results

3.1   Data

Abdominal CT data on 60 patients from two clinical datasets were randomly retrieved in de-identified form under IRB approval (40 patients from PHC and 20 from GIONC). Specifically, 20 scans from PHC were used for training, and the remaining 20 PHC scans and 20 GIONC scans were for testing. The FOVs of PHC scans ranged from $335 \times 335 \times 390\,mm^3$ to $500 \times 500 \times 708\,mm^3$, with resolutions ranging from $0.65 \times 0.65 \times 2.50\,mm^3$ to $0.98 \times 0.98 \times 5.00\,mm^3$. The FOVs of GIONC scans were from $346 \times 346 \times 165\,mm^3$ to $412 \times 412 \times 505\,mm^3$, with resolutions from $0.65 \times 0.65 \times 1.50\,mm^3$ to $0.85 \times 0.85 \times 5.00\,mm^3$. All 60 scans were manually labeled by an experienced rater and HU values were used to

---

[1] https://www.nitrc.org/project/showfiles.php?group_id=385&release_id=3557.

generate ground truth of skeletal muscle, psoas, VAT and SAT. Specifically, for the 40 PHC scans, essential biomarkers, i.e., xiphoid process, pubic symphysis, and umbilicus were identified, and the abdominal wall and psoas muscle were delineated on axial slices spaced every 5 cm, generating 177 and 184 axial slices for training and testing, respectively. Besides, 40 axial slices at the L3 position of the 40 testing scans were extracted and labeled. Axial slices from the same patient for training were not used for testing.

3.2   Experimental Setting

For all training and testing slices, a body mask was obtained by thresholding the image to remove the background, then selecting the largest 3D connected component to ensure that the CT table was excluded before image analysis. All the images were centered after body extraction. A leave-one-out approach that excluded slices from the same patient was used to optimize the parameters in PCA dimension reduction on the training slices from PHC dataset. As a result, 9 modes of variation in the low-dimensional space and $k = 3$ neighboring images are chosen to estimate the target image class.

In the AASM-based abdominal wall segmentation, 177 labeled axial slices from 20 patients were used as training set (also atlases) to build the active shape model with default parameters as in [9]. The parameters in energy function (1) of psoas refinement were empirically set as $\lambda_1 = 0.1$, $\lambda_2 = 0.01$, $\beta = 0.2$.

3.3   Results

Automated results were validated against the manual labels on 184 axial slices taken at different positions in 20 scans (Fig. 3). The Spearman's rank correlation coefficients between estimated cross-sectional tissue area (cm^2) and the truth were 0.91, 0.75, 0.99, and 0.99 for skeletal muscle, psoas, VAT and SAT, respectively. Figure 4 shows qualitative segmentation results at different positions from one CT. Although there are large shape variations in axial slices taken at different positions, the automated segmentations of the skeletal muscle, VAT and SAT region match well with the manual label. Failures of the psoas segmentation occur on the slices taken at the bottom position, where the psoas muscle region is very small and difficult to detect (see Fig. 4, row 1, column 3).

In Fig. 5, we used the Spearman rank correlation to compare the estimated tissue area by the proposed method with the ground truth on axial slices taken at L3 position from 40 testing scans. Average tissue areas of three and five central L3 slices were also measured.

In Table 1, we compared our method with the baseline method [8] on 40 L3 axial slices from testing scans. Both the proposed method and baseline focused on whole CT scan segmentation and used slice-wise algorithms. The main difference is that the baseline method used an active contour model to refine the initial segmentation of the atlas method. As shown in Table 1, our method achieved significantly ($p < 0.001$) higher Dice similarity index (Dice) values for the skeletal muscle, VAT and SAT using Wilcoxon signed rank test.

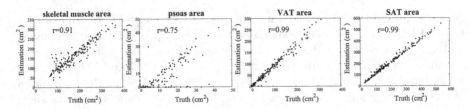

Fig. 3. Scatter plots showing the correlation between estimated tissue area by the proposed method and the ground truth on 184 axial slices.

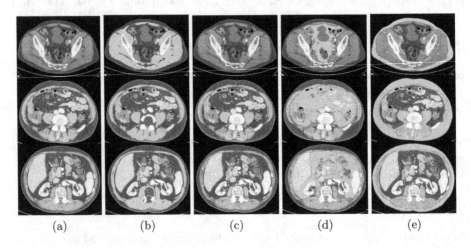

(a)   (b)   (c)   (d)   (e)

Fig. 4. Qualitative segmentation results on different axial slices from one subject: manual label (green), automated label (red) and overlap (yellow). (a) Original image. (b) Skeletal muscle. (c) Psoas muscle. (d) VAT. (e) SAT. (Color figure online)

Table 1. Comparison of tissue area estimation by the proposed method and Zhang et al. [8] on 40 L3 axial slices.

Tissue	Skeletal muscle	Psoas muscle	VAT	SAT
Manual area (cm^2)	142.7 ± 35.0	15.6 ± 5.9	168.4 ± 97.5	224.6 ± 126.5
Proposed Dice	0.854 ± 0.110	0.740 ± 0.259	0.887 ± 0.075	0.933 ± 0.046
Proposed area error (cm^2)	17.1 ± 14.9	4.5 ± 7.1	12.0 ± 14.0	15.5 ± 14.4
Zhang et al. [8] Dice	0.758 ± 0.128	–	0.828 ± 0.054	0.852 ± 0.054
Zhang et al. [8] area error (cm^2)	46.8 ± 27.7	–	46.6 ± 22.1	44.0 ± 21.7
Proposed vs. Zhang et al. [8] Dice p-value	3.3×10^{-5}	–	2.4×10^{-5}	5.6×10^{-8}
Proposed vs. Zhang et al. [8] area error p-value	3.8×10^{-6}	–	7.6×10^{-7}	1.6×10^{-6}

Automated Characterization of Body Composition   33

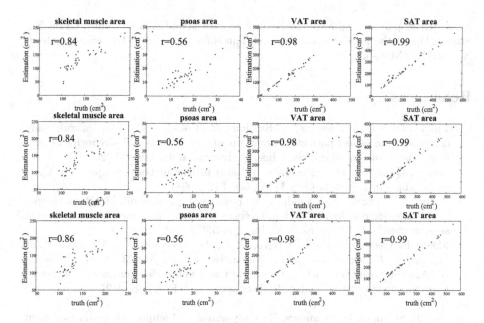

Fig. 5. Scatter plots showing the correlation between estimated tissue area by the proposed method and the ground truth. The first row shows tissue area estimated on one slice at middle L3 position. The second and third row show the average tissue area estimated at three and five slices at the L3 position, respectively.

4 Conclusions

We presented a segmentation pipeline to quantitatively measure the skeletal muscle, psoas muscle, visceral adipose tissue and subcutaneous adipose tissue from clinically acquired abdominal CT scans. The results on 40 subjects from two separate clinical datasets demonstrated that the proposed framework was able to achieve 0.854, 0.740, 0.887 and 0.933 Dice similarity coefficient for the skeletal muscle, psoas muscle, VAT and SAT, respectively. This method is fully automated, without the need of interaction or parameter adjustment, which gives it potential to be applied in a clinical environment. Future work can be the improvement of the proposed method by using shape prior in psoas muscle segmentation.

Acknowledgements. This research was supported by NIH 1R03EB012461, NIH 2R01 EB006136, NIH R01EB006193, NIH P30 CA068485, NIH R01 HL 098445 (PI - Carr), and AUR GE Radiology Research Academic Fellowship, and in part using the resources of the Advanced Computing Center for Research and Education (ACCRE) at Vanderbilt University, Nashville, TN. This project was supported in part by VISE/VICTR VR3029 and the National Center for Research Resources, Grant UL1 RR024975-01, and is now at the National Center for Advancing Translational Sciences, Grant 2 UL1 TR000445-06. The content is solely the responsibility of the authors and does not necessarily represent the official views of the NIH. This research was supported in part by the National Natural Science Foundation of China (Grant No. 91630311) and the Fundamental Research Funds for the Central Universities (Grant No. 2017XZZX007-02).

References

1. Yip, C., Dinkel, C., Mahajan, A., Siddique, M., Cook, G., Goh, V.: Imaging body composition in cancer patients: visceral obesity, sarcopenia and sarcopenic obesity may impact on clinical outcome. Insights Imaging 6(4), 489–497 (2015)
2. Lee, S., Gallagher, D.: Assessment methods in human body composition. Curr. Opin. Clin. Nutr. Metab. Care 11(5), 566–572 (2008)
3. Popuri, K., Cobzas, D., Esfandiari, N., Baracos, V., Jagersand, M.: Body composition assessment in axial CT images using FEM-based automatic segmentation of skeletal muscle. IEEE Trans. Med. Imaging 35(2), 512–520 (2016)
4. Idoate, F., Cadore, E., Casas-Herrero, A., Zambom-Ferraresi, F., Marcellán, T., de Gordoa, A., Rodriguez-Mañas, L., Bastarrika, G., Marques, M., Martínez-Velilla, N.: Adipose tissue compartments, muscle mass, muscle fat infiltration, and coronary calcium in institutionalized frail nonagenarians. Eur. Radiol. 25(7), 2163–2175 (2015)
5. Yao, J., Sussman, D., Summers, R.: Fully automated adipose tissue measurement on abdominal CT. In: Weaver, J., Molthen, R. (eds.) Proceedings of the SPIE Medical Imaging 2011: Biomedical Applications in Molecular, Structural, and Functional Imaging, vol. 7965, p. 79651Z. SPIE (2011)
6. Inoue, T., Kitamura, Y., Li, Y., Ito, W., Ishikawa, H.: Psoas major muscle segmentation using higher-order shape prior. In: Menze, B., Langs, G., Montillo, A., Kelm, M., Müller, H., Zhang, S., Cai, W., Metaxas, D. (eds.) MCV 2015. LNCS, vol. 9601, pp. 116–124. Springer, Cham (2016). https://doi.org/10.1007/978-3-319-42016-5_11
7. Chung, H., Cobzas, D., Birdsell, L., Lieffers, J., Baracos, V.: Automated segmentation of muscle and adipose tissue on CT images for human body composition analysis. In: Miga, M., Wong, K. (eds.) Proceedings of the SPIE Medical Imaging 2009: Visualization, Image-Guided Procedures, and Modeling, vol. 7261, p. 72610K. SPIE (2009)
8. Zhang, W., Liu, J., Yao, J., Summers, R.: Segmenting the thoracic, abdominal and pelvic musculature on CT scans combining atlas-based model and active contour model. In: Novak, C., Aylward, S. (eds.) Proceedings of the SPIE Medical Imaging 2013: Computer-Aided Diagnosis, vol. 8670, p. 867008. SPIE (2013)
9. Xu, Z., Conrad, B., Baucom, R., Smith, S., Poulose, B., Landman, B.: Abdomen and spinal cord segmentation with augmented active shape models. J. Med. Imaging 3(3), 036002 (2016)
10. Modat, M., Ridgway, G., Taylor, Z., Lehmann, M., Barnes, J., Hawkes, D., Fox, N., Ourselin, S.: Fast free-form deformation using graphics processing units. Comput. Methods Programs Biomed. 98(3), 278–284 (2010)
11. Wang, H., Suh, J., Das, S., Pluta, J., Craige, C., Yushkevich, P.: Multi-atlas segmentation with joint label fusion. IEEE Trans. Pattern Anal. Mach. Intell. 35(3), 611–623 (2013)

12. Yuan, J., Bae, E., Tai, X.C.: A study on continuous max-flow and min-cut approaches. In: Proceedings of the IEEE Conference on Computer Vision and Pattern Recognition - CVPR 2010, pp. 2217–2224. IEEE (2010)
13. Yuan, J., Ukwatta, E., Tai, X., Fenster, A., Schnörr, C.: A fast global optimization-based approach to evolving contours with generic shape prior. UCLA Technical Report, pp. 12–38. CAM (2012)

Unfolded Cylindrical Projection for Rib Fracture Diagnosis

Catalina Tobon-Gomez[1]([✉]), Tyler Stroud[1], John Cameron[1], Dave Elcock[1],
Andrew Murray[1], Daniel Wyeth[1], Chris Conway[1], Steven Reynolds[1],
Pedro Augusto Gondim Teixeira[2], Alain Blum[2], and Costas Plakas[1]

[1] Toshiba Medical Visualization Systems, Edinburgh, UK
ctobon-gomez@tmvse.com
[2] Service d'Imagerie Guilloz, CHRU, Nancy, France

Abstract. The recommended exam for assessing chest trauma is a computed tomography (CT) chest scan. Using multi-planar reconstructions to evaluate a CT volume to assess the ribcage is a tedious and time-consuming task. We have designed an application that provides an automatically rendered unfolded unobstructed view of the entire ribcage using an *unfolded cylindrical projection*. This paper describes the underlying algorithm which has two main steps: ribcage segmentation and ribcage unfolding. The unfolding technique we developed preserves the relative size and location of the ribs and surrounding tissue, providing a natural anatomical reference for the reader. It also demonstrated usefulness to identify other musculoskeletal conditions such us scoliosis, calcified cartilage, bone tumours. To evaluate the usefulness of the application, we evaluated it on 70 representative CT chest scans. The evaluation was performed by a clinical expert who graded the specialized unfolded cylindrical projection view on a 5 point Likert scale according to the level of diagnostic confidence. Results showed that 84% of the studies were clinically useful (above grade 3). The algorithm is fully automatic and it runs in an average time of 24 s. The evaluation described in this paper gives positive initial feedback on the usefulness of the application. A recent multi-reader clinical study showed that using the specialized unfolded cylindrical projection view obtains similar diagnostic accuracy to conventional multi-planar reconstructions while reducing the reading time.

Keywords: Rib fractures · Clinical application · Unfolded ribcage

1 Introduction

1.1 Clinical Motivation

Injury-related emergency hospital visits reach up to 37 million in the United States [1] and 39 million in the European Union [2] each year. Fractured ribs are the most common injury in chest trauma. Therefore, it is mandatory to evaluate all ribs in any computed tomography (CT) image of the chest, and it is

© Springer International Publishing AG 2018
B. Glocker et al. (Eds.): MSKI 2017, LNCS 10734, pp. 36–47, 2018.
https://doi.org/10.1007/978-3-319-74113-0_4

of particular importance in trauma patients as 25% of injury-related deaths are caused by chest trauma [3].

According to radiological guidelines the recommended exam for assessing chest trauma is a CT chest scan. Diagnosing rib fractures using a CT scan is a convenient single diagnostic exam, but it is tedious and time-consuming for the reader. Each rib follows a diagonal orientation covering multiple CT slices. Conventional tools require the user to continually create and adjust oblique multi-planar reconstructions (MPRs) due to the curvature of the ribs. Moreover, the full evaluation is performed one rib at a time from side to side.

This has motivated us to develop a clinical application that provides an automatically rendered unfolded unobstructed view of the entire ribcage using an unfolded cylindrical projection (UCP). This specialized UCP view can be browsed as a volume, allowing the clinician to quickly assess the ribcage [4]. The clinical application is interactive, allowing the user to triangulate the position of suspected fractures from the unfolded view to the conventional MPR views to confirm diagnosis.

1.2   State of the Art

Currently there are two commercial applications with a similar purpose. On the one hand, Siemens' syngo. CT application traces the centreline of each rib to define a curved planar reformation (CPR) image for each rib [5]. The displayed image is a composite of the collection of CPR images of the ribs plus a CPR of the spine. The advantage of this approach is that non-displaced fractures are easily visible. The disadvantage is that straightening the ribs complicates the understanding of their relative position and hides other musculoskeletal conditions (e.g. scoliosis).

On the other hand, Carestream's Radial View application provides an unfolded maximum intensity projection of the ribcage. The advantage of this approach is that a projection gives an excellent overview of ribcage. The disadvantage is that maximum intensity projection of ribs hides non-displaced fractures.

Our solution makes improvements on the state of the art by: (1) removing obstructing objects from the projection, (2) improve sensitivity to subtle non-displaced fractures, and (3) preserving the relative size and location of the ribs and surrounding tissue.

2   Data

Landmarks Classifier Training. We used a retrospective in-house database of 369 CT datasets for landmark classifier training. On these datasets, key anatomical markers were collected as ground truth. The ground-truth covers a wide range of anatomies, contrast and non-contrast acquisitions, from multiple scanner vendors.

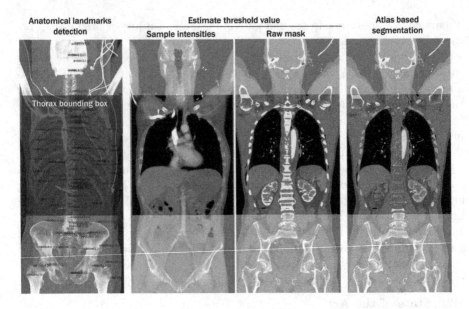

Fig. 1. Overview of the ribcage segmentation process (part 1). See Sect. 3.1 for details.

Segmentation Atlas. Since the main requirement for this tool is computational efficiency, we used a single non-contrast CT dataset as segmentation atlas. We selected an average size individual with no fractures or other evident pathology. On this atlas, several structures were manually segmented by a clinical expert: ribs, spine, sternum, scapulae, clavicles, kidneys. Additionally, anatomical markers were manually collected in the thorax to aid initial alignment (Sect. 3.1).

Testing Database. We used a database of 70 CT studies provided by our clinical collaborators. From this database, we used 44 datasets for algorithm optimisation (*seen datasets*), leaving 26 datasets for blinded evaluation (*unseen datasets*). From the *seen datasets*, six datasets were manually labelled for ribs and spine to provide a quantitative reference.

3   Methods

3.1   Ribcage Segmentation

Anatomical Landmarks Detection. Using technology developed within our research group [6,7], we are able to accurately and efficiently detect anatomical landmarks on novel datasets of any anatomical location (Fig. 1). The method localizes landmarks using a random forest classifier comprising long-range intensity features [8], histogram of oriented gradients (HOG) features [9], and atlas location features. The classifier was trained off-line on a large sample of data (Sect. 2).

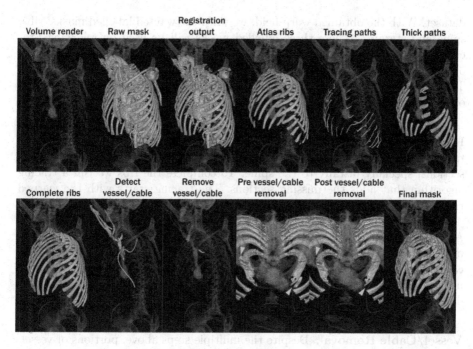

Fig. 2. Overview of the ribcage segmentation process (part 2). Note in the bottom row the areas where vessels/cables were removed (yellow arrows). See Sect. 3.1 for details. (Color figure online)

Thorax Bounding Box. To bound the segmentation of the ribs, we predefine a thorax box in a synthetics atlas. Using the landmarks detected on the novel volume (previous step), we compute a transformation from synthetic atlas space to novel patient space. The bounds are mapped using this transformation. Everything outside the thorax bounds is discarded from subsequent processing (Fig. 1).

Estimate Threshold Value. Even though CT intensity values are relatively calibrated, the values may change in the presence of contrast or pathology. To obtain an initial mask with a raw segmentation of the bone, we vary the threshold value in a case-by-case basis. To define this value, we create a sphere centred at each of the thorax skeletal landmarks and sample intensity values within it. We then compute the 70th percentile of the sampled values. Using this value as a lower threshold, we obtain a mask that contains everything from bones to vessels/cables. In certain cases, it also includes lung fluid, heart chambers, kidneys and/or liver (Fig. 1).

Atlas Based Segmentation. The landmarks detected on the novel dataset are used to initialize the atlas based segmentation. We use non-rigid registration based on a demons algorithm [10] to warp the segmentation atlas to the novel dataset. With the obtained warp field, we warp the wanted labelled masks: ribs, spine and sternum. These three labelled masks will be used on following processing steps. Additionally, we remove from the initial raw mask any identified object that is not a rib: clavicles, scapulae, kidneys, spine and sternum (Fig. 1). This outputs a clean mask that contains mainly ribs with other non-identified objects (e.g. vessels/cables).

Rib Tracing. Due to the similarity of ribs with each other, it is a challenging task for the registration alone. As a result, the warped ribs will be missing sections, specially distally to the spine. To complete the ribs we run a tracing algorithm that adds the missing sections. The tracing starts with the warped ribs as seeds and searches for a path forwards (i.e. away from the spine) and downwards. This naive tracing approach allows to keep computation time low. As a disadvantage, the tracing will stop at the presence of fractures. This is mitigated by seeding all possible sections of ribs with the wrapped rib. The path can follow any location along the full thickness of the potential rib (i.e. it is not constrained to the centrelines). As a final stage, the paths are thickened by dilation and intersection with the input mask (Fig. 2).

Vessel/Cable Removal. Despite the multiple steps above, portions of vessels and/or cables may remain in the rib mask (specially in contrasted studies). To remove this portions of vessel/cables, we run a vesselness filter [11] and extract only areas with very high response. We then find connected components with very high intensity values and remove them from the initial rib mask. We finalize with morphological operations to polish the ribs after removal (Fig. 2).

3.2   Ribcage Unfolding

In order to unfold the ribcage, we want to find a three-dimensional manifold that intersects all the structures of interest and defines the points to be sampled from the volume. To generate this manifold, we define a camera axis along the patient's superior-inferior axis. The axis is located inside the thorax. We use the segmented spine and sternum to define a top coordinate and a bottom coordinate of the camera axis.

Along this axis, we define a collection of points $O_{(1...n)}$. Each point corresponds to a horizontal row of pixels in the output image. For each point O_i, we define a perpendicular plane P_i and tilt it based on an angle α. The tilting makes the ribs more horizontal in the output image. We then define a collection of rays R_j in plane P_i, rotating in the plane around O_i. Each ray corresponds to a column of pixels in the output image. We intersect each ray with the segmented ribs (Sect. 3.1) and choose a mid point. At that position the intensity is sampled and displayed in the two-dimensional (2D) image. Rays that do not intersect are interpolated from neighbouring positions (Fig. 3).

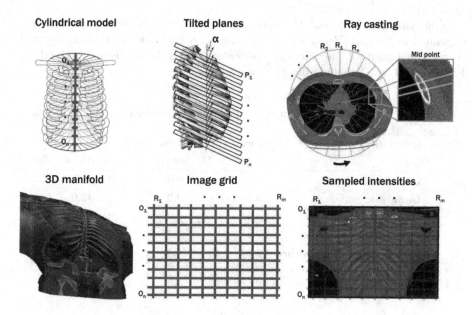

Fig. 3. Overview of the ribcage unfolding process. See Sect. 3.2 for details.

4   Evaluation

4.1   Qualitative Results

We evaluated the clinical application in 70 representative CT chest scans. The qualitative evaluation was performed by a clinical expert who graded the specialized rib view on a 5 point Likert scale according to the level of diagnostic confidence. This grading scale followed the criteria below.

- **Gold standard - grade 5:** The reader can confidently make a diagnosis without any review of the MPRs. No artifacts present.

- **Diagnostic confidence - grade 4:** The reader can confidently make a diagnosis with limited or no review of the MPRs. Little to no artifacts present and there are no artifacts obstructing any relevant anatomy.

- **Moderate confidence - grade 3:** Helpful to make a diagnosis but a clinician would need the MPRs for confirmation. Some artifacts are present but do not obscure significant areas of relevant anatomy.

- **Low level of confidence - grade 2:** Unacceptable. Minimally helpful and artifacts render the projection unacceptable.

- **Very low level of confidence - grade 1:** Indisputably unacceptable.

The evaluation database was split in *seen datasets* and *unseen datasets* (as explained in Sect. 2). Results of the grading can be found in Table 1. Figure 4 shows the layout of the clinical application. This layout is maintained on Figs. 5 and 6 which include illustrative example cases.

Table 1. Summary of qualitative evaluation.

Grade	Description	Scoring results on datasets[a]		
		Seen ($n = 44$)	Unseen ($n = 26$)	All ($n = 70$)
5	Gold standard	0.0	0.0	0.0
4	Diagnostic confidence	59.1	69.2	**62.9**
3	Moderate confidence	29.5	7.7	**21.4**
2	Low level of confidence	11.4	7.7	10.0
1	Very low level of confidence	0.0	15.4	5.7

[a] in percentage w.r.t. total number of cases.
Bolded cases considered clinically useful = 84.3%.

4.2 Quantitative Results

From the *seen datasets*, six cases were manually labelled to provide a quantitative reference. The labels were separated as ribs and spine. We compared the automatically generated masks with the manually generated masks using the following metrics: DICE (overlap), sensitivity and specificity. The masks were clipped to the same thorax bounding box for metric calculation. The results are summarized in Table 2.

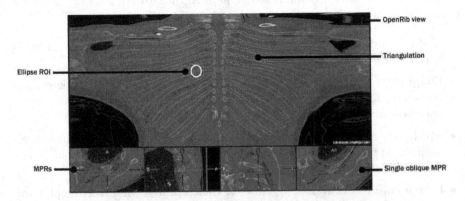

Fig. 4. Layout of the clinical application: the top displays the unfolded cylindrical projection view. The bottom displays three conventional multi-planar reconstructions (axial, sagittal, coronal) and a single oblique multi-planar reconstruction. Use this figure as guidance for Figs. 5 and 6.

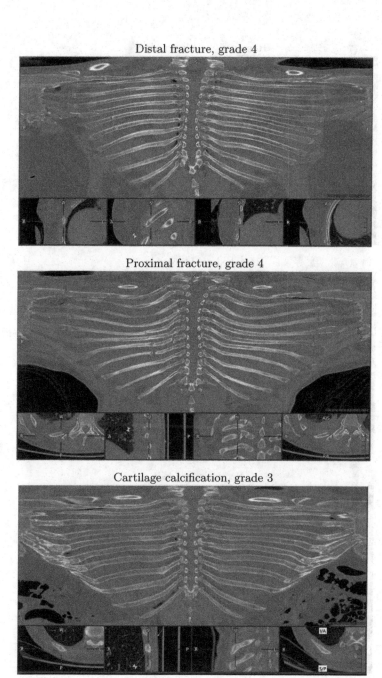

Fig. 5. Snapshots of two cases with fractures (top and middle) and a case with cartilage calcification (bottom).

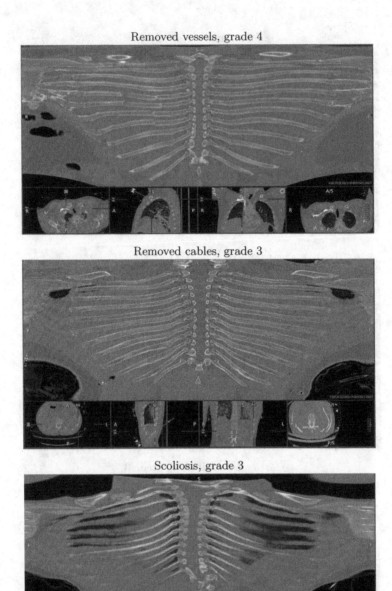

Fig. 6. Snapshot of a case with successfully removed vessels (top), a case with successfully removed cables (middle) and a case with scoliosis (bottom).

4.3   Discussion

Unfolded cylindrical projection views were obtained for all cases without any user interaction. Results showed that overall 84% of the studies were clinically useful (summing cases above grade 3 in all datasets). Low scores were mainly due to segmentation inaccuracies. Some cases still include remains of the scapulae or contrast bolus (vessels) that obscure the ribs. We plan to add editing tools for the user to remove these type of segmentation errors. Finally, the unfolding generates a new type of view unfamiliar to clinicians. This explains the lack of gold standard cases (grade 5). Therefore, the application was designed to use the specialized rib view for quick assessment and navigation, while the fractures can be confirmed on the conventional MPR views.

Regarding the quantitative results, the dice scores for the spine were higher than scores for the ribs. However, the sensitivity and specificity values of the ribs were high. This can be explained by two aspects: (1) the automatic segmentation obtained slightly thicker ribs than the manual segmentation, and (2) the stopping point of the rib (towards the sternum) can be arbitrarily decided, hence including more or less of the costal cartilage (Fig. 7).

As with any clinical application, computation time is a very important factor. Our application runs in an average time of 24 s, as measured in 48 cases in a personal computer with similar specifications to a radiology work-station.

A clinical study using this application has been recently completed. The study found that using UCP allows for similar diagnostic performance with respect to conventional MPRs for the detection of rib fractures, good inter-reader agreement and an important reduction in evaluation time [12].

Axial	Coronal	Sagittal

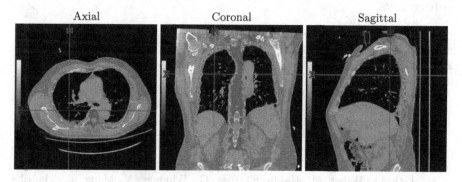

Fig. 7. Case 1 from Table 2. We show the manual labels of the spine (blue) and ribs (green). The differences between the automatic and the manual labels are displayed in yellow. Notice that most of the differences are due to thickness, costal cartilage and morphological operations (specially in the spine). (Color figure online)

Table 2. Summary of quantitative evaluation.

Case	Ribs			Spine		
	DICE	Sensitivity	Specificity	DICE	Sensitivity	Specificity
1	0.692	0.982	0.982	0.843	0.837	0.974
2	0.748	0.994	0.987	0.897	0.944	0.983
3	0.663	0.995	0.981	0.910	0.932	0.989
4	0.758	0.995	0.987	0.936	0.933	0.991
5	0.688	0.996	0.984	0.920	0.933	0.986
6	0.722	0.993	0.985	0.923	0.915	0.990

Masks clipped to the same thorax bounding box for metric calculation.

5 Conclusion

We developed an application that generates a 2D image that displays the entire ribcage. The application was evaluated in 70 chest CT datasets.

The unfolding technique we developed preserves the relative size and location of the ribs and surrounding tissue, providing a natural anatomical reference for the reader. It also demonstrated usefulness to identify other musculoskeletal conditions such us scoliosis, calcified cartilage, bone tumours.

A recent multi-reader clinical study showed that using the specialized UCP view obtains similar diagnostic accuracy as conventional MPRs while reducing the reading time.

References

1. Hospital ambulatory medical care survey: 2013 emergency department summary tables (2013)
2. EuroSafe: Injuries in the European Union: summary of injury statistics for the years 2008–2010 (2013)
3. Calhoon, J., Trinkle, J.: Pathophysiology of chest trauma. Chest Surg. Clin. N. Am. 7(2), 199–211 (1997)
4. Gondim Teixeira, P.A., Blum, A.: Clinical Application of Musculoskeletal CT: Trauma, Oncology, and Postsurgery. MR, pp. 1–27. Springer, Heidelberg (2017). https://doi.org/10.1007/174_2017_25
5. Ringl, H., Lazar, M., Töpker, M., Woitek, R., Prosch, H., Asenbaum, U., Balassy, C., Toth, D., Weber, M., Hajdu, S., Soza, G., Wimmer, A., Mang, T.: The ribs unfolded - a CT visualization algorithm for fast detection of rib fractures: effect on sensitivity and specificity in trauma patients. Eur. Radiol. 25(7), 1865–1874 (2015)
6. Dabbah, M., Murphy, S., Pello, H., Courbon, R., Beveridge, E., Wiseman, S., Wyeth, D., Poole, I.: Detection and location of 127 anatomical landmarks in diverse CT datasets. In: Ourselin, S., Styner, M. (eds.) Proceedings of SPIE Medical Imaging 2014: Image Processing, vol. 9034, p. 903415. SPIE (2014)
7. O'Neil, A.: Image analysis of noisy 3D/4D medical datasets. Ph.D. thesis, Heriot-Watt University, UK (2015)

8. Criminisi, A., Shotton, J. (eds.): Decision Forests for Computer Vision and Medical Image Analysis. Advances in Computer Vision and Pattern Recognition. Springer, London (2013)
9. Dalal, N., Triggs, B.: Histograms of oriented gradients for human detection. In: Proceedings of IEEE Conference on Computer Vision and Pattern Recognition - CVPR 2005, vol. 1, pp. 886–893. IEEE (2005)
10. Crum, W., Griffin, L., Hill, D., Hawkes, D.: Zen and the art of medical image registration: correspondence, homology, and quality. NeuroImage **20**(3), 1425–1437 (2003)
11. Frangi, A.F., Niessen, W.J., Vincken, K.L., Viergever, M.A.: Multiscale vessel enhancement filtering. In: Wells, W.M., Colchester, A., Delp, S. (eds.) MICCAI 1998. LNCS, vol. 1496, pp. 130–137. Springer, Heidelberg (1998). https://doi.org/ 10.1007/BFb0056195
12. Urbaneja, A., De Verbizier, J., Formery, A., Tobon-Gomez, C., Nace, L., Blum, A., Gondim Teixeira, P.: Automatic rib cage unfolding with CT cylindrical projection reformat in polytraumatized patients for rib fracture detection and characterization: diagnostic performance and clinical application (Under review)

3D Cobb Angle Measurements from Scoliotic Mesh Models with Varying Face-Vertex Density

Uroš Petković[1], Robert Korez[1($\boxtimes$)], Stefan Parent[2],
Samuel Kadoury[3], and Tomaž Vrtovec[1]

[1] Faculty of Electrical Engineering, University of Ljubljana, Ljubljana, Slovenia
robert.korez@fe.uni-lj.si
[2] CHU Sainte-Justine, University of Montréal, Montreal, Canada
[3] CHU Sainte-Justine, Polytechnique Montréal, Montreal, Canada

Abstract. To evaluate spinal deformities, the Cobb angle is the main diagnostic parameter that is usually measured on two-dimensional coronal radiographic (X-ray) images. In this paper, we propose a method for the evaluation of the three-dimensional (3D) Cobb angle from 3D spine mesh models with varying face-vertex density. For the upper-end and lower-end vertebra mesh models, the location of the vertebral body center and mesh faces that belong to the vertebral body surface are identified by unsupervised classification of mesh faces of the vertebral body, which serve only as training data, and subsequent supervised classification of all mesh faces. Adjacent mesh faces are then labeled with the same class, and after comparison to mesh faces in the training data, we label the mesh faces of the superior and inferior vertebral endplate. Finally, planes are fitted to the superior endplate of the upper-end vertebra and the inferior endplate of the lower-end vertebra, which define the 3D Cobb angle. The method was tested on 60 triangular mesh models of the scoliotic spine, and each mesh model was generated at 17 different face-vertex densities. For meshes with the mean face edge length below 6 mm, the proposed method was accurate, with the mean absolute error of $3.0°$ and the corresponding standard deviation of $2.2°$ when compared to reference measurements.

Keywords: Spine modeling · Adolescent idiopathic scoliosis
Triangular mesh models · Automated measurements

1 Introduction

Scoliosis is one of the most common spinal deformities, described as an abnormal lateral and rotational curvature of the spine [1]. One of the earliest methods for the quantitative evaluation of spinal curvature was proposed by Cobb in 1948 [2], and is referred to as the Cobb angle. It is usually evaluated from two-dimensional (2D) anteroposterior radiographic (X-ray) images of the spine as the angle between the line along the superior endplate of the upper-end vertebra and

© Springer International Publishing AG 2018
B. Glocker et al. (Eds.): MSKI 2017, LNCS 10734, pp. 48–58, 2018.
https://doi.org/10.1007/978-3-319-74113-0_5

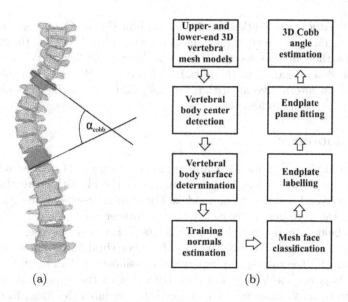

(a)   (b)

Fig. 1. (a) An illustration of the Cobb angle measurement between the superior end-plate of the upper-end vertebra and the inferior endplate of the lower-end vertebra. (b) A flowchart of the proposed algorithm. The inputs of the algorithm are triangular mesh models of the upper-end and lower-end vertebra. For each model we estimate the parameters of the planes that are fitted to superior and inferior endplate of the upper-end and lower-end vertebra, respectively, and the Cobb angle is then estimated from the normal vectors of the corresponding planes.

the line along the inferior endplate of the lower-end vertebra of the deformity (Fig. 1(a)). Although several other methods for quantitative evaluation of spinal curvature have been proposed since [3], the Cobb angle is still the most preferred and established diagnostic parameter for evaluating scoliotic deformities.

Adolescent idiopathic scoliosis is the most common type of scoliosis, and it appears more likely to girls than boys with a 6 : 1 ratio, and with a 10 : 1 ratio in severe cases [4]. The main diagnostic criterion for scoliosis is that the Cobb angle exceeds $10°$ on an anteroposterior spine radiograph. Nowadays, however, with the availability and common usage of three-dimensional (3D) imaging techniques, such as computed tomography (CT) or magnetic resonance (MR), measurements of the Cobb angle are often performed in 3D, which proved to be superior to measurements performed in 2D [3]. To address this issue, planes are, instead of lines, defined along the vertebral endplates, which may be very challenging considering the 3D nature of the images and a relatively complex structure of the spine. On the other hand, automated measurements based on image analysis and processing techniques usually require prior segmentation of vertebrae to perform quantitative measurements. As the results of vertebra segmentation are binary masks that can be represented as triangular mesh models in 3D, it is also valuable to develop algorithms that perform measurements based on 3D mesh models.

Recently, Huo et al. [5] described a method for the 3D Cobb angle measurement from CT images using a mesh model of the spine. However, their method is limited by the manual selection of end vertebrae of the deformity as well as by the manual determination of the initial seed vertex of the mesh. In this paper, we propose an alternative algorithm for the evaluation of the 3D Cobb angle from 3D spine mesh models.

2   Methodology

The proposed algorithm for 3D Cobb angle measurement is divided into seven steps that are shown in Fig. 1(b). The inputs of the algorithm are the upper-end and lower-end vertebra mesh models. For each mesh model we estimate the location of the vertebral body center that is further used to identify the mesh faces that belong to the vertebral body surface. For this purpose, we perform unsupervised classification of mesh faces of the vertebral body that serve only as training data for the subsequent supervised classification of all mesh faces of the vertebra. Adjacent mesh faces are then labeled with the same class, and after comparison to mesh faces in the training data, we label the mesh faces of the superior and inferior vertebral endplate. Finally, planes are fitted to the superior endplate of the upper-end vertebra and the inferior endplate of the lower-end vertebra, which define the 3D Cobb angle.

2.1   Vertebral Body Center Detection

The proposed detection of the vertebral body center is, with the difference that it is adapted for a 3D mesh model, based on the work of Štern et al. [6], who proposed an automated algorithm for the detection of the spinal centerline in CT and MR spine images. As a 3D mesh model of the vertebral body is a closed surface, any line orthogonal to any mesh face intersects with the vertebral surface at least twice, i.e. in a pair of two opposite faces that intersect with this line when it passes inside and outside of the vertebral body. As the vertebral body is approximately a cylindrical structure, these opposite mesh faces have normal vectors with approximately opposite directions. Moreover, it is expected that the centerline of the vertebral body is in the middle of each line connecting any two opposite vertebral body mesh faces. However, as an arbitrary line can intersect with the vertebral surface more than twice (i.e. passes further through pedicles and processes), more candidates for the opposite face can exist.

The 3D mesh model of the k-th vertebra is a triangular mesh structure composed of a vertex set V_k and a face set F_k:

$$V_k = \left\{ v_i \mid i = 1, 2, \ldots, N_v \right\},$$
$$F_k = \left\{ f_i \mid i = 1, 2, \ldots, N_f \right\}, \quad f_i = \left\{ v_p, v_q, v_r \right\}. \tag{1}$$

For each mesh face f_i we perform a search in 3D for the opposite mesh face f_i^*, and the candidates for the opposite mesh face are all faces $f_j \in F_{C,i}$ that fulfill the following three criteria:

- normal vector n_j of the candidate opposite face f_j is oriented in the approximate opposite direction of normal vector n_i of face f_i;
- the Euclidean distance from the center c_i of the face f_i to c_j is between $d_{vb,min}$ and $d_{vb,max}$;
- the Euclidean distance from c_j to line $l_i = c_i + t \cdot n_i$, $t \in \mathbb{R}$, is less then $r_{vb,min}$.

Among all candidates in $F_{C,i}$, the opposite mesh face f_i^* is the one that yields the minimal dot product between normal vectors n_i and n_j of faces f_i and f_j, respectively:

$$f_i^* = \arg \min_{n_j \to f_j} \Big(\mathrm{dot}(n_i, n_j) \Big), \quad j = 1, 2, \ldots, J, \tag{2}$$

where J is the number of candidate mesh faces in $F_{C,i}$. The vertebral body center is located where the lines connecting every pair $\{f_i, f_i^*\}$ of opposite mesh faces most often intersect. For the purpose of finding the location of these intersections, a new 3D image is initialized with zero values in the same coordinate system as the observed vertebra – the 3D accumulator A. Each line connecting a pair of opposite mesh faces $\{f_i, f_i^*\}$ is first transformed with the Bresenham algorithm [7] to determine M discrete points $p_m = (x_m, y_m, z_m)$, $m = 1, 2, \ldots, M$, along the line, and then assigned a weighting function, which is normally distributed according to the Euclidian distance D between the centers c_i and c_i^* of the opposite mesh faces, and scaled by the dot product $\mathrm{dot}(n_i, n_i^*)$ between the corresponding normal vectors n_i and n_i^*. The 3D accumulator value $A(p_m)$ is then increased by the value of the weighting function at each point p_m, $m = 1, 2, \ldots, M$, along the connecting line:

$$A(p_m) = A(p_m) - \mathrm{dot}(n_i, n_i^*) \cdot \exp\left(-\frac{(d(c_i, p_m) - D/2)^2}{2(D/6)^2} \right), \tag{3}$$

where $d(c_i, p_m)$ is the Euclidian distance between c_i and p_m. The resulting 3D accumulator A represents a probability map of likelihoods of image voxels to belong to the vertebral body center. However, the highest likelihoods may be located also within the vertebral processes due to their cylindrical shape. To address this issue, the 3D accumulator is filtered with a mean filter of size $K_X \times K_Y \times K_Z$, determined according to the minimal average size of the human vertebral body. The center of the vertebral body c_b is identified as the voxel with the highest filtered value of the 3D accumulator.

2.2   Superior and Inferior Endplate Labeling

Mesh vertices are first transformed from the image-based coordinate system V to the coordinate system of the mesh V^* by means of the principal component analysis (PCA). Vectors $\{e_x^*, e_y^*, e_z^*\}$ that define the new coordinate system are principal components estimated by PCA, which rotates the vertebra mesh model so that e_z^* is nearly parallel with normal vectors to the vertebral body endplates.

For the purpose of labeling the superior and inferior endplate of the given 3D vertebra mesh model, mesh faces that belong to the vertebral body surface have to be identified. By following a set of rays that are represented as cylinders originating from the detected vertebral body center, we can identify whether the vertebral body center is located within these cylinders. By using the spherical Fibonacci mapping, we first yield a set of points on a unit sphere with a nearly uniform distribution. This point set represents unit vectors of the set of rays, and each unit vector defines the orientation of the corresponding cylinder of radius r_c and height h_c, where h_c is the maximum Euclidean distance from the detected vertebral body center c_b. As mesh faces $f_{cyl,j} \in F_{cyl}$ with corresponding centers $c_{cyl,j}$ that are located within the cylinder are also candidates for the vertebral body surface, we select for each i-th ray face $f_{body,i}$, which is the face with the minimal Euclidean distance between its center and the detected vertebral body center c_b:

$$f_{body,i} = \underset{c_{cyl,i} \to f_{cyl,i}}{\arg \min} \left(d(c_b, c_{cyl,j}) \right), \quad j = 1, 2, \ldots, J. \tag{4}$$

The resulting mesh faces $f_{body,i} \in F_{body}$ represent the boundaries of the vertebral body, i.e. its surface.

However, as the vertebral body is not a fully closed surface, some faces may not belong to the vertebral body but to other vertebral structures. On the other hand, there are mesh faces of the vertebral body that may not be detected. We can predict where the vertebral body surface is by least square ellipsoid fitting to the set of centroids C_{body} of mesh faces F_{body} in the PCA-based coordinate system, resulting in three eigenvectors $\{e_1, e_2, e_3\}$ and ellipsoid radii $\{r_1, r_2, r_3\}$. Due to the elliptical shape of vertebral endplates, ellipsoid fitting is most accurate in the $X^* - Y^*$ plane. From the cross products of all pairs of eigenvectors, we find the pair for which its cross product is most parallel to the Z^*-axis, i.e. to the unit vector $(0, 0, 1)$, by:

$$\{e_i^*, e_j^*\} = \underset{\{e_i, e_j\}}{\arg \max} \left(|\mathrm{dot}\,(\mathrm{cross}(e_i, e_j), (0, 0, 1))| \right), \quad i, j \in \{1, 2, 3\}, \quad i \neq j. \tag{5}$$

From the projecting ellipse, defined by eigenvectors $\{e_i^*, e_j^*\}$ and corresponding radii $\{r_i^*, r_j^*\}$ to the $X^* - Y^*$ plane, we determine the vertebral body surface. Each mesh $f_{body,i} \in F_{body}$ (4), for which the projection of the center $c_{body,i}^*$ to the $X^* - Y^*$ plane is located within the projecting ellipse, is included the training set of mesh faces F_{train} for the determination of vertebral endplates (Fig. 2(a)).

Mesh faces F_{train} (5) can be, again by assuming that the vertebral body is cylindrically shaped, classified in three groups: faces $F_{B,TOP}$ of the top elliptical planar surface (i.e. the superior endplate), faces $F_{B,BOTTOM}$ of the bottom elliptical planar surface (i.e. the inferior endplate), and faces $F_{B,SIDE}$ of the curved surface (i.e. the vertebral body wall). If the main axis of the cylinder representing the vertebral body is aligned with the direction of the Z^* axis, then normal vectors $(n_{B,x}^*, n_{B,y}^*, n_{B,z}^*)$ of $F_{B,TOP}$, $F_{B,BOTTOM}$ and $F_{B,SIDE}$ are represented by $(0, 0, 1)$, $(0, 0, -1)$ and $(x^*, y^*, 0)$, respectively. The appropriate feature for classification of mesh faces F_{train} is therefore $n_{B,z}^*$, i.e. the Z^* component of

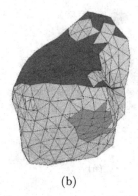

(a)   (b)

Fig. 2. (a) An illustration of mesh faces F_{body} (green and blue) and F_{train} (gray and blue). [Note that the blue color represents the intersection of F_{body} and F_{train}.] (b) An illustration of mesh faces $F_{B,TOP}$ (blue), $F_{B,BOTTOM}$ (green) and $F_{B,SIDE}$ (gray) estimated with k-Means++. (Color figure online)

the normal vector, which is performed by the unsupervised learning method k-Means++ [8]. However, as the vertebral body is not perfectly cylindrical and not perfectly aligned with the Z^* axis, values $n^*_{B,z}$ are arranged around corresponding cluster centers with some variance. To avoid poor clustering, we seed the initial values of clusters by choosing $(1, -1, 0)$ for the initial cluster centers as the main axis of the vertebral body is nearly aligned with the Z^* axis. To emphasize the distances between cluster centers, we transform $n^*_{B,z} \to n'_{B,z}$ with a function $f:\ \ n'_{B,z} = f(n^*_{B,z})$, which should be an odd function to preserve the sign of $n^*_{B,z}$. By applying k-Means++ classification we therefore yield three clusters and corresponding cluster centers. The cluster with the highest value of the cluster center represents faces $F_{B,TOP}$, while the cluster with lowest value of the cluster center represents faces $F_{B,BOTTOM}$ (Fig. 2(b)).

In the next step, we classify mesh faces that belong to the whole vertebra in sets $F_{VB,TOP}$, $F_{VB,BOTTOM}$ and $F_{VB,SIDE}$ according to $n'_{VB,z}$ (Fig. 3(a)). By applying a linear classifier, adjacent faces (i.e. faces that share a common edge) that belong to the same class are collected into groups of faces $F_{A,1}, F_{A,2}, \ldots, F_{A,J}$. The groups that results in the largest number of adjacent faces from the training data represent the superior and inferior endplate (Fig. 3(b)):

$$F_{SUP} = \arg \max_{F_{A,j}} \Big(\text{count}(F_{A,j} \cap F_{B,TOP}) \Big), \quad j = 1, 2, \ldots, J,$$

$$F_{INF} = \arg \max_{F_{A,j}} \Big(\text{count}(F_{A,j} \cap F_{B,BOTTOM}) \Big), \quad j = 1, 2, \ldots, J. \tag{6}$$

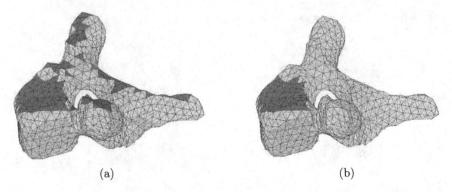

(a)   (b)

Fig. 3. (a) An illustration of mesh faces $F_{VB,TOP}$ (blue), $F_{VB,BOTTOM}$ (green) and $F_{VB,SIDE}$ that were estimated with a linear classifier. (b) An illustration of mesh faces F_{SUP} (blue) and F_{INF} (green) estimated from faces $F_{VB,TOP}$ and $F_{VB,SIDE}$. (Color figure online)

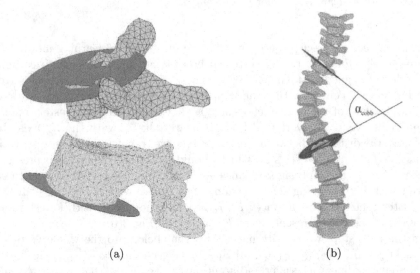

(a)   (b)

Fig. 4. (a) An illustration of the plane estimated with the random sample consensus (RANSAC) algorithm on mesh faces F_{SUP} of the superior endplate of the upper-end vertebra (top) and F_{INF} of the inferior endplate of the lower-end vertebra (bottom). (b) An illustration of the 3D Cobb angle measurement.

2.3   3D Cobb Angle Measurement

By applying the random sample consensus (RANSAC) algorithm [9] with error tolerance e_d on mesh faces F_{SUP} and F_{INF} (6), we estimate the parameters of the planes along the superior endplate of the upper-end vertebra (Fig. 4(a)) and the inferior endplate of the lower-end vertebra, resulting in normal vectors n_{sup} and n_{inf}, respectively. The 3D Cobb angle is finally measured as (Fig. 4(b)):

$$\alpha_{Cobb} = \arccos\left(\text{dot}(\boldsymbol{n}'_{sup}, \boldsymbol{n}'_{inf})\right), \tag{7}$$

where $\boldsymbol{n}'_{sup}$ is the projection of $\boldsymbol{n}_{sup}$ to the $Y-Z$ plane of the upper-end vertebra, and $\boldsymbol{n}'_{inf}$ is the projection of vector $\boldsymbol{n}_{inf}$ to the $Y-Z$ plane of the lower-end vertebra.

3   Experiments and Results

The performance of the proposed method was evaluated on 60 spines that were diagnosed with adolescent idiopathic scoliosis (Sainte-Justine Hospital Research Center, Montréal, Quebec, Canada), with mean reference Cobb angle measurements of 48.8° (range: 15.2–80.9°). The spines were imaged with biplanar radiography and corresponding triangular mesh models between vertebral levels T1 and L5 were obtained by biplanar stereo-reconstruction [10] and kriging interpolation method [11]. For each spine, 17 mesh models with different face-vertex density (i.e. with a different mean face edge length ranging from 1.58 to 6.85 mm) were generated and used for the performance evaluation.

For the vertebral body center detection (Sect. 2.1), $d_{vb,min} = 12\,\text{mm}$, $d_{vb,max} = 60\,\text{mm}$, $r_{vb,min} = 1.2 \times$ mean face edge length were used for the opposite mesh face determination, and mean filter of size $K_X \times K_Y \times K_Z = 15 \times 9 \times 9\,\text{mm}^3$ for the accumulation of lines between the opposite mesh faces. For superior and inferior endplate labeling (Sect. 2.2), $r_c = 1.2 \times$ mean face edge length for cylinders representing rays, function $f: n'_{B,z} = f(n^*_{B,z}) = (n^*_{B,z})^5$ for emphasizing the distances between cluster centers, and $e_d = 1.35\,\text{mm}$ for RANSAC error tolerance.

The proposed method was successfully applied to the 3D mesh models of all 60 spines. Detailed statistical analysis of the obtained results is presented in Table 1.

4   Discussion

In this work, we described a semi-automated method for measuring the Cobb angle from 3D mesh models of the spine. The only manual input to the method is the selection of the upper-end and lower-end vertebra in the (scoliotic) deformity. Apart from that, the method is fully automated, and, according to the obtained results, yields relatively accurate 3D Cobb angle measurements.

From the results in Table 1 we can conclude that the results of the proposed method are comparable to reference manual measurements at different face-vertex densities that correspond to the mean face edge length ranging between 1.58 and 5.90 mm, as the comparison resulted in an average mean absolute error (MAE) of 3.0° and corresponding standard deviation (SD) of 2.2°. Once the mean face edge length exceeds approximately 6 mm, the agreement with reference measurements is lower, which can be observed in a higher MAE, maximal error and the corresponding SD. It appears that at such face-vertex density there

Table 1. Statistical analysis of the obtained 3D Cobb angle measurements at different mean face edge lengths of corresponding 3D spine mesh models, and comparison against reference Cobb angle measurements.

$N = 60$ scoliotic spines		Comparison to reference Cobb angles		
Mean face edge length (mm)	Mean Cobb angle (°)	Mean absolute error (°)	Maximal error (°)	Standard deviation (°)
1.58	48.0	2.9	7.7	2.1
1.91	48.3	3.2	9.0	2.1
2.26	48.2	3.0	7.1	2.0
2.60	48.1	3.1	8.1	1.9
2.93	48.1	2.7	7.6	2.0
3.28	48.3	2.8	9.4	2.0
3.61	47.9	2.7	9.0	2.0
3.94	48.5	2.9	8.4	2.0
4.27	48.7	2.8	10.3	2.1
4.60	48.5	3.3	9.7	2.2
4.93	48.5	3.3	9.0	2.4
5.25	48.9	2.8	8.7	2.3
5.57	47.9	2.9	10.2	2.3
5.90	48.1	3.5	11.8	2.9
6.21	49.0	4.0	25.4	4.0
6.53	48.5	4.0	13.7	3.0
6.85	47.0	4.1	31.3	4.7

are few spine mesh models in the database that do not fit well the vertebral body. Considering that the smallest vertebral body is T1 with a mean width of 23.5 mm, length of 15.0 mm and height of 15.1 mm height for females [12], it is expected the that the mesh model with a mean face edge length in the range of vertebral body dimensions would be inaccurate, and consequently the resulting Cobb angle measurements would also be incorrect. Nevertheless, the accuracy and robustness of the proposed method at lower face-vertex densities, i.e. of up to 6 mm of face edge length, are valuable in terms of reducing the running time of the algorithm due to its quadratic time complexity. On average, the running time was estimated to 40 s (Intel(R) Core(TM) i7 - 4720HQ processor) for a single spine mesh model at the highest face-vertex density.

A method that performs Cobb angle measurements from 3D mesh models of the spine was also proposed by Huo et al. [5], however, the obtained results cannot be directly compared to their method due to the different spine database, different techniques for mesh model reconstruction, and different face-vertex densities of the mesh models. However, Huo et al. obtained SD between 4.56 and 4.67° when measuring the Cobb angle on a database of 22 spines, which is higher than SD of around 2.0° that was obtained by the proposed method. Nevertheless, the most noticeable difference is in the level of automation of both methods. While both methods require manual identification of the upper-end and lower-end vertebrae, the method of Huo et al. additionally requires manual selection of the seed vertex to estimate the parameters of each plane that represents a vertebral endplate. The proposed method, on the other hand, is after the identification of the upper-end and lower-end vertebrae completely automated.

5   Conclusion

We presented a method for measuring the 3D Cobb angle from a 3D triangular mesh model of the spine. The results obtained on a database for 60 scoliotic spines indicate that the method is relatively accurate and robust, and up to a certain level also relatively insensitive to the face-vertex density of the spine mesh model.

Acknowledgements. This work was supported by the Slovenian Research Agency under grants P2-0232, J2-5473, J7-6781 and J2-7118.

References

1. Stedman's Medical Dictionary. http://www.medilexicon.com/dictionary/80286. Accessed 4 June 2017
2. Cobb, J.: Outline for the study of scoliosis. Am. Acad. Orthop. Surg. Instr. Course Lect. **5**, 261–275 (1948)
3. Vrtovec, T., Pernuš, F., Likar, B.: A review of methods for quantitative evaluation of spinal curvature. Eur. Spine J. **18**(5), 593–607 (2009)
4. Trobisch, P., Suess, O., Schwab, F.: Idiopathic scoliosis. Dtsch. Arztebl. Int. **107**(49), 875–884 (2010)
5. Huo, X., Tan, J., Qian, J., Cheng, L., Jing, J., Shao, K., Li, B.: An integrative framework for 3D Cobb angle measurement on CT images. Comput. Biol. Med. **82**, 111–118 (2017)
6. Štern, D., Likar, B., Pernuš, F., Vrtovec, T.: Automated detection of spinal centrelines, vertebral bodies and intervertebral discs in CT and MR images of lumbar spine. Phys. Med. Biol. **55**(1), 247–264 (2010)
7. Bresenham, J.: Algorithm for computer control of a digital plotter. IBM Syst. J. **4**(1), 25–30 (1965)
8. Arthur, D., Vassilvitskii, S.: k-means++: the advantages of careful seeding. In: Proceedings of 18th Annual ACM-SIAM Symposium on Discrete Algorithms - SODA 2007, pp. 1027–1035. SIAM (2007)
9. Fischler, M., Bolles, R.: Random sample consensus: a paradigm for model fitting with applications to image analysis and automated cartography. Commun. ACM **24**(6), 381–395 (1965)
10. Kadoury, S., Cheriet, F., Laporte, C., Labelle, H.: A versatile 3-D reconstruction system of the spine and pelvis for clinical assessment of spinal deformities. Commun. ACM **45**(6), 591–602 (2007)

11. Kadoury, S., Cheriet, F., Labelle, H.: Personalized X-ray 3-D reconstruction of the scoliotic spine from hybrid statistical and image-based models. IEEE Trans. Med. Imaging **28**(9), 1422–1435 (2009)
12. Masharawi, Y., Salame, K., Mirovsky, Y., Peleg, S., Dar, G., Stemberg, N., Hershkovitz, I.: Vertebral body shape variation in the thoracic and lumbar spine: characterization of its asymmetry and wedging. Clin. Anat. **21**(1), 46–54 (2008)

Automatic Localization of the Lumbar Vertebral Landmarks in CT Images with Context Features

Dimitrios Damopoulos[1]([✉]), Ben Glocker[2], and Guoyan Zheng[1]

[1] Institute for Surgical Technology and Biomechanics,
University of Bern, Bern, Switzerland
dimitrios.damopoulos@istb.unibe.ch
[2] Faculty of Engineering, Imperial College London, London, UK

Abstract. A recent research direction for the localization of anatomical landmarks with learning-based methods is to explore ways to enrich the trained models with context information. Lately, the addition of context features in regression-based approaches has been tried in the literature. In this work, a method is presented for the addition of context features in a regression setting where the locations of many vertebral landmarks are regressed all at once. As this method relies on the knowledge of the centers of the vertebral bodies (VBs), an automatic, endplate-based approach for the localization of the VB centers is also presented. The proposed methods are evaluated on a dataset of 28 lumbar-focused computed tomography images. The VB localization method detects all of the lumbar VBs of the testing set with a mean localization error of 3.2 mm. The multi-landmark localization method is tested on the task of localizing the tips of all the inferior articular processes of the lumbar vertebrae, in addition to their VB centers. The proposed method detects these landmarks with a mean localization error of 3.0 mm.

Keywords: Regression · Localization · Lumbar · Vertebral body
Inferior articular process

1 Introduction

Back pain in general and low back pain in particular constitutes a major public health problem, exhibiting epidemic proportions [1]. The computer-assisted diagnosis of pathologies of the lumbar spine involves the analysis of images coming from a series of standard imaging modalities. Computed tomography (CT) images can be used for the diagnosis of spondylolysis, spondylolisthesis and osteoporosis, as this imaging modality permits the measurement of the bone mineral density of the vertebral bodies (VBs). This work focuses on the task of the localization of the lumbar VBs in CT images and the localization of key land-marks on the vertebral processes.

© Springer International Publishing AG 2018
B. Glocker et al. (Eds.): MSKI 2017, LNCS 10734, pp. 59–71, 2018.
https://doi.org/10.1007/978-3-319-74113-0_6

The proposed framework can facilitate subsequent automated procedures, such as the segmentation of the vertebrae, the automatic assessment of skeletal vertebral pathologies and the analysis of the spinal shape. In the case of vertebral segmentation, a large number of proposed methods employ some form of active shape models or active appearance models [2, 3]. The initialization step of these model-based approaches is typically based on the localization of the centers of the VBs. Using more landmarks than just the center of the VBs can add robustness to this initialization step. Furthermore, the detection of vertebral landmarks can function as the building block for the automated assessment of pathologies concerning the global spinal shape (scoliosis, lordosis) and the grading of spondylolisthesis: In [4], an automated method for the measurement of spondylolisthesis was presented, based on the identification of the endplate regions. For this application, the localization of the edges of the endplates in the coronal direction could provide a more direct method for the measurement of the anterior shift.

Localization of anatomical landmarks is a fundamental problem in medical image analysis and a plethora of methods have been proposed in the literature. In recent years, these tend to be based on machine learning tools and they can be roughly categorized into classification-based methods and regression-based methods. A popular research direction is the addition of context information in the model that is constructed by these learning-based methods. For the problem of object segmentation, a principled method for achieving so is the auto-context framework [5]. Recently, there have been attempts to apply this framework for the localization of landmarks with random forest regressors. In particular, in [6] the authors showed that the extraction of context features from the distance maps of a traditional random forest regressor can improve the landmark localization accuracy. Following this research direction, in the present work this method of adding context information is applied to a multiple-landmark localization task, where the locations of more than one landmark are regressed all at once by random forest regressors. We show that the proposed method is able to detect robustly key landmarks of the vertebrae, despite the similar appearance of neigh-boring vertebra. As the proposed method assumes that the centers of the VBs have been already detected, we also present an endplate-based method for the detection of the lumbar VB centers. We evaluate both of the methods in a dataset of 28 lumbar-focused CT images.

2 Method

The proposed framework consists of two modules. The first module deals with the localization of the VBs and the estimation of the pose of the vertebrae. It performs this task via the detection of the vertebral endplates on a spline-based unwrapping of the input image. The second module deals with the localization of key landmarks of the vertebrae, based on the estimation of the VB centers and the vertebral pose by the first module. It employs two levels of random forest regressors. The two modules are described in Sects. 2.1 and 2.2. For the rest of this section, it is assumed that a number of CT images of the lumbar spine are available for training. A training image will be referred to using the notation:

$$I_i : \ \Omega_i \subset \mathbb{R}^3 \to \mathbb{R}, \quad i \in \{1, \ldots, N\}. \tag{1}$$

A testing image will be denoted with I_T. Every training image is accompanied with annotations of the centers of all the VBs within the field of view. We denote the set of the annotations of the training image I_i with:

$$A_i = \big\{(\boldsymbol{c}_1, v_1), \ldots, (\boldsymbol{c}_{m_i}, v_{m_i})\big\}, \tag{2}$$

where $\boldsymbol{c}_j \in \Omega_i$, $v_j \in \mathcal{L}$, $\mathcal{L} = \{S_2, S_1, L_5, L_4, L_3, L_2, L_1, T_12, T_11, T_10\}$. We reduce the set of the spinal levels to T10, since the dataset that we used for the experiments does not capture any vertebrae at higher spinal levels. Finally, it is assumed that the field of view covers at least the S1 – L1 region.

2.1 Localization of Vertebral Bodies and Estimation of Their Pose

The localization of the lumbar VBs is performed in four steps, summarized in Fig. 1. Firstly, a first-level detection of the centers is performed using the method proposed in [7]. This method employs a random forest classifier and in the present work it is used for a first-level detection of the VB centers of the levels $\mathcal{L}$. At training time, it constructs a label-map for every training image,

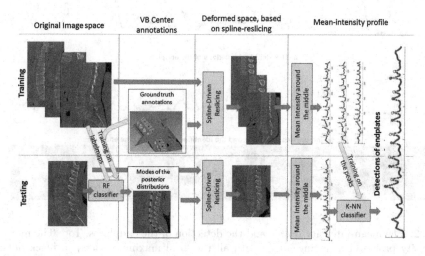

Fig. 1. A flowchart of the steps of proposed pipeline for the localization of the lumbar vertebral bodies (VBs). From left to right: a first-level detection of the VB centers is performed using the method of [7]; the original image is resliced along the curve that passes through the first-level detections; a mean-intensity profile is calculated along the axial center of the resliced image and the peaks of the mean-intensity profile that correspond to endplate locations are identified using a k-nearest neighbors classifier.

using the ground-truth annotations of the VB centers. A random forest multi-label classifier is trained on the label-maps, using as features the mean intensity of displayed boxes (Haar-like features). At testing time, the generated probability map for every vertebral level is assumed to follow a normal distribution. The mode of the distribution for every generated probability map separately is retrieved with the mean-shift mode-seeking algorithm [8].

Secondly, the original CT image is resliced along the curve that passes through a set of VB center locations by performing an image deformation known as *curved planar reformation*[9]. At training time, these locations are the ground truth VB center annotations whereas at testing time they are the first-level VB center detections. The reslicing is carried out using the method of [10], which firstly calculates a B-spline that passes through the first-level detections and then constructs a local coordinate system (LCS) on every point of the B-spline. In the rest of this paper, the resulting deformed image will be referred to as the *spline-unwrapped image*.

Thirdly, for every slice of the spline-unwrapped image, the mean intensity of a region around the middle point of the slice is calculated. The result of this operation is a univariate signal, referred to as the mean-intensity profile (shown in the top plot of Fig. 2). For the training phase, it is denoted with $s_i : O_i \subset \mathbb{N} \to \mathbb{R}$. For a testing image, it is denoted with s_T.

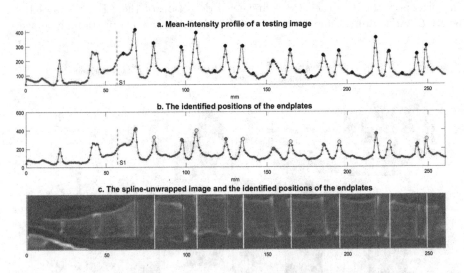

Fig. 2. The mean-intensity profile and the detection of the endplates. Top: The mean-intensity profile of a testing image with all the local maxima (peaks) in black dots; Middle: The out-put of the k-nearest neighbors classifier, which classifies the peaks in "endplate" and "non-endplate". Bottom: The same endplate positions, on the spline-unwrapped image. The prediction of the vertebral body center is the average position of the bottom and top endplate on every lumbar level.

Lastly, the locations of VB centers are inferred from the positions of the vertebral endplates in the mean-intensity profile, using an approach very similar to those of [11,12]. Unlike [11], we do not attempt to detect periodic patterns in the mean intensity profile but we just locate its local maxima. As in [12], the basic observation for the detection of the endplates is that their locations correspond to local maxima (peaks) in the mean-intensity profile. Unlike [12], we do not make any assumptions concerning the orthogonal symmetry of the vertebrae in order to fine tune the VB center estimations and we just average the locations of the bottom and top endplates. Furthermore, we attempt to add robustness to the identification of the peaks that correspond to endplates by training a k-nearest neighbors classifier specifically for this task. In detail:

- **At training time**, for every mean-intensity profile s_i, we locate the positions of those peaks $P_i = \{p_1, \ldots, p_{q_i}\}$, $p_1 \in O_i$ which are anatomically superior to the annotation c_{S_1}. Hence, S1 is used as an anchor vertebra. For every peak position p_ξ we compute three simple features: (a) the value of the peak $s_i(p_\xi)$; (b) its left prominence e_ξ and (c) its right prominence E_ξ. The left prominence is defined as:

$$e_\xi = \max \left\{ s_i(p_\xi) - s_i(\rho), \rho \in O_i, s_i \nearrow [\rho, p_\xi] \right\}, \tag{3}$$

where the $\nearrow$ denotes that s_i is increasing in the specified interval. The right prominence E_ξ is defined symmetrically. A binary label is provided for every peak, marking whether it corresponds to an endplate position or not. A k-nearest neighbors classifier is fit to this training set.
- **At testing time**, the peaks of mean-intensity profile s_T after the S1 first-level detection are identified (Fig. 1) and the three features are computed as in training. The trained k-nearest neighbors classifier classifies these peaks as corresponding to endplates or not. Finally, the estimates for the centers of the lumbar VBs are given by simply averaging the endplate positions. The pose of every vertebra is given by the LCS (computed at the second step) of the point of the B-spline which is closest to the VB center estimation.

2.2   Localization of Vertebral Landmarks

The objective of the second module is to locate a given number of vertebral landmarks on each level of the lumbar spine separately. We are interested in the lumbar spinal levels $\mathcal{L}' = \{L_5, L_4, L_3, L_2, L_1\}$. Let $v \in \mathcal{L}'$ be one such level. For simplicity, it is assumed that same number $M_v = M$ of landmarks is desired to be found on all the levels. Therefore, it is assumed that the annotations B_i^v of the M landmarks of the vertebra at level v of every training image I_i are available. This ordered set of annotations is denoted as:

$$B_i^v = (c_1^v, \ldots, c_M^v), \quad c_j \in \Omega_i. \tag{4}$$

The VB center annotations for the lumbar region of (2) are incorporated in the ordered sets B_i as its first elements, i.e. $c_1^v = c_v$ for all the levels, where c_v is annotation for the VB center. Hence, given a testing image I_T, the task is to localize the M landmarks on each level $v \in \mathcal{L}'$. This is accomplished with two layers of random forest regressors, combined in an auto-context fashion [5]. The two layers are described in detail in the following two sections. The pipeline is summarized in Fig. 3.

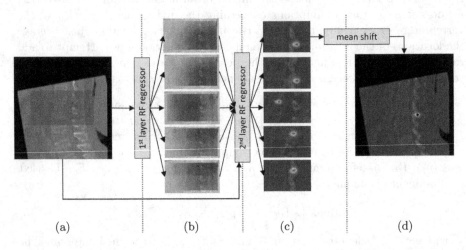

(a)   (b)   (c)   (d)

Fig. 3. Overview of the second module. (a) The image is aligned according the pose of the vertebra and a region of interest around the vertebra is isolated. (b) First layer: a random forest generates the distance maps to the landmarks of this spinal level. (c) Second layer: similarly to the first layer, distance maps are generated by a random forest. The distance maps of the first layer are used as additional images for the calculation of context features. Also, a vote map for every landmark is calculated. (d) The mode of each vote map is located using the mean shift algorithm.

First Layer: Multi-landmark Localization Using Appearance Features.
The first layer employs a traditional multi-landmark regression-based method. One random forest regressor is trained for each lumbar level. Since each of these regressors is being utilized independently of all the others, let's assume that interest is on a specific level $v \in \mathcal{L}'$.

- **At training time**, the images I_i are rotated according to the poses of the vertebrae at level v, so that all the vertebrae at level v are aligned, and a region of interest ROI is constructed around the VB center. The training set is sampled from all the ROIs. For every training sample, the displacements to the M landmarks are computed, hence it is paired with $3 * M$ continuous values. A random forest is trained to regress these displacements. The traditional Haar-like features are used (as in [6,7,13]), which are based on the mean intensity value of randomly displayed boxes. The following feature types are considered:

$$f(x; B_1, B_2, o_1, o_2, s) = \frac{1}{|B_1|} \sum_{y \in B_1} I(x+o_1+y) - \frac{s}{|B_2|} \sum_{y \in B_2} I(x+o_2+y), \quad (5)$$

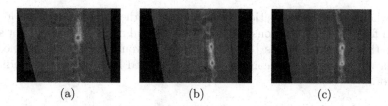

(a)   (b)   (c)

Fig. 4. Illustration of the problem with the single regressor approach on three testing cases. In cases (a) and (c) the level of interest is L1, and in (b) it is L2. The region of interest is represented by a red overlay. The blue-red colormap corresponds to the vote maps. On (a), the vote map retains its maximum value around the correct location. On (b), the vote map still gets its maximum on the correct location (the bottom peak), but it can no longer be considered unimodal. On (c), the problem is clear, as the mode with the highest value (top peak) does not correspond to the ground truth location (bottom peak).

where $s \in \{0,1\}$, B_1, B_2 are the sizes of two 3D boxes and o_1, o_2 are 3D offsets. A specific number of these features is sampled at the beginning of the random forest training and the parameters of the features are sampled uniformly from an interval of allowed values. In each leaf node of the decision trees of the trained random forest, two vectors of dimension $3 * M$ are stored: the mean displacements of the training samples that arrived on this leaf and their variance along every dimension.

- **At testing time**, the first module estimates the VB center of I_T at level v and the relevant pose. Then, I_T is aligned according the detected pose, a ROI is generated around the detected VB center and a testing set is sampled from inside this ROI. In a traditional single-layer approach, every testing sample would be parsed by every tree of the forest and it would cast M votes for the locations of each of the M landmarks. The aggregation of the votes from all the testing samples results in M maps, which in this work will be referred to as *vote maps*. The location of the each of the M landmarks would be inferred from its vote map, via a mode-seeking algorithm. A drawback of this approach is that the vote maps are not guaranteed to be unimodal. In fact, it is to be expected that the vote map will have a high value on not only the target landmark at level v but possibly on the homologous location of neighboring vertebra. This is partially addressed by the fact that only a ROI around the detected VB center of the testing image is considered. However, the problem is not fully eliminated, since it is not possible to know in advance how large this ROI should be. This is illustrated in Fig. 4. The problem is most apparent in Fig. 4(c), where the maximum of the vote map occurs on the wrong level. A mode-seeking algorithm would fail in that case.

Second Layer: Addition of Context Features. The problem of the concurrent appearance of modes on neighboring spinal levels is addressed by the addition of context features. These context features are similar to the ones introduced in [6], where context information is extracted from the distance maps. In [6] one random forest regressor is constructed for every landmark. This would not scale well to the current task, as $|\mathcal{L}'| * M$ regressors would have to be trained on every layer. Therefore, the context features are used here by a multi-landmark regressor.

- **At training time**, every tree of the first layer makes three predictions (one for each spatial dimension) for the displacement of each training sample to each of the M landmarks. The mean value of Euclidean distance of these three predictions over all the trees is called a distance map. At this point, an important decision to be made is which part of the training image should be considered for the computation of the distance maps. A simple choice is to use the same ROI as the one used for the training of the first layer. However, such a setup will bias the second layer into expecting that the VB center lies exactly at the center of the sampling ROI. In order to remove this bias, a modification to the standard Auto-context framework is introduced. For every ground truth annotation c_1^v of the VB centers, W randomly displaced locations are generated:

$$\tilde{c}_{1,w}^v = c_1^v + d_w, \quad d_w \in [-d, d]^3, \quad w \in \{1, \ldots, W\}. \tag{6}$$

The displacements d_w are sampled randomly from the space $[-d, d]^3$. Then, W ROIs $R_w \subseteq \Omega_w$, $w \in \{1, \ldots, W\}$ around each $\tilde{c}_{1,w}^v$ are generated. The regions R_w of the training image I_i are parsed by the random forest of the first layer in order to compute the $W * M$ distance maps $D_{i,w}^m : \Omega_i \to \mathbb{R}^+$. The value of distance maps $D_{i,w}^m$ outside of R_w is set to a fixed, large value. For the training of the second layer, each training image I_i is taken into account

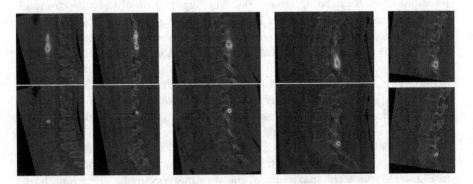

Fig. 5. Qualitative comparison of the voting maps of a single random forest layer (top row) with the voting maps after the second layer of the proposed method (bottom row). From left to right: sagittal cuts of different testing images for levels L1 to L5, respectively. Notice that the images have been automatically aligned around the vertebra of interest. In can be observed that the voting map is more concentrated in the two-layered approach and it is has exactly one mode around the correct landmark location.

W times, each time paired with the M distance maps $D^m_{i,w}$. As in the first layer, a pool of Haar-like features is sampled before the training of the forest starts, with the difference that the intensity image $I(\cdot)$ of (5) can be replaced by one of the $D^m_{i,w}$. When this happens, the resulting Haar-like feature is able to capture context information from the distance maps of the first layer (context feature). The total number of context features is set beforehand as a hyperparameter.

- **At testing time**, the distance maps of the testing image are generated by the first layer, using the same testing ROI as in the first layer. The testing image is paired with the generated distance maps and it is passed to the second layer, so that both appearance features (computed on the original testing image) and context features (computed on the distance maps) can be calculated. The testing pipeline proceeds with the computation of the vote maps. For every testing sample, the vote generated by each tree of the forest for each landmark is taken into account separately, provided that the variance of the displacement is below a certain threshold. As it is illustrated in the second row of Fig. 5, the resulting vote map is unimodal. The mode of every vote map is estimated using the mean-shift algorithm [8]. Finally, the estimated modes are rotated back to the original image space in order to provide the localization of the landmarks.

3   Experiments and Results

3.1   Dataset and Experimental Setup

The proposed methods are evaluated on a dataset of 28 CT images. The intra-slice slice spacing is in the 0.29–0.42 mm range, the inter-slice spacing is 0.7 mm and the slice size is 512×512. All of the images capture at least the S1 – L1 levels, which is typical for scans of the lumbar spine. The thoracic region is captured up to the T10 level some cases. No implants are presented in any of the images. There are cases with mild scoliosis, osteophytes and fractures vertebrae. For every lumbar vertebra, five manual annotations are made: the center of the VB and the tips of the four inferior articular processes. There are four inferior articular process on a typical lumbar vertebra: a bottom-left, a bottom-right, a top-right and a top-left. We will refer to their tips as landmarks A, B, C and D respectively. Sagittal and coronal view of two example annotations for landmarks A and B are shown on Fig. 6(a) and (b).

All of the images are resampled to an isotropic spacing of $1 \times 1 \times 1$ mm. We randomly select 20 images to be used for the training phase of the proposed methods. The held-out eight images will be used for evaluation. The hyperparameters are set through a leave-one-out cross-validation iteration on the training set. The K parameter of the k-nearest neighbors classifier of the first module is set to 15. For the second module, they are as following: for the random forest of the first layer, 50 trees are trained, the size of the feature pool is 10000 and on every node the search space is 200 features. The size of the ROI around every vertebra is $120 \times 150 \times 80$ mm. The training set of every tree is a random 1%

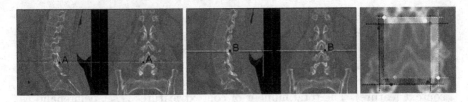

Fig. 6. (a) The sagittal and the coronal views of the annotation of the tip of the bottom-left inferior articular process (landmark A) of an L3 vertebra. (b) The sagittal and coronal views of the annotation of a bottom-right inferior articular process (landmark B) of an L2 vertebra. (c) The three-dimensional bounding boxes of the manual annotations for the inferior articular process (blue dots) and their detections (red dots). The localization errors have been exaggerated. (Color figure online)

subset of the voxels inside the ROIs. At testing time, all the voxels inside the ROI are used. For the second layer, the parameters W, d of (6) are set to 5 and 8 mm, respectively. The size of the feature pool of the random forest is now 11000 features: 10000 intensity-based plus 200 from the each of the five distance maps. For the vote maps, votes with a predicted variance of more than 15 mm in any spatial dimension are ignored.

3.2 Evaluation

For the evaluation of the first module, two metrics are used: (a) the **rate of successful detections** and (b) the displacements to the manual annotations of the VB centers of the lumbar spine (**localization error**). A VB center detection is considered successful when it lies within 10 mm from the respective manual annotation. The detailed evaluation for every lumbar spinal level is presented in Table 1, where the rate of successful detections is labeled as "Id. rate". All of the lumbar VB of the eight testing images are detected successfully. The mean localization error is 3.2 mm, with a standard deviation of 2.0 mm and a median value of 2.8 mm. The evaluation of the first-level detections obtained with the method of [7] is also presented in Table 1.

Table 1. Localization performance of the first module for the vertebral body centers. A detection is considered successful if it lies within 10 mm from the manual annotation (Id. rate). The mean, standard deviation and median of the localization errors are computed on the successful detections only. The first-level detections are the output of the method [7]. The endplate-based detections are the output of the first module.

	First-level detections					Endplate-based detections				
	L1	L2	L3	L4	L5	L1	L2	L3	L4	L5
Id. rate (%)	75.0	62.5	62.5	75.0	100	100	100	100	100	100
Mean (mm)	3.7	6.7	8.1	7.6	5.0	2.8	3.4	3.8	3.1	2.9
Std. (mm)	2.1	3.5	3.3	3.2	1.8	1.3	2.3	1.5	2.6	1.5
Median (mm)	3.4	6.1	6.9	7.6	5.2	2.4	2.4	4.0	1.7	2.7

Table 2. Localization errors of the second module for the five landmarks of L1 – L5. In the case of L4, one testing case has been omitted because it was not possible to annotate all its articular processes due to a vertebral fracture. Hence, there are seven testing images on this spinal level.

	VB center	A	B	C	D	Overall
L1-level landmarks						
Loc. error < 6 mm (%)	100	100	100	100	100	100
Mean (mm)	1.8	2.8	3.0	2.6	3.4	2.7
Std. (mm)	0.6	1.4	1.3	1.1	1.5	1.3
Median (mm)	1.7	2.6	2.7	2.6	2.9	2.7
L2-level landmarks						
Loc. error < 6 mm (%)	100	100	100	100	100	100
Mean (mm)	2.4	2.2	2.1	3.1	2.6	2.5
Std. (mm)	1.1	0.8	0.8	1.2	1.4	1.1
Median (mm)	2.8	2.2	2.0	2.8	2.4	2.3
L3-level landmarks						
Loc. error < 6 mm (%)	100	100	87.5	87.5	100	95.0
Mean (mm)	2.7	3.4	3.7	3.6	2.8	3.2
Std. (mm)	0.9	1.6	1.5	1.9	0.9	1.5
Median (mm)	2.4	3.1	3.1	3.1	2.7	2.9
L4-level landmarks						
Loc. error < 6 mm (%)	100	87.5	87.5	87.5	87.5	88.6
Mean (mm)	1.9	4.0	3.4	3.5	3.4	3.2
Std. (mm)	1.0	1.7	2.3	1.9	2.9	2.2
Median (mm)	1.7	3.2	2.1	3.5	2.4	2.4
L5-level landmarks						
Loc. error < 6 mm (%)	100	75.0	100	100	100	92.5
Mean (mm)	2.7	4.5	3.4	3.4	2.9	3.4
Std. (mm)	1.6	1.6	1.3	1.3	1.1	1.5
Median (mm)	2.4	4.7	3.8	3.3	2.9	3.0

For the evaluation of the second module, the localization error metric is also used. The localization errors for each lumbar level are presented in Table 2, along with the rate of the detections with a localization error of less than 6 mm. Overall, the proposed method achieves a mean localization error of 3.0 mm, with a 1.6 mm standard deviation and a median value of 2.7 mm. 95.4% of the detections have a localization error of below 6 mm. Regarding the training of the second layer, we experimented with removing the randomly displaced ROIs of (6) and train instead using ROIs centered around the VB centers. With that setup, the localization error increases to 3.4 ± 1.8 mm.

Table 3. Dice coefficients for the bounding boxes from the five landmarks over each spinal level.

Dice coefficients	L1	L2	L3	L4	L5	Overall
Mean	0.87	0.90	0.90	0.90	0.87	0.89
Min.	0.80	0.86	0.87	0.80	0.82	0.80
Max.	0.94	0.95	0.96	0.95	0.92	0.96

As an additional metric for the quality of the detections, their bounding boxes are also considered. In particular, the extreme locations of the five landmarks in the each of the three spatial dimensions define six bounding planes and therefore a 3D bounding box. Coronal projections of such bounding boxes are depicted in Fig. 6(c) for both the manual annotations (blue box) and the automatic detections (red box). The evaluation metric is the Dice overlap coefficient of the bounding box of the manual annotations and the bounding box of the detections. The achieved scores on this metric are presented in Table 3. The mean dice coefficient, across all the spinal levels, is 88.8%.

4   Conclusion

The repetitive nature of the spine poses an additional difficult to the task of landmark localization, as neighboring vertebrae often have very similar appearance. However, a fully automatic method for localizing vertebral landmarks is highly desirable, as it can provide as a robust initialization step for model-based segmentation methods and it can facilitate the assessment of certain vertebral pathologies. In this work, a pipeline for the detection of lumbar vertebral landmarks is proposed. The proposed pipeline starts with the detection of VB centers and proceeds with the localization of landmarks on each lumbar level. For evaluation, the pipeline was applied for the localization of the VB centers and the inferior articular processes on a dataset of lumbar-focused CT images. The experimental results suggest that the proposed method can detect reliably the vertebral landmarks on all the levels of the lumbar spine. Even though in our experiments we focused on the articular processes, we expect that the proposed method can be applied for different vertebral landmarks as well, such as key endplate landmarks for the measurement of spondylolisthesis. In the future, we plan to explore such a direction. Future research also includes the more extensive evaluation of the proposed methods on larger datasets and the investigation of ways to improve the localization accuracy, for example by fine-tuning the detections in a multi-scale fashion and by introducing context features from different vertebral levels.

References

1. Reginster, J.: The prevalence and burden of arthritis. Rheumatology **41**(Supp 1), 3–6 (2002)
2. Al Arif, S.M.M.R., Gundry, M., Knapp, K., Slabaugh, G.: Improving an active shape model with random classification forest for segmentation of cervical vertebrae. In: Yao, J., Vrtovec, T., Zheng, G., Frangi, A., Glocker, B., Li, S. (eds.) CSI 2016. LNCS, vol. 10182, pp. 3–15. Springer, Cham (2016). https://doi.org/10.1007/978-3-319-55050-3_1
3. Roberts, M.G., Cootes, T.F., Adams, J.E.: Automatic location of vertebrae on DXA images using random forest regression. In: Ayache, N., Delingette, H., Golland, P., Mori, K. (eds.) MICCAI 2012. LNCS, vol. 7512, pp. 361–368. Springer, Heidelberg (2012). https://doi.org/10.1007/978-3-642-33454-2_45
4. Liao, S., Zhan, Y., Dong, Z., Yan, R., Gong, L., Zhou, X., Salganicoff, M., Fei, J.: Automatic lumbar spondylolisthesis measurement in CT images. IEEE Trans. Med. Imaging **35**(7), 1658–1669 (2016)
5. Tu, Z.: Auto-context and its application to high-level vision tasks. In: Proceedings of the IEEE Conference on Computer Vision and Pattern Recognition, CVPR 2008. IEEE (2008)
6. Gao, Y., Shen, D.: Context-aware anatomical landmark detection: application to deformable model initialization in prostate CT images. In: Wu, G., Zhang, D., Zhou, L. (eds.) MLMI 2014. LNCS, vol. 8679, pp. 165–173. Springer, Cham (2014). https://doi.org/10.1007/978-3-319-10581-9_21
7. Glocker, B., Zikic, D., Konukoglu, E., Haynor, D.R., Criminisi, A.: Vertebrae localization in pathological spine CT via dense classification from sparse annotations. In: Mori, K., Sakuma, I., Sato, Y., Barillot, C., Navab, N. (eds.) MICCAI 2013. LNCS, vol. 8150, pp. 262–270. Springer, Heidelberg (2013). https://doi.org/10.1007/978-3-642-40763-5_33
8. Cheng, Y.: Mean shift, mode seeking, and clustering. IEEE Trans. Pattern Anal. Mach. Intell. **17**(8), 790–799 (1995)
9. Kanitsar, A., Fleischmann, D., Wegenkittl, R., Felkel, P., Gröller, M.: CPR: curved planar reformation. In: Proceedings of the IEEE Visualization Conference, VIS 2002, pp. 37–44. IEEE (2002)
10. Velut, J.: A spline-driven image slicer. VTK J. (2011)
11. Štern, D., Likar, B., Pernuš, F., Vrtovec, T.: Automated detection of spinal centrelines, vertebral bodies and intervertebral discs in CT and MR images of lumbar spine. Phys. Med. Biol. **55**(1), 247–264 (2010)
12. Forsberg, D., Lundström, C., Andersson, M., Vavruch, L., Tropp, H., Knutsson, H.: Fully automatic measurements of axial vertebral rotation for assessment of spinal deformity in idiopathic scoliosis. Phys. Med. Biol. **58**(6), 1775–1787 (2013)
13. Criminisi, A., Robertson, D., Konukoglu, E., Shotton, J., Pathak, S., White, S., Siddiqui, K.: Regression forests for efficient anatomy detection and localization in computed tomography scans. Med. Image Anal. **17**(8), 1293–1303 (2013)

Joint Multimodal Segmentation of Clinical CT and MR from Hip Arthroplasty Patients

Marta Bianca Maria Ranzini[1(✉)], Michael Ebner[1,3], M. Jorge Cardoso[1,3], Anastasia Fotiadou[2], Tom Vercauteren[1,3], Johann Henckel[2], Alister Hart[2,3], Sébastien Ourselin[1,3], and Marc Modat[1,3]

[1] Translational Imaging Group, CMIC, University College London, London, UK
marta.ranzini.15@ucl.ac.uk
[2] Royal National Orthopaedic Hospital NHS Foundation Trust, Stanmore, UK
[3] Wellcome/EPSRC Centre for Interventional and Surgical Sciences,
UCL, London, UK

Abstract. Magnetic resonance imaging (MRI) is routinely employed to assess muscular response and presence of inflammatory reactions in patients treated with metal-on-metal hip arthroplasty, driving the decision for revision surgery. However, MRI is lacking contrast for bony structures and as a result orthopaedic surgical planning is mostly performed on computed tomography images. In this paper, we combine the complementary information of both modalities into a novel framework for the joint segmentation of healthy and pathological musculoskeletal structures as well as implants on all images. Our processing pipeline is fully automated and was designed to handle the highly anisotropic resolution of clinical MR images by means of super resolution reconstruction. The accuracy of the intra-subject multimodal registration was improved by employing a non-linear registration algorithm with hard constraints on the deformation of bony structures, while a multi-atlas segmentation propagation approach provided robustness to the large shape variability in the population. The suggested framework was evaluated in a leave-one-out cross-validation study on 20 hip sides. The proposed pipeline has potential for the extraction of clinically relevant imaging biomarkers for implant failure detection.

Keywords: Muscoloskeletal imaging · Multimodal segmentation
Multimodal registration · CT · MR · Arthroplasty

1 Introduction

In the past 20 years, metal-on-metal (MoM) hip arthroplasty has been one of the most effective surgical interventions for improving life quality. However, this implant type is associated with a non-negligible rate of failure (8% at 12 years from primary surgery [1]), due to adverse tissue inflammatory reactions and increased muscle atrophy [2]. Routine assessment of periprosthetic muscle response to the implant is performed on magnetic resonance (MR) images [3],

© Springer International Publishing AG 2018
B. Glocker et al. (Eds.): MSKI 2017, LNCS 10734, pp. 72–84, 2018.
https://doi.org/10.1007/978-3-319-74113-0_7

whereas computed tomography (CT) imaging is preferred for surgical planning and post-operative follow-up, thanks to its improved contrast for bone and implant [4]. The two modalities provide complementary skeletal and muscular information, which are presently assessed independently in clinical practice. In this context, a single framework merging this information by means of joint automated segmentation could be beneficial for both early detection of implant failure and planning of revision surgery. By providing spatial relationship between muscle, bone and implant simultaneously, the combination of the two imaging modalities could help link implant position (not MR visible) with muscle damage (estimated on MR) to better characterise pain origin. Moreover, it could favour a patient-specific planning of surgical approach to minimise damage to healthy bone and muscular tissue.

In the musculoskeletal clinical field, manual segmentation is still the most frequently adopted solution in clinical routine for delineating regions of interest [5], despite the variety of image-based anatomical models and segmentation techniques presented in the literature. Methods for automated segmentation of hip bony structures in CT images are typically based on statistical shape models [6,7], atlas-based segmentation propagation [8] or, more recently, hybrid approaches [9]. Segmentation of muscles on MR images is more problematic, because of their large inter-subject shape variability and the lack of image contrast between different muscular structures. A common approach for thigh muscles is the incorporation of atlases as priors into conventional segmentation techniques such as active contours or level-set algorithms [10,11]. Remarkable results were also presented by Gilles et al. [12], who introduced a method to automatically segment hip muscles and bones on MR images by means of deformable multi-resolution simplex meshes. The performances of all discussed methods are strongly reliant on the variability encompassed in the training data set and they are often not suitable for pathological conditions. Klemt et al. [13] addressed this issue by developing a robust automated segmentation framework for abductor muscles on MR in both healthy subjects and patients with MoM prostheses. However, little work combining multimodal imaging for the segmentation of musculoskeletal structures has been proposed so far and it is often limited only to spine applications. An example is the method presented by Castro-Mateos et al. [14], which is based on a fast mesh-to-image registration to extract a surface model of CT-derived vertebrae and MR-derived intervertebral discs. Whilst being very suitable for bony structures, the applicability of this method to patients with hip arthroplasty would be hindered by the presence of metal artefact in the images and by the greater morphological and textural variability of muscles.

Taking advantage of the complementary information derived from CT and MR, we propose a fully automated joint segmentation framework of both modalities from patients treated with MoM arthroplasty. Our processing pipeline was designed to handle clinical data, characterised by highly anisotropic resolution and presence of severe metal artefact induced noise, and allows for a three-dimensional representation of patient-specific musculoskeletal hip anatomy.

Key contributions of this work include the use of super resolution reconstruction (SRR) to improve clinical MR image quality; moreover, the development of a robust intra-subject multimodal registration allowed preservation of the rigid structure of bones, while deforming the muscles. Finally, a multi-channel multi-atlas based segmentation propagation guaranteed robustness to the large shape variability in the population.

2   Materials and Methods

2.1   Dataset and Templates Creation

Our dataset includes retrospectively collected images of 11 MoM hip implanted patients (7 females and 4 males, 10 unilateral and 1 bilateral replacement) who had both a CT and an MR scan acquired on the same day. For the MR acquisitions, a Siemens MAGNETON Avanto 1.5T scanner was employed for all patients, using the MARS MRI protocol proposed in [15], which is characterised by rapid 2D MRI acquisition but high voxel resolution anisotropy. This includes the collection of two T1-weighted Turbo Spin Echo (TSE) images: a high-resolution axial acquisition (TE = 8 ms, TR = 509 ms, typical imaging resolution = $0.78 \times 0.78 \times 7.02$ mm^3) and a high-resolution coronal acquisition (TE = 7.1 ms, TR = 627 ms, typical imaging resolution = $1.25 \times 1.25 \times 6.00$ mm^3). Eight CT images were acquired on a Siemens SOMATOM Sensation 16 CT Scanner, while three on a Siemens SOMATOM Definition AS machine (tube voltage in [80, 120] kVp). The images were processed (see Sect. 2.2), split along the left-right axis of symmetry and separated according to the presence of implant. Manual segmentation of pelvic bones, femora and implant were performed on CT, while Gluteus Maximus (GMAX), Gluteus Medius (GMED), Gluteus Minimus (GMIN) and Tensor Fasciae Latae (TFL) were individually manually delineated on the MR. As a result of these processes, we built two template data sets, composed of 10 implanted and 10 non-implanted hip sides respectively - for the sake of simplicity we will refer to the latter as the healthy data set despite the presence of metal artefact generated by the implanted side. Each template includes a CT image, a registered super-resolution reconstructed MR image and the respective joint manual segmentation of bones, muscles and implant. Within each dataset, the templates were robustly aligned onto the average space based on the method proposed in [13].

2.2   Pipeline for Automated Segmentation

A schematic representation of our processing framework is presented in Fig. 1. The pipeline was implemented in NiPype [16], combining registration and segmentation utilities of NiftyReg[1], NiftySeg[2] and FSL[3] software packages with

---

[1] https://cmiclab.cs.ucl.ac.uk/mmodat/niftyreg.
[2] http://cmictig.cs.ucl.ac.uk/wiki/index.php/NiftySeg.
[3] https://fsl.fmrib.ox.ac.uk/fsl/fslwiki.

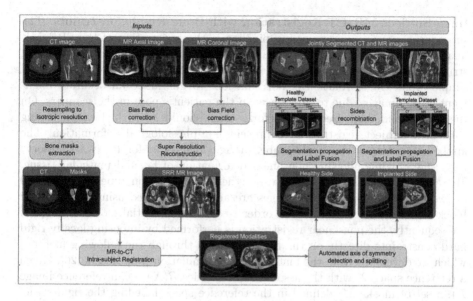

Fig. 1. Proposed pipeline for joint automated segmentation of computed tomography (CT) and magnetic resonance (MR) pelvic images. The two modalities are first processed independently to enhance the image quality. Intra-subject multimodal registration is then performed to align them through a non-linear deformation with rigid constraints in bony structures. The registered CT and MR are split along the axis of symmetry and a multi-atlas based segmentation propagation approach is applied to obtain the automated segmentations of each side, which are finally recombined into the full field of view.

super-resolution reconstruction and the proposed novel multimodal registration framework. Our method is composed of three main blocks which are performed sequentially: image quality enhancement of each modality, intra-subject MR-to-CT registration, and atlas-based segmentation.

Image Quality Enhancement. In the first block, we aim at improving the quality of the clinical images for improved registration steps. The axial and the coronal MR images are first corrected for bias field effects [17]. In order to compensate for the highly anisotropic resolution of clinical MR images (up to a factor of 10), we combine both MR acquisitions into a $1 \times 1 \times 1\,\mathrm{mm}^3$ resolution image using the SRR algorithm presented in [18]. To ease the subsequent registration, the CT is also resampled to the same resolution using a cubic interpolation scheme. An initial estimate of bones segmentation on the CT is extracted by registering the templates to the target space and consequently propagating and fusing their segmentation, allowing the creation of masks for femur, pelvis and implant to be used in the intra-subject registration.

Intra-Subject MR-CT Registration with Bone Rigid Constraints. The subsequent step in our processing pipeline is the registration of the SRR MR image to the respective CT. Multimodal registration for hip musculoskeletal structures is challenging and no standard method has been proposed yet. A simple affine transformation is not sufficient to guarantee an accurate alignment of the images, due to differences in the patient's pose in the scanners. On the other hand, high frequency deformations should be curbed when dealing with intra-subject registration to prevent non-physiological deformation. The applied transformation should embed a rigid behaviour for bones to preserve their shape, while allowing non-linear deformation of fat and muscular tissue. To tackle the discussed issues, we designed a registration pipeline composed of two steps. Firstly, the two images are affinely registered using a symmetric block-matching algorithm [19], in order to provide an initial global alignment. Subsequently, the non-linear registration is performed by imposing locally rigid hard constraints directly on the transformation through the following method, which we developed from the mathematical formulation proposed in [20]. Given a reference space X with the associated intensities $R(X)$ (i.e. a reference image R), a set of masks M_j defined in the reference space labelling the rigid structures, and a floating image F defined in the floating space Y, we defined our registration problem as the optimisation of the transformation $\phi : X \to Y$ such that:

$$\max_{\phi} \quad \left[(1-\alpha-\beta)\,\mathcal{D}(F(\phi(X)),\,R(X)) - \alpha P_L - \beta P_B\right]$$

$$\text{subject to } \phi(x) - A_j x = 0 \quad \forall x \in M_j \subset X, \tag{1}$$

$\mathcal{D}$ is a measure of similarity between the reference and the warped floating image, while P_L and P_B represent the linear elasticity and the bending energy penalty terms [21], whose contribution to the total cost function is weighted by α and β respectively; A_j refers to a rigid transformation applied within the j-th mask. In order to guarantee inverse-consistency and symmetry of the registration [22], we exploit a scaling-and-squaring exponentiation of a stationary velocity field encoded by a cubic B-spline parametrisation defined over a set of control points $\{\mu\}$. The transformation is optimised within a conjugate gradient scheme, and the rigid behaviour in the mask areas is ensured through the following steps:

Algorithm 1. Apply rigid constraints

Compute the gradient $G(\mu)$ of the cost function $\forall \mu \in \{\mu\}$,
for each mask M_j **do**
    Least square regression of $G(\mu), \forall \mu \in M_j$ to fit a rigid transformation A_j
    Set the gradient to $A_j(\mu) \,\forall \mu \in M_j$
end for
Perform a line search along the direction of G.

Differently to current approaches such as [23] where a locally rigid behaviour can be promoted by the addition of a penalty term to the cost function (soft constraint), in our approach the rigid constraints are strictly embedded into the transformation model, not in the optimisation scheme (hard constraint). Thus, chain rule provides an analytical formulation of the conjugate gradient thereby avoiding constrained optimisation. Using the proposed method on a coarse-to-fine pyramidal approach, smooth transitions in the deformation field are maintained by the cubic B-spline parametrisation and the stationary velocity field exponentiation, while forcing rigid behaviours within the masks. To reduce the effect of undesired high-frequency components in the transformation, we set one control point every five voxels, and the masks are dilated at each pyramidal level to account for the local support of the control points. We underline that we extract the robust range of the intensity distributions for both the reference and the floating image, and we perform all the registration steps by flooring or ceiling all intensities outside this range, so as to decrease the influence of metal artefact induced noise.

Once registered with the proposed method, the CT and the MR are merged into a single four-dimensional (4D) volume. In order to employ the appropriate template dataset for the atlas-based segmentation – i.e. healthy or implanted – we developed a symmetry and implant detection algorithm. Based on left-right axis flip and rigid registration, it extracts the sagittal axis of symmetry from the inertia tensor of the image intensities. The 4D volume is split along this axis and each hip side is automatically classified according to the presence of implants.

Atlas-Based Segmentation. Each split hip side is segmented by means of multi-atlas segmentation propagation and label fusion. All the templates are registered to the target 4D image in a three-step process (rigid, affine and non-linear registration as implemented in NiftyReg). The transformation of the affine and the non-linear steps is initialised as the least trimmed squares average affine from all the template transformations estimated at the previous step. Since our templates were previously aligned to their mid-space (Sect. 2.1), this initialisation provides robustness against global failed registration. Notably, the non-linear step is a multi-channel registration, where both modalities contribute jointly and equally to the optimisation of the transformation. Using the estimated transformation, the segmentation of each template is propagated onto the target space. The candidate segmentations are then fused into a consensus through the STEPS algorithm [24], specifically modified to manage a multi-channel local similarity measure. The final segmentation is obtained by merging back the two hip sides and their estimated segmentation, providing a multi-label image that highlights different bones, muscles and implants on both the CT and the MR.

3   Validation and Experiments

3.1   Intra-Subject Registration Evaluation

The first set of experiments we performed aimed at identifying the optimal set of regularisation parameters α and β as shown in (1) for the intra-subject registration. Normalised mutual information (NMI) was used as measure of similarity,

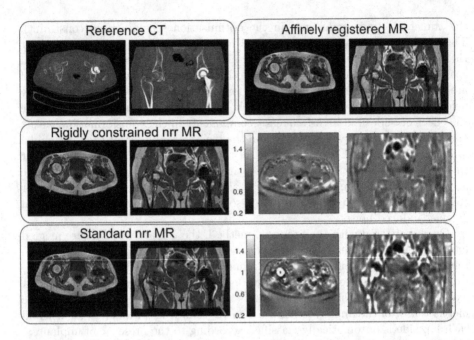

Fig. 2. Example of qualitative registration assessment with default NiftyReg regularisation parameters. The same axial and coronal slices are reported for the reference computed tomography, the super-resolution reconstructed magnetic resonance (MR) after affine registration, the super resolution reconstruction (SRR) MR after rigidly constrained non rigid registration and the SRR MR after standard non-linear registration. For these latter cases, the transformation Jacobian determinant maps are also displayed, showing the effect of the rigid constraints. Yellow arrows indicate exemplary areas where the proposed approach visually recovers a better alignment than the standard fully non-linear registration (e.g. in the femoral head size). (Color figure online)

since it is best suited for multimodal registration. For the sake of comparison, we performed the same study using the standard non-linear registration without the application of the rigid constraints, while keeping all the other parameters unchanged. Although this variant would assume non-rigid deformation of the bones, which is neither anatomically nor clinically correct, such a comparison allows us to verify whether our implementation also improved the registration results compared to the classical approach.

The choice of the best parameters was based on both qualitative and quantitative analysis. The former included visual assessment of the alignment between the CT and the registered MR and of the transformation Jacobian maps. An example of this comparison is reported in Fig. 2, where the Jacobian determinant maps clearly show how the standard registration algorithm fails in recovering a rigid behaviour within the bones, as opposed to the proposed method.

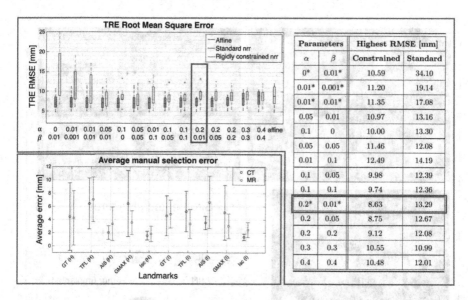

Parameters		Highest RMSE [mm]	
α	β	Constrained	Standard
0*	0.01*	10.59	34.10
0.01*	0.001*	11.20	19.14
0.01*	0.01*	11.35	17.08
0.05	0.01	10.97	13.16
0.1	0	10.00	13.30
0.05	0.05	11.46	12.08
0.01	0.1	12.49	14.19
0.1	0.05	9.98	12.39
0.1	0.1	9.74	12.36
0.2*	0.01*	8.63	13.29
0.2	0.05	8.75	12.67
0.2	0.2	9.12	12.08
0.3	0.3	10.55	10.99
0.4	0.4	10.48	12.01

Fig. 3. Target registration error (TRE) analysis. Top figure: comparison of TRE root mean square error (RMSE) values obtained from the rigidly constrained non-linear registration and the standard one with varying regularisation parameters α - linear elasticity weight - and β - bending energy weight. TRE RMSE from affine registration is shown as well. Table: highest RMSE for each set of parameters. Starred values indicate the sets for which the rigidly constrained registration provided significantly lower RMSE than the standard (Wilcoxon rank sum test, $p < 0.05$). Highlighted in red are the results for the selected best set of parameters. Bottom figure: manual selection reproducibility error for the 10 landmarks and for the two modalities. List of landmarks abbreviations: greater trochanter (GT), tensor fasciae latae (TFL), anterior-inferior iliac spine (AIS), gluteus maximus (GMAX), ischium (Isc). Each landmark is identified in each side and it is categorized as healthy (H) or implanted (I) side. (Color figure online)

A quantification of the registration accuracy was obtained through landmarks analysis. Specifically, we labeled 5 landmarks (3 in bone, 2 in muscles) per hip side which could be conveniently located in both modalities and which cover the full field of view. The target registration error (TRE) was computed as the distance between the CT and the respective warped MR landmark. In order to limit the bias from the manual landmark choice, we repeated the selection twice at different times, we estimated the TRE for each selection and then computed the average TRE for each landmark and for each subject (reproducibility errors for the manual selection are shown in the bottom-left panel of Fig. 3). For each subject we extracted the root mean square error (RMSE) of the TRE across the ten landmarks and we compared the distribution of the RMSE with respect to the registration parameters. A summary of the obtained results is presented in Fig. 3. Overall the proposed method not only provided clinically plausible registration results, but also produced a more accurate alignment of the considered

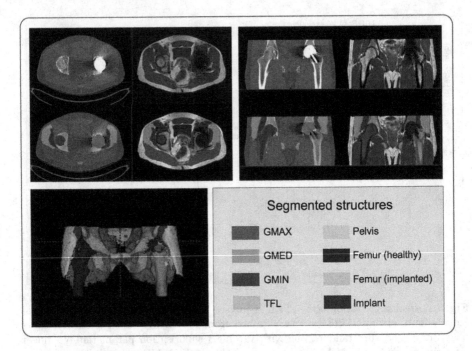

Fig. 4. Example of automated segmentation obtained with the proposed automated pipeline. Top row shows the central axial and coronal slices for one of the subjects for both computed tomography and magnetic resonance, while the second row reports the same images overlaid with the segmentation result. A three-dimensional rendering of the full segmentation is also displayed on the bottom left for the same subject.

landmarks compared to a standard non-linear registration algorithm. The best set of parameters was identified as the one minimising the highest TRE RMSE among all the landmarks, so as to guarantee a reasonably good alignment across the whole field of view. We therefore concluded that the optimal results for the intra-subject registration resulted from the use of normalised mutual information with $\alpha = 0.2$ and $\beta = 0.01$.

3.2   Leave-One-Out Cross Validation

The proposed pipeline was validated through a leave-one-out cross-validation (LOOCV) experiment on the template datasets, by calculating the Dice score between the automated segmentation result and the corresponding manual ground truth for each label and for each subject. The goal of the LOOCV was to compare the achieved results using both modalities jointly to those obtained using only the CT or only the MR images. We recall that the manual segmentation of muscles was not available for the CT, and similarly bones and implant labelling on the MR. Therefore only the available labels were considered in the single-modality experiments. For each analysed type – i.e. only CT, only MR, combined modalities for healthy and for implanted sides – the segmentation propagation and label fusion parameters were tuned to maximise the lowest average Dice Score across subjects and across labels. An example of the obtained automated segmentation is shown in Fig. 4.

The median Dice score for bones, muscles and implant extracted from the three LOOCV experiments are reported in Table 1. It can be observed that the multimodal and the single-modality approaches perform similarly with comparable Dice score values. Overall bone structures were better segmented than muscular ones, due to their lower shape and texture variability. Although the obtained results appear slightly lower with the proposed approach, the observed differences were statistically significant only in one case – i.e. for muscular structures in the healthy side – while for all the other cases the null hypothesis of same underlying distribution was accepted (Wilcoxon rank sum test with 5% significance level). This difference could arise from the need of finding a trade-off in the segmentation propagation and label fusion parameters to achieve a good accuracy in both skeletal and muscular structures for the 4D case. This might go at the expense of a slight reduction of performances with respect to the single-modality case, where the parameters are tuned only for the bones and implant (CT) or for the muscles (MR). Nonetheless, only the proposed framework is able to provide consistent and unified solution to the segmentation of both the CT and the MRI. The use of independent approaches to segment the muscles in the MR images and the bones and implants in the CT image would indeed not guarantee non-overlapping regions of interest. As an example, on our dataset we evaluated that on average 2% of the voxels labeled as muscle on the MR overlapped with CT-labeled bone voxels in our manual segmentation, while the proposed method guarantees no overlap by design. Without the use of

Table 1. Median Dice score values and 95% confidence intervals for bones, implant and muscles: comparison between single- and multimodality results. Wilcoxon rank sum test was performed to test the null hypothesis of same distribution for the multimodality- and the respective single-modality-derived Dice scores (obtained p-values are reported and starred (*) are the cases of rejection of the null hypothesis with 5% significance level). N.A. indicates cases where the manual segmentation was not available.

Healthy side			
	CT	MR	Multimodal	p-value
Bones	0.95 [0.74, 0.97]	N.A	0.94 [0.74, 0.96]	0.164
Muscles	N.A	0.88 [0.74, 0.95]	0.85 [0.70, 0.92]	0.007*
Implanted side			
	CT	MR	Multimodal	p-value
Bones	0.87 [0.63, 0.93]	N.A	0.85 [0.53, 0.90]	0.365
Muscles	N.A	0.84 [0.60, 0.93]	0.77 [0.41, 0.90]	0.054
Implant	0.91 [0.77, 0.95]	N.A	0.91 [0.69, 0.93]	0.970

a registration framework able to deal with the rigid nature of the bones while non-linearly deforming the surrounding soft tissue, it would be more challenging to accurately highlight the muscles in the CT space or the bones in the MR space, due to their poor contrast for these structures.

4   Conclusion

We presented a fully automated processing pipeline for the joint segmentation of bones, abductor muscles and implant on CT and MR images from hip arthroplasty patients. The combination of the two modalities enables accurate joint delineation of healthy and pathological musculoskeletal structures and of their spatial relationship.

As for other atlas-based approaches, the performance of our method could be improved by enlarging the template data sets to better encompass the population variability. Moreover, the presence of metal artefact-induced noise strongly affects the accuracy of both intra- and inter-subject registration; hence future developments of the processing pipeline will introduce novel metal artefact reduction techniques as an image quality enhancement step for the CT. In conclusion, the proposed pipeline is a promising tool towards patient-specific 3D visualisation of musculoskeletal structures, and towards the extraction of clinically relevant imaging biomarkers to detect implant failure. Thanks to our processing steps, the implant can be outlined also on the MR image, where it is typically obscured by the metal artefact. This could help identify the muscles that are at greater risk of developing atrophy due to the presence of the implant, and therefore inform the decision-making process for revision surgery.

Acknowledgements. This work is supported by the EPSRC-funded UCL Centre for Doctoral Training in Medical Imaging [EP/L016478/1], the Royal National Orthopaedic Hospital NHS Trust, the Department of Healths NIHR-funded Biomedical Research Centre at University College London Hospitals and Innovative Engineering for Health award by the Wellcome Trust [WT101957] and EPSRC [NS/A000027/1], and by Wellcome/EPSRC [203145Z/16/Z].

References

1. UK National Joint Registry: 13th Annual Report (December 2015) (2016)
2. Berber, R., Khoo, M., Cook, E., Guppy, A., Hua, J., Miles, J., Carrington, R., Skinner, J., Hart, A.: Muscle atrophy and metal-on-metal hip implants: a serial MRI study of 74 hips. Acta Orthop. **86**(3), 351–357 (2015)
3. MHRA of the Department of Health: Medical Device Alert. MHRA Database, pp. 1–7 (2012). http://www.mhra.gov.uk
4. Bogner, E., Sofka, C.: CT evaluation of total hip arthroplasty complication: Dissociation of acetabular component. HSS J. **3**(1), 112–114 (2007)
5. Pedoia, V., Majumdar, S., Link, T.: Segmentation of joint and musculoskeletal tissue in the study of arthritis. Magn. Reson. Mater. Phy. **29**(2), 207–221 (2016)

6. Seim, H., Kainmüller, D., Heller, M., Lamecker, H., Zachow, S., Hege, H.C.: Automatic segmentation of the pelvic bones from CT data based on a statistical shape model. In: Proceedings of the 1st Eurographics Conference on Visual Computing for Biomedicine - EG VCBM 2008, pp. 93–100 (2008)
7. Yokota, F., Okada, T., Takao, M., Sugano, N., Tada, Y., Tomiyama, N., Sato, Y.: Automated CT segmentation of diseased hip using hierarchical and conditional statistical shape models. In: Mori, K., Sakuma, I., Sato, Y., Barillot, C., Navab, N. (eds.) MICCAI 2013. LNCS, vol. 8150, pp. 190–197. Springer, Heidelberg (2013). https://doi.org/10.1007/978-3-642-40763-5_24
8. Pettersson, J., Knutsson, H., Borga, M.: Automatic hip bone segmentation using non-rigid registration. In: Proceedings of the 18th International Conference on Pattern Recognition - ICPR 2006, vol. 3, pp. 946–949. IEEE (2006)
9. Chu, C., Chen, C., Liu, L., Zheng, G.: FACTS: fully automatic CT segmentation of a hip joint. Ann. Biomed. Eng. 43(5), 1247–1259 (2015)
10. Prescott, J., Best, T., Swanson, M., Haq, F., Jackson, R., Gurcan, M.: Anatomically anchored template-based level set segmentation: application to quadriceps muscles in MR images from the osteoarthritis initiative. J. Digit. Imaging 24(1), 28–43 (2011)
11. Ahmad, E., Yap, M., Degens, H., McPhee, J.: Atlas-registration based image segmentation of MRI human thigh muscles in 3D space. In: Mello-Thoms, C.R., Kupinski, M. (eds.) Proceedings of the SPIE Medical Imaging 2014: Image Perception, Observer Performance, and Technology Assessment, vol. 9037, p. 90371L. SPIE (2014)
12. Gilles, B., Magnenat-Thalmann, N.: Musculoskeletal MRI segmentation using multi-resolution simplex meshes with medial representations. Med. Image Anal. 14(3), 291–302 (2010)
13. Klemt, C., Modat, M., Pichat, J., Cardoso, M., Henckel, J., Hart, A., Ourselin, S.: Automatic assessment of volume asymmetries applied to hip abductor muscles in patients with hip arthroplasty. In: Ourselin, S., Styner, M. (eds.) Proceedings of the SPIE Medical Imaging 2015: Image Processing, vol. 9413, p. 94131M. SPIE (2015)
14. Castro-Mateos, I., Pozo, J., Lazary, A., Frangi, A.: Automatic construction of patient-specific finite-element mesh of the spine from IVDs and vertebra segmentations. In: Gimi, B., Krol, A. (eds.) Proceedings of the SPIE Medical Imaging 2016: Biomedical Applications in Molecular, Structural, and Functional Imaging, vol. 9788, p. 97881U. SPIE (2016)
15. Sabah, S., Mitchell, A., Henckel, J., Sandison, A., Skinner, J., Hart, A.: Magnetic resonance imaging findings in painful metal-on-metal hips: a prospective study. J. Arthroplasty 26(1), 71–76 (2011)
16. Gorgolewski, K., Burns, C., Madison, C., Clark, D., Halchenko, Y., Waskom, M., Ghosh, S.: Nipype: a flexible, lightweight and extensible neuroimaging data processing framework in python. Front. Neuroinf. 5, 13 (2011)
17. Van Leemput, K., Maes, F., Vandermeulen, D., Suetens, P.: Automated model-based bias field correction of MR images of the brain. IEEE Trans. Med. Imaging 18(10), 885–896 (1999)
18. Ebner, M., Chouhan, M., Patel, P.A., Atkinson, D., Amin, Z., Read, S., Punwani, S., Taylor, S., Vercauteren, T., Ourselin, S.: Point-spread-function-aware slice-to-volume registration: application to upper abdominal MRI super-resolution. In: Zuluaga, M.A., Bhatia, K., Kainz, B., Moghari, M.H., Pace, D.F. (eds.) RAMBO/HVSMR -2016. LNCS, vol. 10129, pp. 3–13. Springer, Cham (2017). https://doi.org/10.1007/978-3-319-52280-7_1

84   M. B. M. Ranzini et al.

19. Modat, M., Cash, D., Daga, P., Winston, G., Duncan, J., Ourselin, S.: Global image registration using a symmetric block-matching approach. J. Med. Imaging **1**(2), 024003 (2014)
20. Haber, E., Heldmann, S., Modersitzki, J.: A computational framework for image-based constrained registration. Linear Algebra Appl. **431**(3–4), 459–470 (2009)
21. Ashburner, J., Ridgway, G.: Symmetric diffeomorphic modeling of longitudinal structural MRI. Front. Neurosci. **6**, 197 (2013)
22. Modat, M., Daga, P., Cardoso, M., Ourselin, S., Ridgway, G., Ashburner, J.: Parametric non-rigid registration using a stationary velocity field. In: Proceedings of the IEEE Workshop on Mathematical Methods in Biomedical Image Analysis - MMBIA 2012, pp. 145–150 (2012)
23. Staring, M., Klein, S., Pluim, J.: A rigidity penalty term for nonrigid registration. Med. Phys. **34**(11), 4098–4108 (2007)
24. Cardoso, J., Leung, K., Modat, M., Keihaninejad, S., Cash, D., Barnes, J., Fox, N., Ourselin, S.: STEPS: similarity and truth estimation for propagated segmentations and its application to hippocampal segmentation and brain parcelation. Med. Image Anal. **17**(6), 671–684 (2013)

Reconstruction of 3D Muscle Fiber Structure Using High Resolution Cryosectioned Volume

Yoshito Otake[1]([⊠]), Kohei Miyamoto[1], Axel Ollivier[1,2], Futoshi Yokota[1], Norio Fukuda[1], Lauren J. O'Donnell[3], Carl-Fredrik Westin[3], Masaki Takao[4], Nobuhiko Sugano[4], Beom Sun Chung[5], Jin Seo Park[6], and Yoshinobu Sato[1]

[1] Graduate School of Information Science,
Nara Institute of Science and Technology, Ikoma, Japan
otake@is.naist.jp
[2] Ecole Nationale Supérieure d'Ingénieurs de Caen, Caen, France
[3] Harvard Medical School, Brigham and Women's Hospital, Boston, USA
[4] Graduate School of Medicine, Osaka University, Suita, Japan
[5] Department of Anatomy, School of Medicine, Ajou University,
Suwon, South Korea
[6] School of Medicine, Dongguk University, Seoul, South Korea

Abstract. Three-dimensional (3D) muscle fiber architecture is important in patient-specific biomechanical simulation. While several in-vivo methods using diffusion tensor imaging and ultrasound have been demonstrated their feasibility in reconstruction of the fiber architecture, the main challenge is the lack of gold standard. Although physical measurement from cadavers has been considered as the accurate way of determining 3D muscle fiber architecture, its downsides include error in the manual tracing and the labor intensive process allowing only sparse sampling of a particular muscle. We propose an alternative method of obtaining a dense fiber architecture of multiple muscles in close proximity using high resolution cryosectioned images. Similar to the diffusion tensor imaging, we first extract the local orientation at each voxel using the structure tensor analysis and then tractography algorithm is applied to obtain stream lines. The proposed method was applied to all muscles around the hip joint and the masticatory muscles. Qualitative comparison with the anatomy textbook indicated that the proposed method reconstructed a plausible muscle fiber architecture. We plan to make the reconstructed fiber architecture of whole body muscles publicly available in order to serve for the biomechanics community.

Keywords: Muscle fiber architecture · Gold standard
High resolution cryosectioned images

© Springer International Publishing AG 2018
B. Glocker et al. (Eds.): MSKI 2017, LNCS 10734, pp. 85–94, 2018.
https://doi.org/10.1007/978-3-319-74113-0_8

1   Introduction

While the Hill-type muscle model that simplifies three-dimensional (3D) muscle architecture as a few strings with the mechanical property of muscle-tendon complex has successfully demonstrated usefulness of biomechanical simulation in a number of applications including human gait [1] and surgical simulation [2], limitations of the simplification include (1) the lack of ability to represent changes of the line-of-action during movement due to wrapping over the bones or other muscles [3] and (2) difficulty in determining the parameters of each string which in reality represents a cluster of muscle fibers [4]. Thus, 3D volumetric muscle models containing the muscle fiber architecture [3,5] have been investigated to improve accuracy in musculoskeletal simulation.

In order to model the patient-specific muscle fiber architecture, diffusion tensor imaging (DTI) and ultrasound [6,7] have been employed and evaluated against a ground truth obtained from cadaveric specimens [8,9]. The direct measurement of a fixed cadaver using a coordinate measurement machine (CMM) provides reliable ground truth, however, it has the following downsides: (1) the number of measurable fibers is limited due to the large amount labors, resulting in a sparsely sampled fiber model, and (2) difficulty in measuring multiple contiguous muscles while keeping their original shape since dissection of the muscle is inevitable. Since muscles often function as a group, the spatial relationship of the fiber architecture between neighboring muscles is important.

In this study, we propose an approach to reconstructing dense muscle fiber architecture of multiple muscles in one subject using a dataset of high resolution cryosectioned images. The method computes the gradient-based structure tensor to obtain local orientation and computes tractography similar to the one

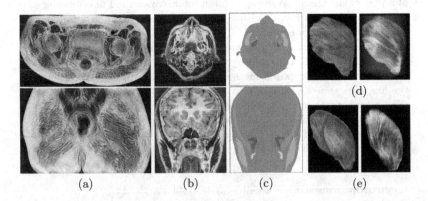

(a)   (b)   (c)   (e)

Fig. 1. Cryo-section images contained in the Visible Korean Human [11,12]. (a) Axial and coronal slices of the female pelvis dataset. (b) Male whole body dataset, and (c) its segmentation mask. The artifact correction (see text for details) has been applied to (a) and (b). Volume rendering and its projection view (ray-sum rendering) of (d) the gluteus maximus and (e) gluteus medius muscles.

proposed by Wang et al. [10] in the optical coherence images of the brain. We demonstrate and qualitatively evaluate the proposed method for muscles in the hip and head regions.

2   Method

2.1   Dataset

The dataset we used in this study is the Visible Korean Human (VKH) [11,12], which consists of a series of photographs of cryosection of human cadavers. Among several datasets in VKH (different genders and type of anatomies), we used two datasets in this study: (1) The male whole body dataset containing 8506 RGB images with 0.2 mm slice interval, 0.2×0.2 mm^2 in-plane resolution, the matrix size of 2468×1407 and covering the entire body from the top of the head to the tip of the foot [11], and (2) female pelvis dataset containing 2508 images with 0.1 mm interval, 0.1×0.1 mm^2 in-plane resolution with 3520×1943 matrix and covering from the top of the pelvis to about 8 cm inferior to the greater trochanter [12]. Both datasets contain segmentation masks of anatomical structures including muscles, bones, vessels and other organs (937 and 154 structures for the male whole body and female pelvis datasets, respectively) which were manually traced by experts at 1.0 mm interval (i.e., every 5 slices for the male dataset and every 10 slices for the female dataset). B-spline interpolation was performed to the segmentation mask to obtain a slice interval corresponding to the RGB images and then the mask was applied to extract the target muscle and stuck to obtain a volume with isotropic voxels (Fig. 1(d), (e)). Note that the structures visible in the cryosection images in this scale are not the individual fibers, but the edges between muscle fascicle (bundle of muscle fibers) and surrounding connective tissues. Our goal is to reconstruct the direction of the fiber fascicle, which is equivalent to the direction of each fiber, by detecting the orientation of those edges.

2.2   Correction of Artifact

Despite careful calibrations in terms of geometry and color to keep the pixel size and color response constant throughout the dataset, we observed a slight discontinuity of the color balance at every few slices as shown in Fig. 2(a), which appears as an artifact in the coronal slice and was enhanced when we observed the dataset in a projection view (Fig. 2(b)). This artifact is likely to be originated from the slice-by-slice color adjustment process. In order to avoid accuracy degradation in our texture analysis to extract the 3D orientation, we propose an artifact correction process as detailed in the following. The repetitive artifact in z-direction (out-of-plane direction) is corrected by applying a low-pass filter in the frequency domain.

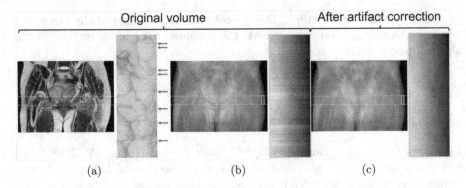

Original volume   After artifact correction

(a)   (b)   (c)

Fig. 2. Example demonstration of the effect of the proposed artifact correction method. (a) Coronal slice of the original RGB volume and a zoomed-in view of the yellow rectangular region. The red arrows indicate the artifact especially distinct in the view. (b) Anterior-posterior projection view, where the artifact appears more distinct. (c) The grayscale converted volume after the proposed artifact correction. The effect of the artifact correction is clearly demonstrated. (Color figure online)

We denote the original image and its Fourier transform as $h(i, j, k)$ and $H(x, y, z)$, respectively. The high frequency region in z-direction near the z-axis of $H(x, y, z)$ was zero-masked by multiplying a mask volume defined as the following:

$$M(x, y, z) = \begin{cases} 0, & \text{if } \sqrt{x^2 + y^2} < t_r \text{ and } |z| > t_z, \\ 1, & \text{otherwise,} \end{cases} \quad (1)$$

which represents a zero-valued cylinder along z-axis with radius of t_r and filled by one in between $-t_z < z < t_z$. t_r and t_z are the cut-off frequency which we experimentally determined as 0.2 and 0.08 (cycles per millimeter) in this study. An inverse Fourier transform of the masked volume, $\mathcal{F}^{-1}(H(x, y, z)M(x, y, z))$, provides a volume after the artifact correction. In this study, we corrected artifact in the R-, G-, and B-plane separately.

2.3 Computation of Structure Tensor

The RGB volume after the artifact correction was then converted into gray-scale using `rgb2gray()` function in Matlab 2016a (The MathWorks Inc., Natick, MA, USA) which follows the equation: $grayvalue = 0.2989R + 0.5870G + 0.1140B$. The local orientation of the muscle fiber around each voxel was estimated by the gradient-based structure tensor [13]. The structure tensor of a volume-of-interest centering at (i, j, k) is defined by:

$$J(i, j, k) = \begin{bmatrix} J_{xx}(i, j, k) & J_{xy}(i, j, k) & J_{xz}(i, j, k) \\ J_{yx}(i, j, k) & J_{yy}(i, j, k) & J_{yz}(i, j, k) \\ J_{zx}(i, j, k) & J_{zy}(i, j, k) & J_{zz}(i, j, k) \end{bmatrix}, \quad (2)$$

where $J_{xy} = \{\frac{d}{dx}G(i,j,k;\sigma_1) * I(i,j,k)\}\{\frac{d}{dy}G(i,j,k;\sigma_1) * I(i,j,k)\}$ represents a multiplication of Gaussian weighted first derivative with respect to the x and y axes. The other element follows the same notation. In order to obtain a smooth tensor field, we apply another Gaussian filter to each element of $J(i,j,k)$ with a standard deviation of σ_2. While σ_1 needs to be adjusted based on the amount of image noise, σ_2 determines smoothness of the tensor field which affects the following tractography algorithm. We empirically found that $\sigma_1 = 1\,\mathrm{mm}$ and $\sigma_2 = 3\,\mathrm{mm}$ are suitable in our dataset, thus are used in the experiment below. An example visualization of the computed structure tensor field is shown in Fig. 3(b). The structure tensor becomes a pin-like shape when the volume-of-interest exhibits a sheet-like texture (the "pin" directs perpendicular to the sheet), while it becomes a disk-like shape for a line-like structure (the disk spreads in the plane perpendicular to the line). When comparing with DTI, since the diffusion happens in the direction along the line for a line-like structure, we proposed the following conversion process of the structure tensor field in order to employ tractography algorithms commonly used in DTI, which we call an *inverse* of the structure tensor:

$$\lambda_1' = \lambda_1, \qquad \lambda_2' = \lambda_1 + \lambda_3 - \lambda_2, \qquad \lambda_3' = \lambda_3, \tag{3}$$

where λ_1, λ_2, λ_3 represent eigenvalues of the original structure tensor ($\lambda_1 > \lambda_2 > \lambda_3$) and λ_1', λ_2', λ_3' represent eigenvalues of the *inverted* structure tensor (which ensures $\lambda_1' > \lambda_2' > \lambda_3'$). Then, the eigenvectors corresponding to the largest and smallest eigenvalues are swapped. The idea behind this *inversion* process is to generate a diffusion-tensor-like tensor from the structure tensor by converting the "pen"-tensor to the disk and the "disk"-tensor to the pen (note that the metric called linear measure [14], $c_l = (\lambda_1 - \lambda_2)/\lambda_1$, becomes the planar measure, $c_p = (\lambda_2 - \lambda_3)/\lambda_1$, and vice versa after this *inversion*).

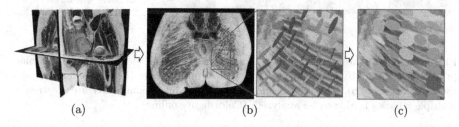

(a)   (b)   (c)

Fig. 3. Computation and visualization of the structure tensor. (a) Grayscale volume after artifact correction. Visualization of the (b) structure tensor and (c) its *inverse* computed in the right gluteus maximus muscle. Each tensor is represented as an ellipsoid whose principal axes correspond to the tensor's eigenvector system (its length shows the absolute value of the tensor's eigenvalue and the orientation is its eigenvector). The color indicates the linear measure, $(\lambda_1 - \lambda_2)/\lambda_1$ [14], of each tensor. (Color figure online)

2.4   Computation of Tractography

From the *inverted* structure tensor field, tractography is computed. In this study, we performed the tractography algorithm and visualization of the results in 3D Slicer[1][15] via the SlicerDMRI project[2].

3   Results

The tractography computed on 24 muscles around the hip joint in the female pelvis dataset is shown in Fig. 4 together with the list of each muscle's name. Figure 5 shows the results of four representative masticatory muscles (masseter, buccinator, lateral and medial pterygoid) from the male whole body dataset. The illustrations from an anatomy textbook [16] are shown next to each visualization in order for the visual evaluation of the validity of the computed fiber bundles. In order to further explore an application of the proposed method, we performed a fiber clustering method [17] which applies the spectral clustering on a similarity metric between fibers. The similarity metric used here is the fiber distance error defined as the mean distance between pairs of corresponding points on the fibers. Figure 6 shows an example where the fibers in the gluteus medius muscle were clustered into five clusters and visualized fibers in each cluster with one color.

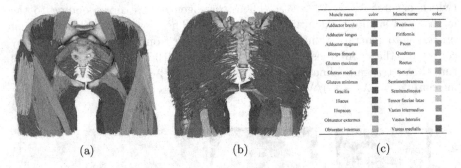

(a)   (b)   (c)

Fig. 4. Results of the computed fiber architecture of the muscles around the hip joint. (a) Anterior view. (b) Posterior view. (c) List of muscles and the corresponding color shown in (a) and (b). The relationship of the three-dimensional fiber architecture of multiple muscles is able to be analyzed. (Color figure online)

---

[1] http://www.slicer.org.
[2] http://dmri.slicer.org.

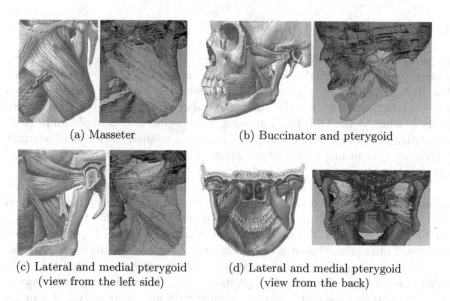

(a) Masseter

(b) Buccinator and pterygoid

(c) Lateral and medial pterygoid
(view from the left side)

(d) Lateral and medial pterygoid
(view from the back)

Fig. 5. Results of the computed fiber architecture of the masticatory muscles. The tractography (right) was visually compared with an anatomy textbook [16] (left). The color of the fibers indicates the fiber's orientation averaged over the entire line (red, green and blue components correspond to the x, y, and z direction, respectively). (Color figure online)

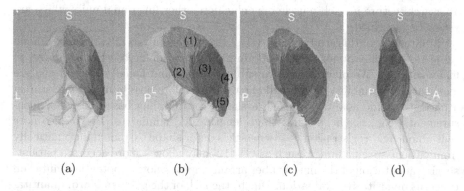

(a)   (b)   (c)   (d)

Fig. 6. Result of the fiber clustering [17] of the right gluteus medius muscle. The muscle fiber bundles computed by the proposed method were clustered into five clusters. (a) to (d) show the views from different angles rotated by 45 degrees each. All fiber bundles in each cluster was visualized with one color. The anterior region acting for flexion and internal rotation is represented as clusters 3, 4 and 5, while the posterior region acting for extension and external rotation is represented as clusters 1 and 2. (Color figure online)

4   Discussion and Conclusion

We proposed a method to reconstruct a dense 3D fiber architecture of multiple muscles in one functional unit using a high resolution cryosectioned volume. The manual tracing in cadaver specimens, which is currently considered as a gold standard, requires a large amount of labor and is subjected to the error in the tracing by the CMM and imposes deformation that is implausible in in-vivo situation. On the other hand, the proposed method allows to reconstruct a large number of fibers of multiple neighboring muscles without the effect of deformation.

A straightforward application of the reconstructed fiber architecture is biome-chanical simulation. The simulation with volumetric muscle models has been drawing attention partly due to the rapid increase of computing power allowing simulation of behavior of more detailed structure. The patient-specific charac-teristics of fiber arrangement is critical in such simulation environment. Patient-specific biomechanical simulation may help, for example, understand the stress balance at the knee joint in loading position by comparing the fiber arrangement in magnetic resonance (MR) images acquired with an open-gantry MR scanner that allows scanning by the standing position.

The result of fiber clustering in Fig. 6 shows several clusters which may be corresponding to each functional unit within a muscle. For example, the anterior fibers in the gluteus medius are argued to help to rotate the hip joint medially, while the posterior fibers help to rotate laterally. Such detailed analysis of the fiber architecture in each muscle may elucidate other functional units which are yet to be identified.

Limitations of this study include the lack of the analysis of variability among subjects. It is clearly not easy to obtain high resolution cryosectioned images of many subjects. We plan to use two subjects (male and female)[18] and analyze inter-subject variability, which will allow us to explore possibility for performing a patient-specific adaptation using a simple local scaling based on a few mea-surements (e.g., height, weight, thigh length, etc.) similar to [1]. We also note that a non-rigid registration of the muscle's outer shape extracted automatically from patient-specific images such as CT [19] may allow a more accurate patient-specific adaptation of the muscle fiber arrangement. Another potential limitation concerns quantitative evaluation. Due to the lack of the gold standard, quantita-tive evaluation of the proposed method is quite challenging. The manual tracing of each fiber in the cryosection volume is one possible solution to obtain the ground truth, though visually tracking one muscle fiber over a number of slices is troublesome due to ambiguous boarders between the neighboring fibers. Ani-mal or cadaver studies subsequent cryosection could be another option though the accuracy of physical tracing of fibers and muscle's deformation become error source in that case. Further investigation on quantitative evaluation is in our future work.

Acknowledgements. This research was supported by MEXT/JSPS KAKENHI 26108004, JST PRESTO 20407, and AMED/ETH the strategic Japanese-Swiss cooperative research program, NIH grant U01CA199459 and P41EB015902.

References

1. Rajagopal, A., Dembia, C., DeMers, M., Delp, D., Hicks, J., Delp, S.: Full-body musculoskeletal model for muscle-driven simulation of human gait. IEEE Trans. Biomed. Eng. **63**(10), 2068–2079 (2016)
2. Marra, M., Vanheule, V., Fluit, R., Koopman, B., Rasmussen, J., Verdonschot, N., Andersen, M.: A subject-specific musculoskeletal modeling framework to predict in vivo mechanics of total knee arthroplasty. J. Biomech. Eng. **137**(2), 020904 (2015)
3. Webb, J., Blemker, S., Delp, S.: 3D finite element models of shoulder muscles for computing lines of actions and moment arms. Comput. Methods Biomech. Biomed. Engin. **17**(8), 829–837 (2014)
4. Hicks, J., Uchida, T., Seth, A., Rajagopal, A., Delp, S.: Is my model good enough? Best practices for verification and validation of musculoskeletal models and simulations of movement. J. Biomech. Eng. **137**(2), 020905 (2015)
5. Blemker, S., Delp, S.: Three-dimensional representation of complex muscle architectures and geometries. Ann. Biomed. Eng. **33**(5), 661–673 (2005)
6. Damon, B., Froeling, M., Buck, A., Oudeman, J., Ding, Z., Nederveen, A., Bush, E., Strijkers, G.: Skeletal muscle diffusion tensor-MRI fiber tracking: rationale, data acquisition and analysis methods, applications and future directions. NMR Biomed. **30**(3), e3563 (2017)
7. Bolsterlee, B., Veeger, H., van der Helm, F., Gandevia, S., Herbert, R.: Comparison of measurements of medial gastrocnemius architectural parameters from ultrasound and diffusion tensor images. J. Biomech. **48**(6), 1133–1140 (2015)
8. Schenk, P., Siebert, T., Hiepe, P., Güllmar, D., Reichenbach, J., Wick, C., Blickhan, R., Böl, M.: Determination of three-dimensional muscle architectures: validation of the DTI-based fiber tractography method by manual digitization. J. Anat. **223**(1), 61–68 (2013)
9. Engelina, S., Robertson, C., Moggridge, J., Killingback, A., Adds, P.: Using ultrasound to measure the fibre angle of vastus medialis oblique: a cadaveric validation study. Knee **21**(1), 107–111 (2014)
10. Wang, H., Lenglet, C., Akkin, T.: Structure tensor analysis of serial optical coherence scanner images for mapping fiber orientations and tractography in the brain. J. Biomed. Opt. **20**(3), 036003 (2015)
11. Park, J., Chung, M., Hwang, S., Lee, Y., Har, D., Park, H.: Visible Korean human: improved serially sectioned images of the entire body. IEEE Trans. Med. Imaging **24**(3), 352–360 (2005)
12. Shin, D., Jang, H., Hwang, S., Har, D., Moon, Y., Chung, M.: Two-dimensional sectioned images and three-dimensional surface models for learning the anatomy of the female pelvis. Anat. Sci. Educ. **6**(5), 316–323 (2013)
13. Bigun, J.: Optimal orientation detection of linear symmetry. In: Proceedings of the 1st IEEE International Conference on Computer Vision - ICCV 1987, pp. 433–438. IEEE (1987)
14. Westin, C., Maier, S., Mamata, II., Nabavi, A., Jolesz, F., Kikinis, R.: Processing and visualization for diffusion tensor MRI. Med. Image Anal. **6**(2), 93–108 (2002)

15. Fedorov, A., Beichel, R., Kalpathy-Cramer, J., Finet, J., Fillion-Robin, J., Pujol, S., Bauer, C., Jennings, D., Fennessy, F., Sonka, M., Buatti, J., Aylward, S., Miller, J., Pieper, S., Kikinis, R.: 3D Slicer as an image computing platform for the Quantitative Imaging Network. Magn. Resonan. Imaging **30**(9), 1323–1341 (2012)
16. Netter, F.: Atlas of Human Anatomy. Netter Basic Science, Elsevier Health Sciences (2010)
17. O'Donnell, L., Westin, C.F.: Automatic tractography segmentationu using a high-dimensional white matter atlas. IEEE Trans. Med. Imaging **26**(11), 1562–1575 (2007)
18. Park, H., Choi, D., Park, J.: Improved sectioned images and surface models of the whole female body. Int. J. Morphol. **33**(4), 1323–1332 (2015)
19. Yokota, F., Takaya, M., Okada, T., Sugano, N., Tada, Y., Tomiyama, N., Sato, Y.: Automated muscle segmentation from 3D CT data of the hip using hierarchical multi-atlas method. In: Proceedings of the 12th Annual Meeting of the International Society for Computer Assisted Orthopaedic Surgery - CAOS 2012 (2012)

Segmentation of Pathological Spines in CT Images Using a Two-Way CNN and a Collision-Based Model

Robert Korez[✉], Boštjan Likar, Franjo Pernuš, and Tomaž Vrtovec

Faculty of Electrical Engineering, University of Ljubljana, Ljubljana, Slovenia
robert.korez@fe.uni-lj.si

Abstract. Accurate boundary delineation and segmentation of pathological spines is indispensable in spine-related applications that rely on the knowledge of vertebral shape. However, exact vertebral boundaries are often difficult to determine due to articulation of vertebrae with each other that may cause vertebral overlaps in segmentations of adjacent vertebrae. To solve this problem, we propose a novel method that consists of two steps. In the first step, the probability maps that determine vertebral boundaries are obtained from a two-way convolutional neural network, trained on normal thoracolumbar spines. In the second step, a collision-based model that consists of (at least two) consecutive vertebra mesh models is initialized close to the observed vertebrae and vertices of each mesh are displaced towards the detected boundaries. As this can lead to mesh collisions in the form of vertices of one mesh penetrating the adjacent one (and/or vice versa), these vertices are efficiently detected and then driven out of the adjacent mesh while locally preserving the shape of the corresponding mesh. By applying the proposed method to 15 three-dimensional computed tomography images of the lumbar spine containing 75 normal and fractured vertebrae, quantitative comparison against reference vertebra segmentations yielded an overall mean Dice similarity coefficient of 93.2%, mean symmetric surface distance of 0.5 mm, and Hausdorff distance of 8.4 mm.

Keywords: Image segmentation · Computed tomography
Pathological spine · Two-way convolutional neural network
Collision-based model

1 Introduction

Accurate boundary delineation and segmentation of vertebrae in three-dimensional (3D) computed tomography (CT) images is essential to the clinical diagnosis and treatment of pathological conditions that affect the spine. However, exact vertebral boundaries are often difficult to determine due to articulation of vertebrae with each other that may cause vertebral overlaps in segmentations of adjacent vertebrae. Thus, despite an increasing interest in vertebra segmentation in recent years, accurate segmentation methods of pathological spines are still lacking.

© Springer International Publishing AG 2018
B. Glocker et al. (Eds.): MSKI 2017, LNCS 10734, pp. 95–107, 2018.
https://doi.org/10.1007/978-3-319-74113-0_9

Related Work. In the past decade, several automated and semi-automated vertebrae segmentation methods that directly or indirectly address the vertebral overlap have been developed. Kim and Kim [1] proposed a fully automated method that was based on constructing 3D fences to separate vertebrae, and then the region growing algorithm was applied within the constructed 3D fences to obtain the final segmentation. Klinder et al. [2] carried out segmentation of vertebrae by using an ensemble of shape-constrained deformable models [3], where vertebrae models were interacting with each other throughout the adaptation to target vertebrae. A statistical multi-vertebrae anatomical model that treated the shape and pose of each vertebra independently was developed by Rasoulian et al. [4], and by the nature of the model definition, vertebral overlap was avoided. Recently, in the work of Castro-Mateos et al. [5], vertebral overlap was addressed with the statistical interspace model, which provides the neighboring relationship between regions in different objects of a multi-object structure by learning the statistical distribution of the interspace between them. The limitations of the aforementioned studies are: (i) manual interactions were often required [4,5], which can be labor-intensive, time-consuming and error-prone, especially when observing large datasets, (ii) statistical shape modeling cannot always capture shape features of pathological samples as they may be suppressed by shape features of a considerably larger number of healthy samples [2,4,5], (iii) the complexity and variability in the appearance of vertebrae and their surroundings cannot be handled by low-level appearance representations, such as intensities [4], valley-emphasized Gaussian intensities [1] or intensity gradients [2,5], and (iv) vertebral overlaps were not completely prevented [2].

To overcome the above mentioned limitations, we combine recent developments in machine learning (i.e. deep learning) and shape modeling (i.e. deformable models), and propose a novel method for fully automated segmentation of vertebrae from 3D CT pathological spine images. In the first step, the probability maps that determine vertebral boundaries are obtained from a two-way convolutional neural network (CNN), trained on normal thoracolumbar spines. In the second step, a collision-based model that consists of (at least two) consecutive vertebra mesh models is initialized close to the observed vertebrae and vertices of each mesh are displaced towards the determined boundaries. As this can lead to mesh collisions in the form of vertices of one mesh penetrating the adjacent one (and/or vice versa), these vertices are efficiently detected and then driven out of the adjacent mesh while locally preserving the shape of the corresponding mesh. The proposed method was evaluated on a publicly available database of 15 CT images of the lumbar spine and demonstrated highly accurate segmentations of 75 normal and fractured vertebrae.

2   Methodology

The proposed method consists of two consecutive steps. In the first step, a testing image of the pathological spine is run through a two-way CNN that is trained on a repository of training images of normal spines, resulting in three probability maps that represent likelihoods of image voxels to belong to the anterior arch (i.e. vertebral body), posterior arch (i.e. spinous, transverse, superior articular and inferior articular processes, and pedicles) and background. By thresholding the anterior arch probability map and using simple morphological operations on the obtained binary image, centroids of vertebral bodies are coarsely determined. In the second step, a collision-based model is initialized as a mesh union of (at least two) consecutive vertebrae with the mean pose and shape obtained from the repository of training meshes of normal vertebrae, and placed in the vicinity of the target vertebrae using the previously determined centroids. The segmentation of target vertebrae is performed by an iterative approach where the model is deformed toward high-magnitude gradients of the augmented background probability map, and mesh collisions in the form of one mesh penetrating the adjacent one (and/or vice versa) are prevented.

2.1   Two-Way CNN

In the field of medical imaging, CNNs are currently one of the main tools used for solving challenging tasks that have traditionally depended on experts for solution [6]. Such tasks include object detection and identification [7], image segmentation [8] and assessment of condition severity [9]. Without relying on handcrafted features, CNNs have the ability to learn features for a specific task directly from the raw image data, and since features are learned in hierarchy of increasing complexity and abstraction, they provide robustness and flexibility. The proposed two-way CNN architecture is, similarly as first proposed in [10] and later adopted in [11–13], made of two paths in order to perform voxel-wise classification based on appearance (i.e. local path) and spatial location (i.e. global path) details around the voxel of interest.

Training. In each epoch of the training stage, thousands of pairs of image patches are extracted around randomly selected voxels from the repository of training images of the normal spines, and sent through a two-way CNN in order to learn its weights and biases $\boldsymbol{\theta}$. In detail, let pair $(\mathcal{L}, \mathcal{G})$ denote the collection of all extracted pairs of image patches in the current epoch. For each randomly selected voxel $\boldsymbol{v}$, two image patches $\boldsymbol{L} \in \mathcal{L}$ and $\boldsymbol{G} \in \mathcal{G}$ of size $27 \times 27 \times 27$ and $55 \times 55 \times 55$, respectively, are extracted around the voxel $\boldsymbol{v}$ and sent through two paths of different operations (i.e. convolution, pooling). In the first (local) path, patch $\boldsymbol{L}$ is sent through nine convolutional layers with small kernels (i.e. of size $3 \times 3 \times 3$) and residual connections, each followed by a parametric rectified linear unit (PReLU). In the second (global) path, patch $\boldsymbol{G}$ is sent consecutively two times through three convolutional layers with kernels of size $5 \times 5 \times 5$, $4 \times 4 \times 4$ and $3 \times 3 \times 3$, respectively, each followed by a PReLU, and a (max) pooling layer with pool of size $2 \times 2 \times 2$ and stride of size $2 \times 2 \times 2$. To achieve that outputs of both paths have the same size, the final layer of the second path is a transposed (convolutional) layer with kernels of size $3 \times 3 \times 3$, followed by a PReLU. The resulting outputs of both paths are jointly sent through three fully connected

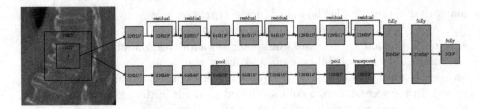

Fig. 1. A schematic illustration of the applied two-way convolutional neural network architecture.

layers, each seen as a convolution one with kernels of size $1 \times 1 \times 1$ and followed by a PReLU. The outputs of the last fully connected layer correspond to particular segmentation classes (i.e. anterior arch, posterior arch and background) and are finally fed to a softmax function to obtain the predicted posterior probabilities that the group of voxels (of size $9 \times 9 \times 9$) around the randomly selected voxel v belongs to each of the segmentation classes. The two-way CNN architecture is in detail illustrated in Fig. 1. By interpreting the probabilities of the CNN as distributions over the segmentation classes, a natural training criteria is to maximize the probability of all classes in the training repository, i.e. to minimize the negative log-likelihood probability for each segmented image in the training repository. The optimal weights and biases $\boldsymbol{\theta}$ of the CNN are obtained using the hybrid scheme [13] between the dense training scheme on a whole image [14] and the commonly used training scheme on individual patches.

Testing. In the testing stage, the two-way CNN with optimally learned weights and biases $\boldsymbol{\theta}$ is applied on the testing image $\boldsymbol{I}$ of the pathological spine in order to obtain three probability maps $\boldsymbol{A}$, $\boldsymbol{P}$ and $\boldsymbol{B}$ that represent likelihoods of image voxels to belong to the anterior arch, posterior arch and background, respectively. In detail, the input image $\boldsymbol{I}$ is first fragmented into I non-overlapping blocks of size $9 \times 9 \times 9$. For each block, two image patches $\boldsymbol{L}_i$ and $\boldsymbol{G}_i$, $i \in I$, of size $27 \times 27 \times 27$ and $55 \times 55 \times 55$, respectively, are extracted around its central voxel. By sending $\boldsymbol{L}_i$ and $\boldsymbol{G}_i$ through the trained two-way CNN, probability maps $\boldsymbol{A}_i$, $\boldsymbol{P}_i$ and $\boldsymbol{B}_i$ are obtained and assembled into probability maps $\boldsymbol{A}$, $\boldsymbol{P}$ and $\boldsymbol{B}$, respectively. A testing image with corresponding probability maps is shown in Fig. 2.

2.2   Collision-Based Model

Initialization. A collision-based model is initialized as a mesh union of two consecutive vertebrae with the mean pose and shape obtained from the repository of training meshes of normal vertebrae, and denoted by $\mathcal{M} = \mathcal{M}_1 \cup \mathcal{M}_2$ with vertices $\boldsymbol{M} = \boldsymbol{M}_1 \cup \boldsymbol{M}_2$ and faces $\boldsymbol{F} = \boldsymbol{F}_1 \cup \boldsymbol{F}_2$. In order to place mesh $\mathcal{M}$ in the vicinity of target vertebrae, the probability map $\boldsymbol{A}$ (Sect. 2.1, Fig. 2(b)), which is obtained from the two-way CNN, is thresholded into vertebral bodies and background. Then, the obtained binary mask is processed with simple

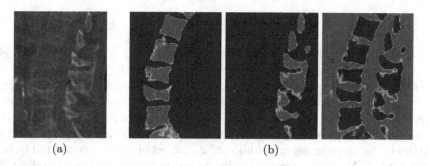

(a)   (b)

Fig. 2. The results of the trained two-way convolutional neural network applied on a testing image of the pathological spine. (a) A testing image, shown in the mid-sagittal cross-section. (b) The corresponding probability maps that represent likelihoods of image voxels to belong to the anterior arch (left), posterior arch (middle) and background (right). The colors range from dark blue for low probabilities to dark red for high probabilities of voxels to belong to each segmentation class. (Color figure online)

morphological operations, such as hole filling, dilation and erosion, to obtain multiple connected components with their centers of masses coarsely defining the centroids of all visible vertebral bodies in image I. Finally, the centers of masses of $\mathcal{M}_1$ and $\mathcal{M}_2$ are jointly repositioned near previously determined centroids of two consecutive vertebral bodies, and the repositioned mesh union is denoted by $\mathcal{X} = \mathcal{X}_1 \cup \mathcal{X}_2$ with vertices $\boldsymbol{X} = \boldsymbol{X}_1 \cup \boldsymbol{X}_2$ and faces $\boldsymbol{F}$.

Segmentation. The segmentation of the target vertebrae is performed by an iterative approach, where vertices $\boldsymbol{X}$ of mesh $\mathcal{X}$ are deformed toward high-magnitude gradients of probability map $\boldsymbol{B}$. However, along the high-magnitude gradients that represent vertebral boundaries, holes or protuberances that are not part of the vertebrae may appear due to the two-way CNN mispredictions. Therefore, probability map $\boldsymbol{B}$ is augmented with image I as $\boldsymbol{B}' = (1+\alpha\cdot\boldsymbol{B})\odot\boldsymbol{I}$, where $\odot$ is the element-wise multiplication and α is the weighting factor.

In each iteration, the deformation of vertices $\boldsymbol{X}$ is represented as an optimization problem, where each vertex is iteratively driven by the information from $\boldsymbol{B}'$ towards vertebral boundaries and constrained by the topology of mesh $\mathcal{M}$ with mean pose and shape. The optimization problem is formulated as

$$\boldsymbol{X}^* = \arg\min_{\boldsymbol{X}\in\mathbb{R}^{|\boldsymbol{X}|\times 3}} \sum_{i=1}^{|\boldsymbol{X}|} \left(w_i \left\| \mathrm{proj}_{\boldsymbol{g}(\boldsymbol{x}_i^*)}(\boldsymbol{x}_i^* - \boldsymbol{x}_i) \right\|^2 \right.$$
$$\left. + \beta \sum_{j\in\mathcal{N}(\boldsymbol{x}_i)} \|(\boldsymbol{x}_i - \boldsymbol{x}_j) - (\boldsymbol{m}_i - \boldsymbol{m}_j)\|^2 \right) \tag{1}$$

and

$$\boldsymbol{x}_i^* = \boldsymbol{x}_i + \arg\max_{j\in\mathcal{J}} \left\{ F_i(\boldsymbol{x}_i + j\,\delta\,\boldsymbol{n}(\boldsymbol{x}_i)) - D\,\delta^2\,j^2 \right\} \delta\,\boldsymbol{n}(\boldsymbol{x}_i), \tag{2}$$

$$F_i(\boldsymbol{x}) = \langle \boldsymbol{n}(\boldsymbol{x}_i), \boldsymbol{g}(\boldsymbol{x}) \rangle, \tag{3}$$

$$w_i = \max\left\{0, \arg\max_{j \in \mathcal{J}} \left\{F_i(\boldsymbol{x}_i^*) - D\,\delta^2\,j^2\right\}\right\}, \tag{4}$$

where $\boldsymbol{x}_i \in \boldsymbol{X}$ is the current vertex position, $\boldsymbol{n}(\boldsymbol{x}_i)$ is the mesh outwards normal at $\boldsymbol{x}_i$, $\mathcal{J}$ is the sampling parcel that represents the discrete search profile along $\boldsymbol{n}(\boldsymbol{x}_i)$, D and δ serve to penalize large distances between $\boldsymbol{x}_i$ and $\boldsymbol{x}_i^*$, $\boldsymbol{g}(\boldsymbol{x})$ is the gradient of the augmented probability map $\boldsymbol{B}'$ at location $\boldsymbol{x}$, $\mathcal{N}(\boldsymbol{x}_i)$ is the set of vertices in the one-ring neighbourhood of $\boldsymbol{x}_i$ (i.e. set of vertices connected to vertex $\boldsymbol{x}_i$), $\boldsymbol{m}_i \in \boldsymbol{M}$, β is the weighting factor and proj is the vector projection [3]. To solve (1) for $\boldsymbol{X}$, the conjugate gradient method is used.

The optimization problem can however lead to mesh collisions in the form of one mesh (e.g. $\mathcal{X}_1$) penetrating the adjacent one (i.e. $\mathcal{X}_2$), and/or vice versa. To avoid such a scenario, we introduce a novel step in the iterative approach where vertices from $\boldsymbol{X}_1$ that penetrate $\mathcal{X}_2$ are efficiently detected and then driven out of $\mathcal{X}_2$ by the as-rigid-as-possible modeling [15] that locally preserves the shape of $\mathcal{X}_1$.

Let vertices $\boldsymbol{Y} = \boldsymbol{Y}_1 \cup \boldsymbol{Y}_2$ denote the solution of the optimization problem (1) at each iteration, and let $\mathcal{Y} = \mathcal{Y}_1 \cup \mathcal{Y}_2$ denote the corresponding mesh with faces $\boldsymbol{F}$. To determine if $\mathcal{Y}_1$ penetrates $\mathcal{Y}_2$, vertices from $\boldsymbol{Y}_1$ have to be tested whether they are inside $\mathcal{Y}_2$. Firstly, for a vertex $\boldsymbol{y}_{1,i} \in \boldsymbol{Y}_1$, a ray $\boldsymbol{r}_{1,i}(t) = \boldsymbol{y}_{1,i} + t\boldsymbol{d}_{1,i}$ is shot out of $\boldsymbol{y}_{1,i}$ in a random direction $\boldsymbol{d}_{1,i}$. Secondly, for each face $\boldsymbol{f}_{2,j} \in \boldsymbol{F}_2$, $j = 1, 2, \ldots, |\boldsymbol{F}_2|$, the matrix equation in the form

$$\left[-\boldsymbol{d}, \boldsymbol{y}_{2,j}^{(2)} - \boldsymbol{y}_{2,j}^{(1)}, \boldsymbol{y}_{2,j}^{(3)} - \boldsymbol{y}_{2,j}^{(1)}\right] \cdot [t, u, v]^T = \boldsymbol{y}_{1,i} - \boldsymbol{y}_{2,j}^{(1)} \tag{5}$$

is solved for $t, u, v \in \mathbb{R}$, where $\boldsymbol{y}_{2,j}^{(k)} \in \boldsymbol{Y}_2$, $k = 1, 2, 3$, are three vertices that define face $\boldsymbol{f}_{2,j}$ [16]. It can be concluded that if $u, v \geq 0$ and $u + v = 1$, then ray $\boldsymbol{r}_{1,i}$ intersects face $\boldsymbol{f}_{2,j}$. Let $N_{1,i}$ denote the number of faces that ray $\boldsymbol{r}_{1,i}$ intersects. Finally, it can be concluded that if $N_{1,i} \equiv 1 \bmod 2$, then vertex $\boldsymbol{y}_{1,i}$ is inside $\mathcal{Y}_2$ (Algorithm 1).

Based on the above, let $\boldsymbol{Y}_1' \subset \boldsymbol{Y}_1$ denote vertices that are inside $\mathcal{Y}_2$. The most straightforward way to drive vertices $\boldsymbol{Y}_1'$ out of $\mathcal{Y}_2$ is an iterative approach where vertices $\boldsymbol{Y}_1'$ are firstly displaced for a small distance in the inward direction along the corresponding vertex normals and then tested whether they are still inside $\mathcal{Y}_2$. However, such primitive deformations of mesh $\mathcal{Y}_1$ can significantly change its topology (e.g. spikes jutting out of the mesh) and the outcome is a mesh that may not represent anatomically correct vertebral boundaries. To avoid such a scenario, vertices $\boldsymbol{Y}_1'$ are rather displaced by the as-rigid-as-possible modeling [15] that locally preserves the shape of $\mathcal{Y}_1$.

The as-rigid-as-possible modeling is a powerful deformation technique that produces anatomically natural-looking results with guaranteed convergence. The main principle used is that small local parts of the mesh change smoothly and as rigidly as possible. Let $\boldsymbol{Z}_1$ denote initial vertices, i.e. $\boldsymbol{Y}_1$, and let $\boldsymbol{Z}_1'$ denote displaced vertices, i.e. $(\boldsymbol{Y}_1 \backslash \boldsymbol{Y}_1') \cup \boldsymbol{Y}_1''$, where $\boldsymbol{Y}_1''$ denotes vertices $\boldsymbol{Y}_1'$ that were

Algorithm 1. Test if a vertex is inside a mesh

input: vertex $y_{1,i} \in Y_1$, mesh $\mathcal{Y}_2$ with vertices Y_2 and faces F_2
output: boolean b

1: set $b = \mathbf{false}$, $N_{1,i} = 0$
2: shot a ray $r(t) = y_{1,i} + td$, $t \in \mathbb{R}$, out of vertex y_1 in a random direction d
3: **for all** faces $f_{2,j} \in F_2$ **do**
4:     solve $\left[-d, y_{2,j}^{(2)} - y_{2,j}^{(1)}, y_{2,j}^{(3)} - y_{2,j}^{(1)}\right] \cdot [t, u, v]^T = y_{1,i} - y_{2,j}^{(1)}$ for $t, u, v \in \mathbb{R}$, where
    $y_{2,j}^{(k)} \in Y_2$, $k = 1, 2, 3$, are three vertices that define face $f_{2,j}$ [16]
5:     **if** $u, v \geq 0$ and $u + v \leq 1$ **then**
6:        set $N_{1,i} = N_{1,i} + 1$
7:     **end if**
8: **end for**
9: **if** $N_{1,i} \equiv 1 \bmod 2$ **then**
10:     set $b = \mathbf{true}$
11: **end if**

---

displaced for a small distance in the inward direction along the corresponding vertex normals. To achieve that the topology is preserved in small local neighbourhoods of displaced vertices, the as-rigid-as-possible modeling of vertices Z'_1 is represented as an optimization problem and formulated as

$$Z'^{*}_1, \{R^*_i\} = \underset{\substack{Z'_1 \in \mathbb{R}^{|Z'_1| \times 3} \\ \{R_i\}, R_i \in \mathbb{R}^{3 \times 3}}}{\arg\min} \sum_{i=1}^{|Z'_1|} \left(\sum_{j \in \mathcal{N}(z'_{1,i})} w_{ij} \left\| (z'_{1,i} - z'_{1,j}) - R_i (z_{1,i} - z_{1,j}) \right\|^2 \right), \tag{6}$$

$$w_{ij} = \frac{1}{2} \left(\cot \alpha_{ij} + \cot \beta_{ij} \right), \tag{7}$$

where $z_{1,i} \in Z_1$, $z'_{1,i} \in Z'_1$, α_{ij} and β_{ij} are the opposite angles of the mesh edge defined between vertices $z_{1,i}$ and $z_{1,j}$, $\mathcal{N}(z'_{1,i})$ is the set of vertices in the one-ring neighbourhood of $z'_{1,i}$ and R_i is the rotation that best approximates the transformation that takes vertex $z_{1,i}$ to $z'_{1,i}$ (Fig. 3). To solve (6) for Z'_1 and $\{R_i\}$, a two-step alternating minimization strategy is used [15]. In the first step, vertices Z'_1 are considered as fixed so that the rigid transformations are the only unknowns, and they are determined by

$$S_i = \sum_{j \in \mathcal{N}(z'_{1,i})} w_{ij}(z_{1,i} - z_{1,j})(z'_{1,i} - z'_{1,j})^T = U_i \Sigma_i V_i^T, \tag{8}$$

$$R_i = U_i V_i^T, \tag{9}$$

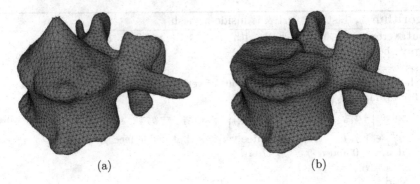

(a)   (b)

Fig. 3. (a) One of the meshes in the mesh union configuration with few vertices (in red) that were penetrating the adjacent mesh (not visible). (b) The resulting mesh after iteratively displacing the penetrated vertices for a small distance in the inward direction along the corresponding vertex normal using the as-rigid-as-possible modeling. [Note that for a clear visualization, we manually displaced a few vertices on the superior endplate, and the demonstrated situation is unlikely to occur.] (Color figure online)

where $U_i\Sigma_iV_i^T$ is the singular value decomposition of S_i. In the second step, with the given set of rigid transformations, vertices Z'_1 are determined by minimizing (6). These interleaved iterations are repeated until the minimum is reached. The resulting mesh $\mathcal{Z}_1\cup\mathcal{Z}_2$ with mesh vertices $Z_1\cup Z_2$ finally represents the segmentation of two consecutive vertebrae.

3   Experiments and Results

3.1   Spine Image Database

The proposed method for segmentation of pathological spines in CT images was trained (i.e. the two-way CNN training and the creation of mesh unions of two consecutive vertebrae with the mean pose and shape) on two and tested on one publicly available databases of 3D CT images that are part of the *Spine Web*,[1] a collaborative platform for research on spine imaging and image analysis. The first (training) database consists of 10 axially reconstructed CT images of the lumbar spine with a total of 50 normal lumbar vertebrae, in-plane voxel size of 0.282–0.791 mm and cross-sectional thickness of 0.725–1.530 mm [17]. The second (training) database consists of 10 axially reconstructed CT images of the thoracolumbar spine with a total of 170 normal thoracic and lumbar vertebrae, in-plane voxel size of 0.313–0.361 mm and cross-sectional thickness of 1 mm [18]. The third (testing) database consists of 15 axially reconstructed CT images of the lumbar spine with a total of 75 normal and fractured lumbar vertebrae, in-plane voxel size of 0.289–0.803 mm and cross-sectional thickness of 1.105–1.892 mm [19]. The incidence of crush, biconcave and wedge fractures is 11% (i.e. eight out

---

[1] Accessible via http://spineweb.digitalimaginggroup.ca.

of 75 vertebrae), 35% (i.e. 26 out of 75 vertebrae) and 11% (i.e. eight out of 75 vertebrae), respectively. For all databases, a reference manually defined binary segmentation mask was available for each vertebra in each image.

3.2   Experimental Setup

Two-Way Convolutional Neural Network. Since the two-way CNN is able to learn useful features from scratch, only minimal image preprocessing was applied (on training and testing databases). Firstly, all images were resampled to an isotropic resolution of $1 \times 1 \times 1 \, \mathrm{mm}^3$ per voxel (using linear interpolation) since the kernels of the CNN need to correspond to the same real-size patterns for all images. Secondly, images were smoothed using a Gaussian kernel of size $0.5 \, \mathrm{mm}$. Finally, the obtained intensities were linearly mapped to interval $[-5, 5]$. To train the two-way CNN, in each out of 40 epochs, 80k pairs of patches were extracted around randomly selected voxels from images in the first and second database. The CNN was trained via the stochastic gradient descent method and accelerated by the Nesterov momentum with its parameter set to 0.9. To avoid overfitting, training was augmented by the dropout (the outputs of last two fully connected layers were randomly set to zero with probabilities of 0.5) and batch normalization.

Mean Pose and Shape Mesh Union. For each i-th lumbar vertebrae pair ($i = 1, 2, \ldots, 5$, corresponding to pairs T11-L1, L1-L2, L2-L3, L3-L4 and L4-L5), the mean pose and shape mesh union $\mathcal{M}_i \cup \mathcal{M}_{i+1}$ of corresponding two consecutive vertebrae was constructed. Firstly, the marching cubes algorithm was applied to each binary mask $\boldsymbol{B}_{jk}$ that represents the reference segmentation of j-th vertebra ($j = 1, 2, \ldots, 6$, corresponding to one thoracic and five lumbar vertebrae) in k-th training image ($k = 1, 2, \ldots, 10$, corresponding to 10 images in the second database). Secondly, each resulting mesh $\mathcal{M}_{j,k}$ was isotropically remeshed [20] so that the number of vertices was independent of the size of j-th vertebra and voxel size of k-th image. Thirdly, the coherent point drift was applied to establish pointwise vertex correspondences among meshes $\{\mathcal{M}_{j,k}\}_{k=1}^{10}$ of j-th vertebra. Finally, the joint pose+shape modeling [21] was used to include, in addition to shape variations, pose variations in i-th vertebrae pair $\{\mathcal{M}_{i,k} \cup \mathcal{M}_{i+1,k}\}_{k=1}^{10}$, yielding the mean pose and shape mesh union $\mathcal{M}_i \cup \mathcal{M}_{i+1}$ for each vertebrae pair.

Collision-Based Model. The collision-based model was initialized as the mean pose and shape mesh union $\mathcal{M}_i \cup \mathcal{M}_{i+1}$ corresponding to i-th observed lumbar vertebrae pair was aligned with the centroids of corresponding vertebral bodies that were determined by processing two-way CNN probability maps (the threshold for the probability map $\boldsymbol{A}$ was experimentally set to 0.9). The segmentation parameters that guide the model toward vertebra boundaries were experimentally set to $\alpha = 1$, $\delta = 1 \, \mathrm{mm}$, $|\mathcal{J}| = 51$, i.e. the length of the discrete search profile was $25 \, \mathrm{mm}$ in the inward and outward direction, $D = 2.5 \, \mathrm{mm}^{-2}$ and

Table 1. The segmentation results of the proposed method with and without collision detection in terms of mean $\pm$ standard deviation of the Dice similarity coefficient (DSC), mean symmetric surface distance (MSD) and Hausdorff surface distance (HD).

Level	With collision detection			Without collision detection		
	DSC (%)	MSD (mm)	HD (mm)	DSC (%)	MSD (mm)	HD (mm)
L1	94.3 ± 2.2	0.4 ± 0.1	6.4 ± 2.2	94.1 ± 2.4	0.4 ± 0.1	6.8 ± 2.7
L2	93.8 ± 2.0	0.5 ± 0.2	8.0 ± 2.6	93.6 ± 2.2	0.5 ± 0.2	11.0 ± 3.3
L3	93.9 ± 1.6	0.5 ± 0.1	7.4 ± 3.5	93.4 ± 2.3	0.5 ± 0.2	10.7 ± 3.6
L4	92.2 ± 2.2	0.6 ± 0.2	10.0 ± 3.9	91.3 ± 3.0	0.7 ± 0.2	14.1 ± 4.5
L5	91.8 ± 1.8	0.6 ± 0.1	10.4 ± 3.2	91.4 ± 2.8	0.6 ± 0.2	12.8 ± 5.0
All (normal)	93.6 ± 2.0	0.5 ± 0.2	8.5 ± 3.8	93.0 ± 2.7	0.5 ± 0.2	10.7 ± 4.6
All (fractured)	92.9 ± 2.3	0.5 ± 0.2	8.4 ± 3.1	92.5 ± 2.8	0.5 ± 0.2	11.4 ± 4.5

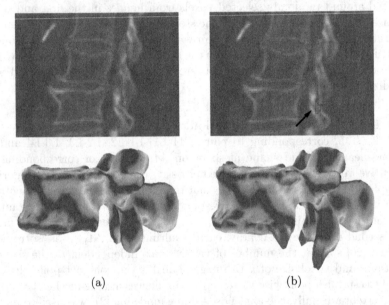

(a)   (b)

Fig. 4. The segmentation results of the proposed method (a) with and (b) without collision detection, shown in mid-sagittal cross-sections (top) and in three dimensions with superimposed color-coded symmetric surface distances against corresponding reference segmentations (bottom). The colors range from blue for short to red for large surface distances (up to 11 mm). The arrow indicates inaccurate delineation of the posterior arch due to the collisions that occur during the deformation of vertices towards vertebral boundaries. (Color figure online)

$\beta = 25$. The number of iterations was set to 5 for the deformation (2)–(4) and as-rigid-as-possible modeling (7)–(9) of mesh vertices. For each resulting mesh pair $\mathcal{Z}_i \cup \mathcal{Z}_{i+1}$, only $\mathcal{Z}_{i+1}$ was used to generate the binary mask of the final segmentation since $\mathcal{Z}_i$ was used to eliminate mesh collisions.

3.3 Results

The vertebrae segmentation performance was evaluated on the third database that consists of lumbar spine images with normal and fractured vertebrae by computing (with respect to the reference manual segmentations) the Dice similarity coefficient (DSC), mean symmetric surface distance (MSD) and Hausdorff surface distance (HD) in terms of mean $\pm$ standard deviation. For all vertebrae, DSC of $93.2 \pm 2.2\%$, MSD of 0.5 ± 0.2 mm and HD of 8.4 ± 3.4 mm were obtained. Detailed results of the proposed method with and without collision detection are presented in Table 1 for all vertebrae levels and in Fig. 4 for a randomly selected vertebra.

4 Discussion

In this paper, we propose a novel method for fully automated segmentation of vertebrae from 3D CT pathological spine images that combines recent developments in machine learning and shape modeling. A two-way CNN is first used to determine vertebral boundaries, and then a collision-based model is used to obtain final segmentations without vertebral overlaps. Similarly as in the method proposed by Castro-Mateos et al. [5], a limitation of the proposed method is that during the segmentation of vertebra L5 (i.e. pair L4–L5), there is no guarantee that L5 segmentation results did not over-segment sacral vertebra S1. A feasible solution would be either to include vertebra S1 as an additional label into the training of the two-way CNN or the lumbosacral vertebra pair L5-S1 into the collision-based model. Despite this minor limitation, the proposed method demonstrated highly accurate segmentations of normal and fractured vertebrae.

Directions for future work include the application of the proposed method for the evaluation of vertebral fractures, as well as its extension to other anatomical structures (e.g. carpal bones or multiple abdominal organs) and imaging modalities (e.g. magnetic resonance).

Acknowledgements. This work was supported by the Slovenian Research Agency (ARRS) under grants P2-0232, J2-5473, J7-6781 and J2-7118.

References

1. Kim, Y., Kim, D.: A fully automatic vertebra segmentation method using 3D deformable fences. Comput. Med. Imag. Graph. **33**(5), 343–352 (2009)
2. Klinder, T., Ostermann, J., Ehm, M., Franz, A., Kneser, R., Lorenz, C.: Automated model-based vertebra detection, identification, and segmentation in CT images. Med. Image Anal. **13**(3), 471–482 (2009)
3. Weese, J., Kaus, M., Lorenz, C., Lobregt, S., Truyen, R., Pekar, V.: Shape constrained deformable models for 3D medical image segmentation. In: Insana, M.F., Leahy, R.M. (eds.) IPMI 2001. LNCS, vol. 2082, pp. 380–387. Springer, Heidelberg (2001). https://doi.org/10.1007/3-540-45729-1_38

4. Rasoulian, A., Rohling, R., Abolmaesumi, P.: Lumbar spine segmentation using a statistical multi-vertebrae anatomical shape+pose model. IEEE Trans. Med. Imaging **32**(10), 1890–1900 (2013)
5. Castro-Mateos, I., Pozo, J., Pereañez, M., Lekadir, K., Lazary, A., Frangi, A.: Statistical interspace models (SIMs): application to robust 3D spine segmentation. IEEE Trans. Med. Imaging **34**(8), 1663–1675 (2015)
6. LeCun, Y., Bengio, Y., Hinton, G.: Deep learning. Nature **521**(7553), 436–444 (2015)
7. Chen, H., Shen, C., Qin, J., Ni, D., Shi, L., Cheng, J.C.Y., Heng, P.-A.: Automatic localization and identification of vertebrae in Spine CT via a joint learning model with deep neural networks. In: Navab, N., Hornegger, J., Wells, W.M., Frangi, A.F. (eds.) MICCAI 2015. LNCS, vol. 9349, pp. 515–522. Springer, Cham (2015). https://doi.org/10.1007/978-3-319-24553-9_63
8. Chen, H., Dou, Q., Wang, X., Qin, J., Cheng, J.C.Y., Heng, P.-A.: 3D fully convolutional networks for intervertebral disc localization and segmentation. In: Zheng, G., Liao, H., Jannin, P., Cattin, P., Lee, S.-L. (eds.) MIAR 2016. LNCS, vol. 9805, pp. 375–382. Springer, Cham (2016). https://doi.org/10.1007/978-3-319-43775-0_34
9. Jamaludin, A., Kadir, T., Zisserman, A.: SpineNet: automatically pinpointing classification evidence in Spinal MRIs. In: Ourselin, S., Joskowicz, L., Sabuncu, M.R., Unal, G., Wells, W. (eds.) MICCAI 2016. LNCS, vol. 9901, pp. 166–175. Springer, Cham (2016). https://doi.org/10.1007/978-3-319-46723-8_20
10. Davy, A., Havaei, M., Warde-Farley, D., Biard, A., Tran, L., Jodoin, P.M., Courville, A., Larochelle, H., Pal, C., Bengio, Y.: Brain tumor segmentation with deep neural networks. In: Proceedings of the 3rd MICCAI Multimodal Brain Tumor Segmentation Challenge - BRATS 2014, pp. 1–5 (2014)
11. Schlegl, T., Waldstein, S.M., Vogl, W.-D., Schmidt-Erfurth, U., Langs, G.: Predicting semantic descriptions from medical images with convolutional neural networks. In: Ourselin, S., Alexander, D.C., Westin, C.-F., Cardoso, M.J. (eds.) IPMI 2015. LNCS, vol. 9123, pp. 437–448. Springer, Cham (2015). https://doi.org/10.1007/978-3-319-19992-4_34
12. Havaei, M., Davy, A., Warde-Farley, D., Biard, A., Courville, A., Bengio, Y., Pal, C., Jodoin, P.M., Larochelle, H.: Brain tumor segmentation with deep neural networks. Med. Image Anal. **35**, 18–31 (2017)
13. Kamnitsas, K., Ledig, C., Newcombe, V.F., Simpson, J.P., Kane, A.D., Menon, D.K., Rueckert, D., Glocker, B.: Efficient multi-scale 3D CNN with fully connected CRF for accurate brain lesion segmentation. Med. Image Anal. **36**, 61–78 (2017)
14. Long, J., Shelhamer, E., Darrell, T.: Fully convolutional networks for semantic segmentation. In: Proceedings of the IEEE Conference on Computer Vision and Pattern Recognition - CVPR 2015, pp. 3431–3440 (2015)
15. Sorkine, O., Alexa, M.: As-rigid-as-possible surface modeling. In: Proceedings of the 5th Symposium on Geometry Processing - SGP 2007, pp. 1–8 (2007)
16. Möller, T., Trumbore, B.: Fast, minimum storage ray-triangle intersection. J. Graph. Tools **2**(1), 21–28 (1997)
17. Ibragimov, B., Likar, B., Pernuš, F., Vrtovec, T.: Shape representation for efficient landmark-based segmentation in 3-D. IEEE Trans. Med. Imaging **33**(4), 861–874 (2014)
18. Yao, J., Burns, J.E., Munoz, H., Summers, R.M.: Detection of vertebral body fractures based on cortical shell unwrapping. In: Ayache, N., Delingette, H., Golland, P., Mori, K. (eds.) MICCAI 2012. LNCS, vol. 7512, pp. 509–516. Springer, Heidelberg (2012). https://doi.org/10.1007/978-3-642-33454-2_63

19. Korez, R., Ibragimov, B., Likar, B., Pernuš, F., Vrtovec, T.: A framework for auto-
    mated spine and vertebrae interpolation-based detection and model-based segmen-
    tation. IEEE Trans. Med. Imaging **34**(8), 1649–1662 (2015)
20. Botsch, M., Kobbelt, L.: A remeshing approach to multiresolution modeling. In:
    Proceedings of the 2nd Eurographics Symposium on Geometry Processing - SGP
    2004, pp. 189–196 (2004)
21. Bossa, M., Olmos, S.: Multi-object statistical pose+shape models. In: Proceedings
    of the 4th IEEE International Symposium on Biomedical Imaging - ISBI 2007, pp.
    1204–1207. IEEE (2007)

Attention-Driven Deep Learning for Pathological Spine Segmentation

Anjany Sekuboyina[1,2(✉)], Jan Kukačka[1,2], Jan S. Kirschke[2], Bjoern H. Menze[1], and Alexander Valentinitsch[1,2]

[1] Department of Informatics, Technische Universität München, Munich, Germany
`anjany.sekuboyina@tum.de`
[2] Department of Diagnostic and Interventional Neuroradiology, Klinikum rechts der Isar, Munich, Germany

Abstract. Accurate segmentation of the spine in computed tomography (CT) images is mandatory for quantitative analysis, e.g. in osteoporosis, but remains challenging due to high variability in vertebral morphology and spinal anatomy among patients. Conventionally, spine segmentation was performed by model-based techniques employing spine atlases or statistical shape models. We argue that such approaches, even though intuitive, fail to address clinical abnormalities such as vertebral fractures, scoliosis, etc. We propose a novel deep learning-based method for segmenting the spine, which does not rely on any pre-defined shape model. We employ two networks: one for localisation and another for segmentation. Since a typical spine CT scan cannot be processed at once owing to its large dimensions, we find that both nets are essential to work towards a perfect segmentation. We evaluate our framework on three datasets containing healthy and fractured cases: two private and one public. Our approach achieves a mean Dice coefficient of ∼0.87, which is comparable but not higher than the state-of-art model-based approaches. However, we show that our approach handles degenerate cases more accurately.

Keywords: Spine segmentation · Automated segmentation
Deep learning · Fully convolutional network

1 Introduction

Spine segmentation is a crucial component in quantitative medical image analysis. It directly allows detection and assessment of vertebral fractures and indirectly supports modelling and monitoring of the spinal ageing process. In this work we propose a method based on "deep-learning", that generates precise spine segmentations on computed tomography (CT) images. It overcomes the drawbacks of earlier segmentation approaches and thus can be used in clinical settings. Particularly, our approach is capable of handling scans with varying fields-of-view (FOV) and degenerate spine or vertebrae.

A. Sekuboyina and J. Kukačka—Contributed equally.

© Springer International Publishing AG 2018
B. Glocker et al. (Eds.): MSKI 2017, LNCS 10734, pp. 108–119, 2018.
https://doi.org/10.1007/978-3-319-74113-0_10

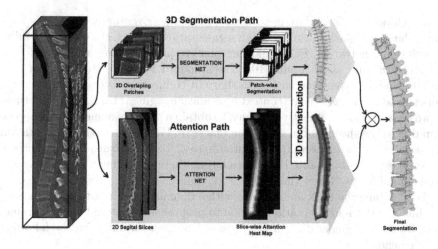

Fig. 1. Schematic outline of the proposed approach.

Previous works often deal with spine segmentation in a multi-step approach incorporating spine localisation and vertebra detection followed by the segmentation [1,2]. Various traditional computer vision techniques have been successfully applied, such as active shape models and snake-based methods [3,4], level sets [5] or graph-based approaches using normalized-cuts [6]. Most of these methods rely on prior knowledge in the form of spine atlases or statistical shape models which are used to provide a good initialisation. Such models reach state-of-the-art performance on healthy spines with no signs of osteoporotic fractures, attaining Dice coefficients (DICE) of over 0.9. However, osteoporotic patients often suffer from severe vertebral fractures in various stages and spinal deformities such as scoliosis. In such cases, model-dependent segmentation might fail due to the high variability of the unique shape of a fracture or deformity that does not resemble a mean shape model. A shape model is also restricted by its mesh interpolation algorithm, which makes extreme deformations unfeasible. Moreover, CT images acquired for preoperative planning due to other diseases in the thoracic or abdominal area have the spine in them as a consequence. Such opportunistic scans have varying FOVs, spatial resolution, and image reconstruction, in addition to variations in scan enhancements due to contrast agents. Model-based approaches, which rely on good initialisations, could fail in such cases either due to lack of landmarks for registration, uneven intensities, and noise. This calls for data-driven approach based on supervised learning that does not rely on pre-defined models, but learns the variability by training on several kinds of contingencies.

Machine learning-based approaches have proven to fulfill these requirements, given that enough data is available for their training. Glocker et al. [7] and Suzani et al. [8] attempt the vertebra detection problem on arbitrary FOVs using random forests and multi-layer perceptrons respectively. More recently, Chen et al. [9] try to make use of the omni-present convolutional neural networks (CNN), with a clever cost formulation, to detect vertebrae. Eventually the CNNs have gained large popularity also for image segmentation through the concept of fully-convolutional networks (FCN) allowing pixel-to-pixel training and inference on (nearly) arbitrary sized inputs [10]. The standard FCN architecture of a contracting and an expanding path with shortcut connections is exploited in recent works on segmentation in the context of medical imaging [11–13]. However, these approaches cannot be directly extended to obtain a dense segmentation of a spine scan due to the sheer spatial resolution of a scan. For instance, the segmentation net used in [10] works on inputs containing $\sim2.5 \times 10^5$ pixels; a typical whole spine CT scan is about 100–1000 times larger, thereby making a straightforward extension of an FCN non-viable.

We combine the FCN architecture with a domain-specific data-preprocessing pipeline and data-augmentation scheme to propose a robust and scalable framework for spine segmentation in CT images. The method builds on the following key elements:

1. A low-resolution attention FCN for spine localisation that works on two-dimensional sagittal slices of a scan.
2. A high-resolution segmentation FCN for fine segmentation that takes three-dimensional patches as input.
3. A smart patch extraction strategy to incorporate the FOV invariance and bypass memory limitations.
4. A domain-specific data augmentation to increase the training set size and incorporate the typical biological variance.

Our approach is free from predefined shape models and is purely data-driven, and is thus highly generalisable across varying FOVs, spinal deformities, and spatial resolutions given sufficiently diverse training data. Methodological details are presented in Sect. 2. We evaluate our method on a large private dataset of 56 (a) healthy and (b) fractured patients. We also compare our approach against the state-of-the-art methods on a publicly available dataset from the 2014 MICCAI Workshop on Computational Methods and Clinical Applications for Spine Imaging (CSI2014) [14]. Our approach achieves a comparable mean DICE of around 87%, while perfectly segmenting fine details of normal as well as deformed vertebrae. Details of the experiments follow in Sect. 3.

2 Methodology

We present our approach to spine segmentation in two stages. Firstly, a two-dimensional (2D) FCN which provides a low-resolution localisation of the spine. Secondly, we present the 2D-three-dimensional (3D) FCN that generates high-resolution binary segmentations. Fusing the predictions of both the networks results in a good segmentation of a spine volume. An overview of our approach is shown in Fig. 1.

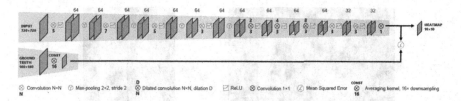

Fig. 2. Attention-net. The network utilizes 10 convolutional layers with stride 1, kernel sizes and dilation factors are denoted in the image. Moreover, the first 4 conv-layers are followed by max-pooling. Numbers above blobs represent number of features in the hidden feature space. Observe the drop in spatial resolution from the input to the output slice, thereby providing a low-resolution attention map for a given sagittal slice. Every n-th sagittal slice from the scan volume is considered for inference, thereby reducing the number of forward passes for scan, which makes the attention generation very fast. Consequently, the original scan resolution is restored by interpolation in all three directions.

2.1 Localization: Attention-Net

We exploit the structure and position of the spine in a scan, that are generally invariant, to obtain a rough localisation of the spine. The network performing this task is called the *attention net*. Since sagittal view provides significant context on the spine's location, the attention net operates fully in 2D on sagittal slices. The net is fully convolutional and outputs a 2D map of lower dimension than the input. Every value ($\in [0, 1]$) in the predicted 2D map corresponds to a 16×16 region in the input, and represents the percentage of foreground voxels ('spine' voxels) in that region. Figure 2 illustrates the architecture of the *attention-net*. A 2D patch of 160×160 (padded to size 720×720) predicts a maps of size 10×10. Since context is of utmost importance for determining the presence of spine, we increase the receptive field with dilated convolutions [15] in the downstream convolutional layers. We incorporate the resolution reduction in the third dimension by working only on every n^{th} sagittal slice. At the end, given an input volume, the attention net works on sagittal slices and predicts a lower-resolution volume (called the *attention map*) whose values indicate the presence of spine. The attention map is then up-sampled to the input dimension for further use.

Training and Inference. The ground truth for training is obtained from the available spine segmentations. Every volume is down-sampled by a factor of $16 \times 16 \times n$ ($n = 8$, in our experiments), each voxel representing the ratio of spine-voxels to total-voxels in its corresponding 16×16 region. The network is trained to minimise the mean-squared error between predicted map and ground truth. During training, given a scan volume, we train on large patches randomly sampled from sagittal slices with data augmentation through rigid transformations (2D rotations by $\pm 20°$ and scaling of these axes by $\pm 40\%$); we advocate the use of patches as incorporation of invariance to arbitrary FOVs. During test

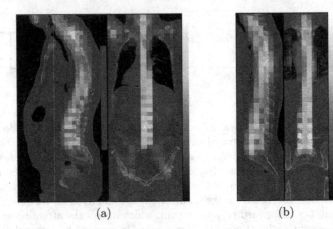

(a)   (b)

Fig. 3. Attention maps. (a) and (b) show two computed tomography scans overlaid with the response of the Attention-Net aggregated over all slices in the direction of view. Notice that the response is focused predominantly on the spine. This attention-map is Gaussian smoothened, thresholded, and converted to a binary mask, which is then fused with the Segmentation-Net's response.

time, the patches are sampled from every n-th sagittal slice with overlap such that the entire slice is covered. The predicted low-resolution attention map for each of these patches is up-sampled to the resolution of the scan volume, and filtered with a 3D Gaussian kernel, $\mathcal{N}(0, \Sigma)$. Figure 3 shows an attention map of two test cases. For better visualisation of the 3D map, the response is aggregated in the direction of view and overlaid on the mid-slice. Observe that the net succeeds in localising the spine. This attention-map is thresholded and converted to a binary mask, which is then fused with the Segmentation-Net's response as elaborated in the following sections. The threshold-value and the covariance of the Gaussian smoothing (Σ) are tuned on the validation set.

2.2 Spine Segmentation: Segmentation-Net

Precise segmentation can be obtained when the receptive field of the network if small enough that it focuses on minute details, while being large enough to capture sufficient context. We achieve this by incorporating a patch-based approach. Such an approach also alleviates the restriction that the limited memory of a GPU imposes on the volume that can be processed by the network. We propose a segmentation net that is fully convolutional and a combination of 2D and 3D convolutions, building on the versatile 'U' architecture commonly used for segmentation [12,16]. A detailed view of the network's architecture is shown in Fig. 4. The input to the network is a 3D block from the scan, having larger receptive field in the sagittal view (for example, an input block could be of size $188 \times 188 \times 12$, with the first two dimensions corresponding to the sagittal view). At an isotropic resolution of $1\,\text{mm}^3$, the receptive field for predicting one voxel's label has a size of $\sim 18.4 \times 18.4 \times 0.8\,\text{cm}^3$. The output is a dense pixel-wise segmentation of dimensions equal to that of the input.

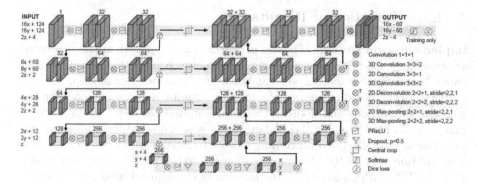

Fig. 4. Segmentation-net. The network has a five-level downsampling path, each level consisting of two convolutions with a ReLU activation and a max-pooling, and a symmetric upsampling path, which are connected by skip connections for recovery of high resolution. Notice the utilisation of a combination of two-dimensional and three-dimensional convolutions to process higher information in the sagittal direction, while conglomerating information from the adjacent slices. The size of the inputs and outputs is parameterised by the dimensions of the smallest blob on the path as $x, y \geq 4, z \geq 3$.

Training and Inference. We use a segmentation-centric loss function of DICE [13] as the objective function. At the training time we randomly sample patches from the input volumes and apply online generated elastic and rigid deformations to them as a form of data augmentation. Specifically, we apply rotations along the sagittal plane by $\pm 2°$ and scaling by $\pm 10\%$ along with minute contrast adjustments. Employing dropout after the convolutions on the lowest level of the contracting path gave a significant performance improvement. At the test time, the patches are extracted uniformly with overlap such that the resulting segmentations cover the entire test scan.

To conclude the approach: given a scan volume, the segmentation-net provides its dense segmentation. Since the latter splits the volume in sub-blocks, we observe that the context in these blocks is insufficient for perfect segmentation. We therefore observe several false positives in the form of *stray* segmentation, wherein, in addition to spine, other regions such as parts of the rib cage, pelvic bone, sacrum etc. are also segmented. The thresholded binary attention-map, which localises only the spine, is used as a mask over the output of the segmentation-net to clear away the stray segmentations[1], resulting in the final segmentation map.

---

[1] A cascaded fusion of these nets was also tried where the patches for the segmentation net are obtained only from the region proposed by the attention map. We observed that the accuracy of this approach was not superior to our approach of late-fusion.

3   Experiments and Results

Implementation Details. The two networks in our approach are implemented as standalone modules. Given a scan, the inference in both the nets run in parallel, and their responses are combined. As a preprocessing step, the CT volumes are subjected to anisotropic diffusion filtering in order to smoothen the homogeneous regions and improve the details around the edges. Both the nets were implemented in Caffe [17]. Adam solver was employed for optimising the loss. The nets were trained till convergence with initial learning rates of 10^{-5} for segmentation net and 10^{-4} for the attention net. When implemented on a Nvidia Titan X GPU with 12 GB RAM, the training of the segmentation net converged in two days while that of the attention net took one day. The convergence was faster in the latter case owing to a significantly lower number of parameters.

Data. We evaluate our framework on three datasets: (Dataset 1) forty five patients without fractures but varying age from 25 to 69 years, (Dataset 2) eleven cases with vertebral fractures, to evaluate the performance on deformed vertebrae, and (Dataset 3) the spine segmentation challenge of the CSI2014 dataset containing twenty CT scans, for comparison with other model-based techniques. Datasets 1 and 2 are private in-house datasets gathered from our picture archiving and communication system. The scans were acquired over a period of two years for various patient examinations and not specifically for the spine analysis, which results in a high diversity in terms of patient-age, abnormalities, FOV, and scanner calibrations. The ground truth segmentation for this data was obtained by first using the approach in [1][2] and then manually corrected by a medical expert. Experiments on these datasets are therefore close to the clinical scenario.

Dataset 1. This is employed to validate the generalisability towards varying BMDs and scanner calibrations. It includes *healthy controls* (HC) with no fractures, which have been acquired with varying scanner settings (fields-of-view, spatial resolution, etc.). Thus, there is a significant variation in the Hounsfield units (HU) of the scans. We reserve three volumes as a validation set and another three volumes for testing, the remaining thirty nine are used for training.

Dataset 2. We utilise this to evaluate the performance on fracture cases (Fx). For this experiment we fused the forty five cases of Dataset 1 with eleven cases from this dataset, all of which have fractures. On top of the splits defined for Dataset 1, we add six fractured cases to the training set, two to the validation set, and two to the test set.

---

[2] We would like to thank Klinder et al., the authors and our industry partners (Philips, Hamburg, Germany), for providing us with the segmentation of Datasets 1 and 2 based on their approach in [1].

Dataset 3. As a final experiment, we intend to compare our algorithm with the other best-performing segmentation algorithms. For this task, we choose the public dataset of the segmentation challenge in CSI2014. This contains a total of 20 scans, 10 for training and 10 for testing. Of the test set, five scans are of healthy subjects less than 35 years old, and five other scans are of osteoporotic spines aged above 55 years. From the 10 training volumes we reserve one for validation and use the remaining nine for fine-tuning of the model pre-trained on the Dataset 2. We refer the reader to [14] for a detailed description of the dataset.

Results. The results of the experiments on the Datasets 1 and 2 are reported in the Table 1. Our method reaches good results both for healthy and fractured cases, proving to generalise well to a wide range of data. In both cases we observed the segmentation net suffer from stray segmentations which were mostly filtered out by the attention net, steadily improving the DICE by 1–10%. The resulting segmentation of our method are visualised in Fig. 5, comparing it to a well-known model-based segmentation approach [1]. Notice the over-segmentation of the vertebral process regions (top row, HC) in the model-based approach. This is expected as the process of a vertebra has very high variability from patient-to-patient. Such a variability cannot be captured by an atlas or a shape model. Such over-segmentation does not occur in our approach. The bottom row illustrates our approaches performance on a fractured vertebra. Observe how the model-based segmentation fails to capture the deformities. This illustrates the restriction the interpolation algorithm in such approaches fails to capture extreme deviations from the mean shape. Our approach, however, successfully segments the degenerate vertebra as it learns to segment on the edges and is not hindered by any shape priors. We attribute the bleeding in the vertebral process regions (Fig. 5, bottom row) to predictions of the neighbouring slices; we do not observe this artefact consistently in our results.

The results of the experiment on Dataset 3 are reported in Table 2. We compare our approach with two methods that have been deemed best performing according to the challenge organisers. Korez et al. [4] use a mean shape model based strategy followed by an efficient interpolation theory oriented mesh deformation, and performed best on healthy cases. Forsberg [2] performed well on fractured cases. It uses a multi-atlas based segmentation followed by a B-spline relaxation to adapt for the variability of vertebral structures. Observe that our algorithm achieves a comparable performance with the state-of-art in the healthy cohort. The performance on the fractured cases is not up to the mark; we identify the cause to be following:

Table 1. DICE for Datasets 1 and 2. The performance of our method is consistent among HC and Fx cases.

Dataset	DICE (%)
Dataset 1 (HC)	87.60 ± 5.0
Dataset 2 (HC+Fx)	85.91 ± 4.8

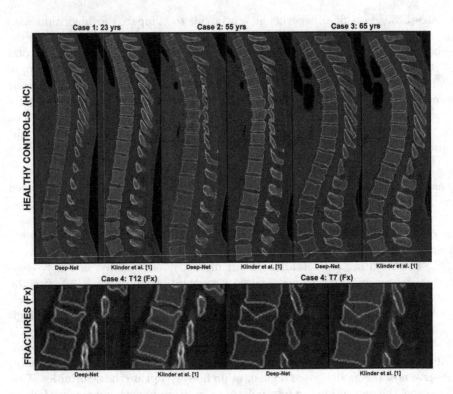

Fig. 5. Comparison of the proposed method (red) and Klinder et al. [1] (blue) to the ground truth (yellow contour). Top row: Test cases from the Dataset 1. Our method performs better in matching the actual vertebra shape and does not suffer from over-segmentation. However, it does not always provide structurally consistent results; for example, the first and the last vertebra in the left-most image are not fully segmented. Bottom row: Fractured cases from the Dataset 2. Our model-free approach is able to capture the unique deformation of the fractured vertebra, opposed to the model-based method. (Color figure online)

Table 2. Comparison of the performance of our approach with other state-of-the-art methods on the benchmark dataset of the 2014 MICCAI Workshop on Computational Methods and Clinical Applications for Spine Imaging, on healthy and osteoporotic test sets.

Approach	DICE (%)	
	HC	Osteoporotic
Forsberg [2][a]	92.1 ± 3.0	87.8 ± 1.5
Korez et al. [4][a]	94.7 ± 4.0	88.2 ± 3.0
Our approach	92.1 ± 1.6	83.7 ± 4.7

[a] In these methods, DICE was computed at vertebra level and aggregated; our DICE is computed on the entire spine.

The fractured vertebra in the test set are treated by cement injection inside the vertebra (for example, case 26 and case 30 have cementing in T12 and L3 vertebrae). This procedure causes distinctive artefacts in the image, as opposed to untreated fractures. As there was not a single case of a cement-treated fracture in our training set and since our approach is purely data-driven, our method does not perform as expected. This can be observed by observing a more detailed view on the performance metric of the osteoporotic set, where we obtain a highest DICE of 89.4% and a median DICE of 85.5%. However, this performance can be easily improved by adding more representative data into the training set.

4   Conclusion

In this paper we propose a model-free deep learning based framework for pathological spine segmentation in CT images. Our method uses a pair of fully-convolutional networks that complement one another: The first network provides a coarse localisation of the spine in the form of an attention map, while the second network provides precise high-resolution segmentations. Both these are fused to obtain the final segmentation map of the spine. We evaluate the method on three datasets and obtain promising results indicating applicability in a clinical setting. Our main conclusions are the following: (1) Our approach based on neural networks is far more robust, generalisable, and precise on fine details as a consequence of its dependence on every voxel and its surrounding, unlike the traditional models that depend on predefined shapes and edges for fine-tuning, (2) our approach successfully segments healthy as well as fractured vertebrae, given both cases are sufficiently represented in the training set, (3) our approach achieves Dice coefficients of above 90% for healthy cases and above 80% for osteoporotic cases on the CSI2014 dataset. We believe that its performance can be further improved with a larger and more representative dataset. Lastly, (4) we remark that our approach fails to incorporate information pertaining to structural consistency of a spine. This results in a peculiar behaviour where our method fails to segment parts of a vertebra or sometimes entire vertebrae at the start or end of a spine. This can be observed in Fig. 5 (top row). We intend to investigate ways in which such global structural regularity can be imposed during the training phase of our networks.

As part of future work, we plan to employ a graphical model to split the binary segmentation into different vertebrae, thereby labeling the segmentation, based on a conditional random field-based approach.

Acknowledgements. This work was funded from the European Research Council (ERC) under the European Union's Horizon 2020 research and innovation programme (GA637164–iBack–ERC–2014–STG).

References

1. Klinder, T., Ostermann, J., Ehm, M., Franz, A., Kneser, R., Lorenz, C.: Automated model-based vertebra detection, identification, and segmentation in CT images. Med. Image Anal. **13**(3), 471–482 (2009)
2. Forsberg, D.: Atlas based segmentation of the thoracic and lumbar vertebrae. In: Yao, J., et al. (eds.) CSI 2014. LNCVB, vol. 20, pp. 215–220. Springer, Cham (2015). https://doi.org/10.1007/978-3-319-14148-0_18
3. Kadoury, S., Labelle, H., Paragios, N.: Spine segmentation in medical images using manifold embeddings and higher-order MRFs. IEEE Trans. Med. Imaging **32**(7), 1227–1238 (2013)
4. Korez, R., Ibragimov, B., Likar, B., Pernuš, F., Vrtovec, T.: Interpolation-based shape-constrained deformable model approach for segmentation of vertebrae from CT spine images. In: Yao, J., et al. (eds.) CSI 2014. LNCVB, vol. 20, pp. 235–240. Springer, Cham (2015). https://doi.org/10.1007/978-3-319-14148-0_21
5. Huang, J., Jian, F., Wu, H., Li, H.: An improved level set method for vertebra CT image segmentation. Biomed. Eng. Online **12**, 48 (2013)
6. Lootus, M., Kadir, T., Zisserman, A.: Automated radiological grading of spinal MRI. In: Yao, J., et al. (eds.) CSI 2014. LNCVB, vol. 20, pp. 119–130. Springer, Cham (2015). https://doi.org/10.1007/978-3-319-14148-0_11
7. Glocker, B., Feulner, J., Criminisi, A., Haynor, D., Konukoglu, E.: Automatic localization and identification of vertebrae in arbitrary field-of-view CT scans. In: Ayache, N., et al. (eds.) Proceedings of 15th International Conference on Medical Image Computing and Computer-Assisted Intervention – MICCAI 2012. LNCS, vol. 7512, pp. 590–598. Springer, Heidelberg (2012). https://doi.org/10.1007/978-3-642-33454-2_73
8. Suzani, A., Rasoulian, A., Seitel, A., Fels, S., Rohling, R., Abolmaesumi, P.: Deep learning for automatic localization, identification, and segmentation of vertebral bodies in volumetric MR images. In: Webster, R., Yaniv, Z. (eds.) Proceedings of SPIE Medical Imaging 2015: Image-Guided Procedures, Robotic Interventions, and Modeling, vol. 9415, p. 941514. SPIE (2015)
9. Chen, H., Shen, C., Qin, J., Ni, D., Shi, L., Cheng, J.C.Y., Heng, P.-A.: Automatic localization and identification of vertebrae in Spine CT via a joint learning model with deep neural networks. In: Navab, N., Hornegger, J., Wells, W.M., Frangi, A.F. (eds.) MICCAI 2015. LNCS, vol. 9349, pp. 515–522. Springer, Cham (2015). https://doi.org/10.1007/978-3-319-24553-9_63
10. Shelhamer, E., Long, J., Darrell, T.: Fully convolutional networks for semantic segmentation. IEEE Trans. Pattern Anal. Mach. Intell. **39**(4), 640–651 (2017)
11. Ronneberger, O., Fischer, P., Brox, T.: U-Net: convolutional networks for biomedical image segmentation. In: Navab, N., Hornegger, J., Wells, W.M., Frangi, A.F. (eds.) MICCAI 2015. LNCS, vol. 9351, pp. 234–241. Springer, Cham (2015). https://doi.org/10.1007/978-3-319-24574-4_28
12. Çiçek, Ö., Abdulkadir, A., Lienkamp, S.S., Brox, T., Ronneberger, O.: 3D U-Net: learning dense volumetric segmentation from sparse annotation. In: Ourselin, S., Joskowicz, L., Sabuncu, M.R., Unal, G., Wells, W. (eds.) MICCAI 2016. LNCS, vol. 9901, pp. 424–432. Springer, Cham (2016). https://doi.org/10.1007/978-3-319-46723-8_49
13. Milletari, F., Navab, N., Ahmadi, S.A.: V-Net: fully convolutional neural networks for volumetric medical image segmentation. In: Proceedings of 4th International Conference on 3D Vision - 3DV 2016, pp. 565–571. IEEE (2016)

14. Yao, J., Burns, J., Forsberg, D., Seitel, A., Rasoulian, A., Abolmaesumi, P., Hammernik, K., Urschler, M., Ibragimov, B., Korez, R., Vrtovec, T., Castro-Mateos, I., Pozo, J., Frangi, A., Summers, R., Li, S.: A multi-center milestone study of clinical vertebral CT segmentation. Comput. Med. Imaging Graph. **49**, 16–28 (2016)

15. Yu, F., Koltun, V.: Multi-scale context aggregation by dilated convolutions. arXiv preprint arXiv:1511.07122 (2015)

16. A three-dimensional U-Net for synaptic cleft detection (2016). https://github.com/zudi-lin/pse-unet

17. Jia, Y., Shelhamer, E., Donahue, J., Karayev, S., Long, J., Girshick, R., Guadarrama, S., Darrell, T.: Caffe: convolutional architecture for fast feature embedding. In: Proceedings of 22nd ACM International Conference on Multimedia, pp. 675–678. ACM (2014)

Automatic Full Femur Segmentation from Computed Tomography Datasets Using an Atlas-Based Approach

Bryce A. Besler[1,2,3], Andrew S. Michalski[2,3], Nils D. Forkert[3,4], and Steven K. Boyd[2,3(✉)]

[1] Biomedical Engineering Graduate Program,
University of Calgary, Calgary, Canada
[2] McCaig Institute for Bone and Joint Health,
University of Calgary, Calgary, Canada
skboyd@ucalgary.ca
[3] Department of Radiology, Cumming School of Medicine,
University of Calgary, Calgary, Canada
[4] Hotchkiss Brain Institute, University of Calgary, Calgary, Canada

Abstract. Automatic segmentation of femurs in clinical computed tomography remains a challenge. Joints degraded by old age are a particularly challenging dataset to segment. The objective of this study is to evaluate existing methods and propose an alternative method for segmentation of femurs in clinical computed tomography datasets for joints degraded by old age. Bilateral hip computed tomography scans of three cadaveric specimens (six femurs) were available for this study. Deformable registration using an affine selection criterion was used for atlas-based segmentation. For comparison, the six femurs were also segmented with two graph-cut algorithms. An automatic graph-cut segmentation algorithm was only able to separate the femur from the pelvis in two of the six femurs due to a limitation of graph-cuts. The atlas-based method produced consistent automatic segmentations for all degraded joints. In conclusion, atlas-based femur segmentation performs considerably better than an automatic graph-cut algorithm when applied to degraded joints.

Keywords: Atlas-based segmentation · Graph-cut · Femur
Computed tomography

1 Introduction

Clinical computed tomography (CT) is a versatile imaging modality used to stage surgery and investigate the source of abdominal pain. During these common applications, quantitative image data of bones are inadvertently captured. As a consequence of its applicability, CT generates a large collection of clinically relevant bone data that is not yet effectively used. This collection of bone

© Springer International Publishing AG 2018
B. Glocker et al. (Eds.): MSKI 2017, LNCS 10734, pp. 120–132, 2018.
https://doi.org/10.1007/978-3-319-74113-0_11

image data can be used to answer population-level questions about bone health and develop novel screening technologies. Of particular interest is the automatic assessment of femurs in clinical CT to opportunistically screen for osteoporosis [1]. Femoral fractures account for 72% of all fracture-related healthcare costs [2], posing a strong incentive to help detect fractures before they happen. A robust and automatic segmentation of the femur would be required for high-throughput assessment of bone health.

Many techniques for segmenting femurs in medical image data have been proposed in the past. For example, Zoroofi et al. [3] proposed a method employing standard image processing techniques. More precisely, the image data is smoothed with a Gaussian filter, histogram-based thresholding is applied, and the segmentation is cleaned using morphological operators. Kang et al. [4] employed a region growing technique using locally adaptive thresholding. The resulting segmentation was cleaned using both morphological closing and slice-wise contour closing.

More advanced techniques based on the energy minimization framework of graph-cuts [5] yield improved segmentations compared to simple intensity thresholding. In Pauchard et al. [6], a user interactively applies brush strokes to the image data enforcing hard constraints on foreground and background voxels. The edges of the bone are segmented using the standard boundary term for graph-cuts. Krčah et al. [7] proposed an automatic graph-cut segmentation method. Here, a modified sheetness measure based on Descoteaux et al. [8] is used to increase the contrast at the surface of the bone. The graph-cut algorithm makes use of this enhanced contrast and the quantitative nature of Hounsfield units to segment bone structures. A morphological erosion is applied to disconnect the femur and the pelvis if they are connected. The boundary between the two articulating bones is determined by another, separate graph-cut algorithm.

However, the aforementioned techniques have difficulty separating well-connected joints, a problem generally seen in older populations. Extensive manual correction is often necessary but not feasible for high-throughput applications. Within this context, atlas-based approaches could overcome the problem of well-connected joints and improve segmentation accuracy by including shape information. The basic idea of atlas-based methods is to register an atlas dataset with a corresponding segmentation of the structure of interest to an individual dataset. The result of the registration is used to transform the segmentation to the reference image.

Previously, Ehrhardt et al. [9] used Thirion's demons [10] to segment full pelvis and femur CT scans and to identify anatomical landmarks. The authors pointed out that the femur-acetabulum connection was particularly difficult to segment. Whitmarsh et al. [11] proposed a multi-atlas-based method using free-form deformations with label fusion to produce a highly accurate segmentation. Local-weighted voting was used to generate the final segmentation. However, the image volumes were artificially restricted to the joint and computed on relatively young subjects, reducing the applicability of the algorithm to clinically relevant scans. Additionally, it has been shown that label fusion with an increasing number of atlas images can have both decreasing performance and increased computation time [12], which was not considered in the work of Whitmarsh et al. [11].

The objective of this study is to develop an automated method for segmenting femurs in clinical CT datasets with a special focus on degraded joints. Two existing segmentation techniques using the graph-cut framework are explored for full femur segmentation. A limitation of graph-cut based methods due to the conformity of the femoroacetabular joint is presented. An atlas-based segmentation method using a selection criterion is proposed.

2   Materials and Methods

2.1   Data Acquisition

Bilateral hip CT scans were acquired from three cadavers using a GE Revolution CT Scanner (GE Healthcare). In-plane resolution was 0.684 mm by 0.684 mm with a slice thickness of 0.625 mm. The scan volume begins above the iliac crest of the pelvis and stops in the proximal tibia containing the entire femur. Reconstructed volumes contained 291 million voxels on average. A slice of the greyscale image data and a direct volume rendering of the image data is shown in Fig. 1.

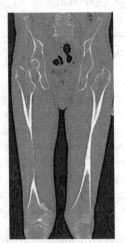
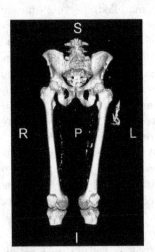

(a) Coronal slice of the greyscale data.   (b) Direct volume rendering.

Fig. 1. Computed tomography scan volume.

The age and sex of the three cadavers were 86, male; 72, female; and 90, female. The cause of death of all cadavers was respiratory and related to old age. No cadavers had metal in the scan volume (such as an implant). All of these specimens display degraded joints due to age (see Fig. 2). As a result of

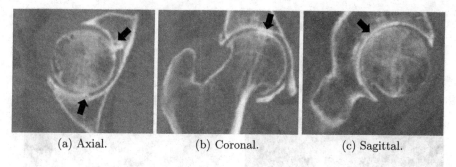

(a) Axial.   (b) Coronal.   (c) Sagittal.

Fig. 2. Contact between femur and pelvis.

this, there is large contact between the femoral head and the acetabulum of the femur in two of the three specimens. In the third case, the contact between the femur and acetabulum is very small, but present. A quantitative measure of joint degeneration was not made.

2.2   Pre-processing

Each CT image was resampled to an isotropic resolution of 0.625 mm using cubic interpolation. After this, the image volume was split sagittally creating two volumes with one volume containing the left femur and the other volume containing the right femur. The left femurs were mirrored in the lateral-medial direction to match the anatomical orientation of right femurs. Similar to a previous study [11], a mask of the subject's body was defined using a threshold of −200 Hounsfield units. This mask of the body was used to restrict the registration domain.

2.3   Manual Segmentations

Each femur was semi-automatically segmented using the graph-cut method described by Pauchard et al. [6], implemented in the freely available software MITK-GEM[1]. In this interactive method, a brush is used to define regions of foreground (femur) and background (tibia, pelvis, muscle, fat, and air). Foreground strokes were interactively placed in each dataset in the diaphyseal cortical bone and in the sagittal, coronal, and axial slices of the proximal and distal femur. Background strokes were placed in the sagittal, coronal, and axial slices of the tibia and pelvis including joint space. Background strokes were also places on muscle, fat, and air. After rough foreground and background definition, a graph-cut algorithm is used to obtain the final segmentation.

Because the segmentations produced by MITK-GEM included joint space (see Fig. 3), the six MITK-GEM segmentations were manually corrected by a medical imaging expert. Furthermore, rough edges in the manual segmentation

---

[1] https://simtk.org/projects/mitk-gem.

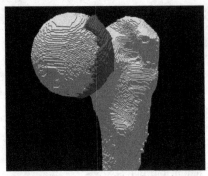

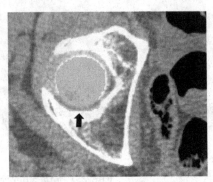

(a) Manual segmentation (white) over-laid with the MITK-GEM segmenta-tion (red).

(b) Axial slice of the MITK-GEM seg-mentation overlaid on the image data.

Fig. 3. Visualization of MITK-GEM segmentation for the specimen with the least contact between femur and pelvis. (Color figure online)

were smoothed with an image-closing operator (spherical kernel of diameter three voxels). These manual segmentations were used as the ground truth for evaluation as well as for multi-atlas segmentation.

2.4 Atlas-Based Segmentations

The objective of atlas-based segmentation is to find a mapping of voxels in an atlas image to voxels in a fixed image. If a correspondence can be found, then a segmentation defined in the atlas image can be mapped to the fixed image and used as a segmentation of the fixed image. This mapping is typically solved for using linear and non-linear (deformable) intensity-based image registration.

The previously described CT datasets of the six femurs and the corresponding manual segmentations were used as the basis for the multi-atlas-based segmentation. The deformation field was solved by applying an affine transform for a rough initialization followed by a deformable registration using B-spline free-from deformation. Normalized cross correlation was used as the image similarity-metric.

A selection criterion was used to rank the affine registered atlases compared to the query image, where only the atlas with the best registration metric after affine registration was selected for subsequent non-linear registration to save computation time while increasing the chance of achieving a good non-linear registration. The final spacing of the B-spline control points was 5 mm. A multi-resolution registration scheme with six levels was used and the spacing between B-spline control points was decreased by half at each level of the pyramid. The registration domain was restricted to a mask of the bone and soft tissue as described in Sect. 2.2. The open-source software Elastix [13] version 4.8[2] was used for registration. Parameter files can be found in the Elastix database[3].

---

[2] http://elastix.isi.uu.nl.
[3] http://elastix.bigr.nl/wiki/index.php/Par0046.

2.5   Evaluation

Leave-one-out-cross-validation was used to evaluate the multi-atlas-based seg-mentation method described in this work. Given a query femur, the remaining five atlas images were used as described in Sect. 2.4 to produce an atlas segmen-tation.

Obviously, a contralateral femur exists for any query image in the multi-atlas dataset, which might bias the evaluation. To investigate this potential bias, leave-one-out-cross-validation of atlas-based segmentation was conducted with and without the contralateral femur in the atlas. Thus, two atlas-based segmentations were generated for each case, one with the contralateral femur in the atlas (con.) and one without the contralateral femur in the atlas (alt.). The two segmentation cases will validate that the affine selection criterion can select the best atlas for a given image while removing evaluation bias.

For comparison purposes, the segmentations resulting from applying the graph-cut algorithm described by Pauchard et al. [6] (MITK-GEM) - prior to manual correction - were also quantitatively evaluated. Finally, all six femurs were segmented using the graph-cut method of Krčah et al. [7], the source code of which is publicly available[4]. Thus, four segmentation results – Atlas (con.), Atlas (alt.), MITK-GEM, and Krčah – were available for each femur and com-pared to the manual segmentation.

For all cases, the Dice similarity coefficient [14] and the Hausdorff distance [15] were used for quantitative comparison to the ground truth segmentation. The Dice similarity coefficient is a measure of mean overlap between two seg-mentations and is expected to be very large (close to 1.0) given the small surface area to volume ratio of a femur [16]. The Hausdorff distance is a complementary statistic to the Dice similarity coefficient because it measures the worst possible error between two segmentations. The Hausdorff distance is regarded as a very harsh metric and identifies segmentations that may have large local differences but are otherwise well segmented.

3   Results

The Dice similarity coefficient and Hausdorff distance comparing the four algo-rithm segmentations to the manual segmentation are presented in Tables 1 and 2, respectively. The MITK-GEM method had the best results with an average Dice similarity coefficient of 0.994 and an average Hausdorff distance of 4.58 mm. The Krčah method had the worst results with an average Dice similarity coefficient of 0.801 and an average Hausdorff distance of 102.40 mm. For the atlas-based method, removing the contralateral femur from the atlas increased the average Hausdorff distance from 5.95 mm to 8.53 mm and decreased the average Dice similarity coefficient from 0.978 to 0.969. The contralateral femur always had the best image similarity metric after the affine registration (data not shown).

---

[4] https://github.com/mkrcah/bone-segmentation.

Table 1. Dice similarity coefficient for each method.

Sample	Leg	Atlas (con.)	Atlas (alt.)	MITK-GEM	Krčah
1	Left	0.982	0.976	0.997	0.988
1	Right	0.983	0.972	0.997	0.987
2	Left	0.978	0.969	0.996	0.674
2	Right	0.977	0.968	0.993	0.657
3	Left	0.974	0.967	0.994	0.745
3	Right	0.973	0.964	0.988	0.755

All four algorithms have Dice similarity coefficients above 0.95 when the pelvis and the femur are separated in the final segmentation.

The Krčah method successfully separated the femur from the pelvis in two of the six femurs, both in the specimen with the least contact between the femur and pelvis. Figure 4 shows an axial slice of the successful Krčah segmentations overlaid on the greyscale data. No joint space between the femur and acetabulum of the pelvis is included in the successful Krčah segmentations. Figure 5 shows each segmentation method overlaid on the image data at the proximal, middle, and distal femur for a specimen with a well-connected joint. Joint space was included in all MITK-GEM segmentations including the specimen with the least contact between the femur and pelvis, visualized in Fig. 2. Figure 5(m) shows a large volume of joint space included in the Krčah segmentation when it fails to separate the femur and pelvis. Figure 5(g) shows a poor atlas-based segmentation result where the segmentation leaks from the femur into the pelvis. A surface rendering for each segmentation overlaid on the manual segmentation is shown in Fig. 6 for a femur that is well-connected to the pelvis. Figure 6(d) shows the full pelvis connected to the femur when the Krčah method fails.

4   Discussion

In this study, an automatic method for segmenting femurs in clinical computed tomography using a multi-atlas-based approach is proposed. The age of the cadavers presented a particularly difficult dataset due to contact between the femur and pelvis. Segmentations obtained using graph-cut methods consistently include joint space in the segmentation. The automatic graph-cut method of Krčah et al. [7] was unsuccessful in separating the femur from the pelvis in four of six femurs. In contrast, the atlas-based segmentation method with a selection criterion generated more consistent results.

Screening technologies and population-level health assessment require robust and automatic segmentation of the femur for high-throughput assessment of bone health. Algorithms for segmenting femurs from clinical CT must be accurate for the full range of anatomical variation expected in the population. The CT dataset used in this study consisted of three cadavers with degraded joints due to age,

Table 2. Hausdorff distance for each method (in mm).

Sample	Leg	Atlas (con.)	Atlas (alt.)	MITK-GEM	Krčah
1	Left	4.19	12.56	4.59	3.42
1	Right	3.59	3.80	4.19	4.38
2	Left	6.03	7.29	3.95	171.45
2	Right	9.56	6.16	5.04	180.64
3	Left	5.63	7.02	4.68	127.13
3	Right	6.73	14.38	5.00	127.36

an expected population when performing opportunistic screening. Two cadavers had large contact areas between the femur and the acetabulum of the pelvis.

The difficulty of segmenting the femur arose from the connection in the femoroacetabular joint. The femoroacetabular joint is a ball-and-socket joint where contact between the femur and the acetabulum of the pelvis has a large surface area with identical voxel intensities. Conceptually, this surface can be visualized as a surface patch on a sphere with a large solid angle. The geometry of the joint makes it particularly difficult to separate the femur from the acetabulum when the joint has been degraded due to age.

Two existing methods using the graph-cut framework were used for femur segmentation in this challenging dataset. The automatic graph-cut method of Krčah et al. [7] failed to separate the femur from the pelvis in four of the six femurs. Both successful segmentations were from the specimen with the least contact between the femur and the acetabulum of the pelvis. No joint space was included in successful Krčah segmentations. The semi-automatic graph-cut method of Pauchard et al. [6] produced femur segmentations with joint space in the segmentation for all six femurs, including the less connected specimen. The discrepancy between graph-cut methods can be explained by the modified

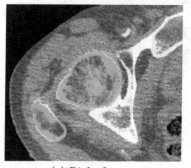
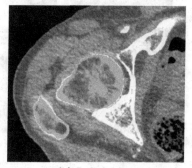

(a) Right femur.   (b) Left femur.

Fig. 4. Visualization of the successful Krčah segmentations.

128   B. A. Besler et al.

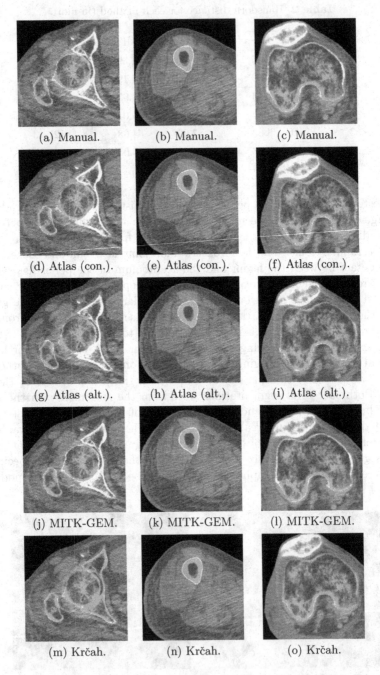

(a) Manual.　　　(b) Manual.　　　(c) Manual.

(d) Atlas (con.).　(e) Atlas (con.).　(f) Atlas (con.).

(g) Atlas (alt.).　(h) Atlas (alt.).　(i) Atlas (alt.).

(j) MITK-GEM.　(k) MITK-GEM.　(l) MITK-GEM.

(m) Krčah.　　　(n) Krčah.　　　(o) Krčah.

Fig. 5. An axial slice from the proximal femur (left), the diaphysis (middle), and the distal femur (right) for each segmentation overlaid on the image data of sample 3, left leg.

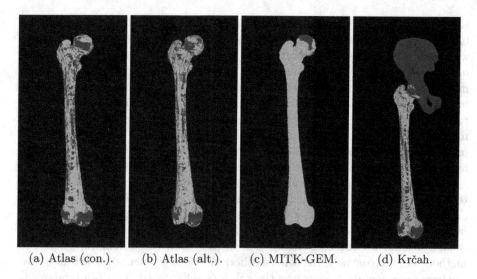

(a) Atlas (con.).   (b) Atlas (alt.).   (c) MITK-GEM.   (d) Krčah.

Fig. 6. Visualization of algorithm segmentations (red) overlaid with manual segmentation (white). (Color figure online)

sheetness filter which increases contrast in the joint space as well as the inclusion of background hard links in the pelvis and joint space.

However, bone structures in contact have identical voxel intensities and contrast cannot be enhanced. This is a limitation of the graph-cut framework where connected bone structures cannot be separately segmented. To overcome this limitation, Krčah et al. [7] implemented a post-processing step to separate connected bone structures. The initial segmentation is eroded with a spherical kernel to separate connected bones. If a segmentation is split into multiple parts after erosion, the boundary between the separated parts is determined by another, separate graph-cut algorithm. However, when the femur and pelvis are segmented as one bone structure, an annulus of joint space can be included in the initial segmentation if the joint space is narrow (see Fig. 5(m)). The thin annulus of joint space between the femur and pelvis is segmented similar to marrow space in the diaphysis. This greatly increases the effective contact area in the joint and makes it impossible for the spherical kernel to separate the connected bone structures. Even if the bone structures could be separated, this large annulus of joint space would be classified as belonging to either the femur or pelvis segmentation, or possibly split between both. The inclusion of joint space is a limitation of graph-cut based femur segmentation when the femoroacetabular joints is well-connected. Formulating the original graph-cut problem as a multi-label problem with neighbouring bones as separate labels may prevent this problem.

The two graph-cut methods and the atlas-based method for femur segmentation with and without a contralateral femur were compared with a corresponding manual segmentation. The semi-automatic method of Pauchard et al. [6] showed the best performance both in terms of Dice similarity coefficient and

Hausdorff distance. However, the method of Pauchard et al. had a systematic bias to include joint space in the femur segmentation. Additionally, this method was used as the basis for generating the ground truth segmentations, thus the metrics are biased towards favouring the method of Pauchard et al. Finally, this method is not automatic and requires user interaction while the proposed atlas-based approach is fully automatic. For high-throughput application to clinically relevant CT datasets with joints degraded by old age, the proposed atlas-based method outperformed the automatic method of Krčah et al. [7]. Atlas-based segmentation with a selection criterion showed more consistent separation of the femur from the pelvis than the automatic graph-cut method of Krčah et al. [7].

The proposed atlas-based method using an affine-registration selection criterion was specifically designed as an alternative to graph-cut based methods and to overcome the segmentation problems arising from large contact areas by including shape information. Overall, the atlas-based method produced more reliable results for the challenging CT dataset than the automatic graph-cut method. On the contrary, the atlas method results in segmentation errors where the femur segmentation leaks into the pelvis (see Fig. 5(g)). This is a fundamental limitation of atlas-based registration for femur segmentation. It is unknown if label fusion can overcome segmentation leakage in degraded joints.

The accuracy of the atlas-based segmentation was seen to depend on the composition of the atlas. The average Hausdorff distance increased by 2.58 mm when the contralateral femur was removed from the atlas. Decreased performance is expected since contralateral femurs are anatomically similar in size and shape, but will vary locally in density, osteophytic growths, and geometric conformity.

It must be highlighted that this is not the first work proposing an atlas-based method for femur segmentation [9,11]. Atlas are a favoured technique for femur segmentation because they can use shape information to better separate the femur from the pelvis. However, using a selection criterion for ranking atlases against a query image is a computationally fast method of utilizing all atlases in a multi-atlas. A selection criterion avoids a full-resolution registration of each atlas image to the query image while selecting the best atlas for the query image. To improve segmentation accuracy, a larger number of images with a broader anatomical range could be included in the atlas. The number of images needed in the atlas would depend on the variability of femur anatomy in the target population under study. For opportunistic screening of osteoporosis, the target population includes healthy individuals across all ages as well as osteoporotic individuals. Furthermore, combining atlas selection with label fusion and a larger atlas could increase the segmentation accuracy of the proposed atlas-based segmentation algorithm while decreasing the computation time relative to naive label fusion techniques [12]. A detailed analysis of computation time is needed.

Finally, the dataset used in this study presents limitations. The dataset was small limiting the generalizability of the method. The cadaveric data was captured under ideal conditions with no motion artifacts, ideal subject positioning, near-isotropic voxel spacing, and at a very high resolution. Future work could look at the sensitivity of this method to the parameters listed above.

In conclusion, multi-atlas-based segmentation with a selection criterion is a promising alternative and provides more consistent femur segmentations than typically used graph-cut methods in a challenging CT cadaveric dataset.

Acknowledgements. The authors would like to thank NSERC CGS-M for funding, the Body Donation Program at the Gross Anatomy Laboratory for access to cadaveric specimens, and the individuals who graciously contributed their bodies. The authors would also like to thank Dr. Sonny Chan from the Department of Computer Science at the University of Calgary for guidance.

References

1. Pickhardt, P., Pooler, B., Lauder, T., del Rio, A., Bruce, R., Binkley, N.: Opportunistic screening for osteoporosis using abdominal computed tomography scans obtained for other indications. Ann. Intern. Med. **158**(8), 588–595 (2013)
2. Burge, R., Dawson-Hughes, B., Solomon, D., Wong, J., King, A., Tosteson, A.: Incidence and economic burden of osteoporosis-related fractures in the United States, 2005–2025. J. Bone Miner. Res. **22**(3), 465–475 (2007)
3. Zoroofi, R., Sato, Y., Sasama, T., Nishii, T., Sugano, N., Yonenobu, K., Yoshikawa, H., Ochi, T., Tamura, S.: Automated segmentation of acetabulum and femoral head from 3-D CT images. IEEE Trans. Inf. Technol. Biomed. **7**(4), 329–343 (2003)
4. Kang, Y., Engelke, K., Kalender, W.: A new accurate and precise 3-D segmentation method for skeletal structures in volumetric CT data. IEEE Trans. Med. Imaging **22**(5), 586–598 (2003)
5. Boykov, Y., Funka-Lea, G.: Graph cuts and efficient N-D image segmentation. Int. J. Comput. Vision **70**(2), 109–131 (2006)
6. Pauchard, Y., Fitze, T., Browarnik, D., Eskandari, A., Pauchard, I., Enns-Bray, W., Pálsson, H., Sigurdsson, S., Ferguson, S., Harris, T., Gudnason, V., Helgason, B.: Interactive graph-cut segmentation for fast creation of finite element models from clinical CT data for hip fracture prediction. Comput. Methods Biomech. Biomed. Eng. **19**(16), 1693–1703 (2016)
7. Krčah, M., Székely, G., Blanc, R.: Fully automatic and fast segmentation of the femur bone from 3D-CT images with no shape prior. In: Proceedings of the 8th IEEE International Symposium on Biomedical Imaging - ISBI 2011, pp. 2087–2090. IEEE (2011)
8. Descoteaux, M., Audette, M., Chinzei, K., Siddiqi, K.: Bone enhancement filtering: application to sinus bone segmentation and simulation of pituitary surgery. Comput. Aided Surg. **11**(5), 247–255 (2006)
9. Ehrhardt, J., Handels, H., Malina, T., Strathmann, B., Plötz, W., Pöppl, S.: Atlas-based segmentation of bone structures to support the virtual planning of hip operations. Int. J. Med. Inform. **64**(2–3), 439–447 (2001)
10. Thirion, J.: Image matching as a diffusion process: an analogy with Maxwell's demons. Med. Image Anal. **2**(3), 243–260 (1998)
11. Whitmarsh, T., Treece, G.M., Poole, K.E.S.: Automatic segmentation and discrimination of connected joint bones from CT by multi-atlas registration. In: Yao, J., Klinder, T., Li, S. (eds.) Computational Methods and Clinical Applications for Spine Imaging. LNCVB, vol. 17, pp. 199–207. Springer, Cham (2014). https://doi.org/10.1007/978-3-319-07269-2_17

12. Aljabar, P., Heckemann, R., Hammers, A., Hajnal, J., Rueckert, D.: Multi-atlas based segmentation of brain images: atlas selection and its effect on accuracy. NeuroImage **46**(3), 726–738 (2009)
13. Klein, S., Staring, M., Murphy, K., Viergever, M., Pluim, J.: Elastix: a toolbox for intensity-based medical image registration. IEEE Trans. Med. Imaging **29**(1), 196–205 (2010)
14. Dice, L.: Measures of the amount of ecologic association between species. Ecology **26**(3), 297–302 (1945)
15. Huttenlocher, D., Klanderman, G., Rucklidge, W.: Comparing images using the hausdorff distance. IEEE Trans. Pattern Anal. Mach. Intell. **15**(9), 850–863 (1993)
16. Rohlfing, T., Brandt, R., Menzel, R., Maurer, C.: Evaluation of atlas selection strategies for atlas-based image segmentation with application to confocal microscopy images of bee brains. NeuroImage **21**(4), 1428–1442 (2004)

Classification of Osteoporotic Vertebral Fractures Using Shape and Appearance Modelling

Paul A. Bromiley[1](✉), Eleni P. Kariki[2], Judith E. Adams[2], and Timothy F. Cootes[1]

[1] Centre for Imaging Sciences, School of Health Sciences, University of Manchester, Manchester, UK
`paul.bromiley@manchester.ac.uk`
[2] Radiology and Manchester Academic Health Science Centre, Central Manchester University Hospitals NHS Foundation Trust, Manchester, UK

Abstract. Osteoporotic vertebral fractures (VFs) are under-diagnosed, creating an opportunity for computer-aided, opportunistic fracture identification in clinical images. VF diagnosis and grading in clinical practice involves comparisons of vertebral body heights. However, machine vision systems can provide a high-resolution segmentation of the vertebrae and fully characterise their shape and appearance, potentially allowing improved diagnostic accuracy. We compare approaches based on vertebral heights to shape/appearance modelling combined with k-nearest neighbours and random forest (RF) classifiers, on both dual-energy X-ray absorptiometry images and computed tomography image volumes. We demonstrate that the combination of RF classifiers and appearance modelling, which is novel in this application, results in a significant (up to 60% reduction in false positive rate at 80% sensitivity) improvement in diagnostic accuracy.

Keywords: Osteoporosis · Vertebral fracture · Shape modelling

1 Introduction

Osteoporosis is a common skeletal disorder characterised by a reduction in bone mineral density (BMD). This is commonly assessed using dual-energy X-ray absorptiometry (DXA); a T-score of < -2.5 (i.e. more than 2.5 standard deviations below the mean in young adults) [1] is used as a criterion suggesting osteoporosis. It significantly increases the risk of fractures, most commonly occurring in the hips, wrists or vertebrae. Approximately 40% of postmenopausal Caucasian women are affected, increasing their lifetime risk of fragility fractures to as much as 40% [1]. Osteoporosis therefore presents a significant public health problem for an ageing population. However, between 30–60% of vertebral fractures (VFs) may be asymptomatic and only about one third of those present on

© Springer International Publishing AG 2018
B. Glocker et al. (Eds.): MSKI 2017, LNCS 10734, pp. 133–147, 2018.
https://doi.org/10.1007/978-3-319-74113-0_12

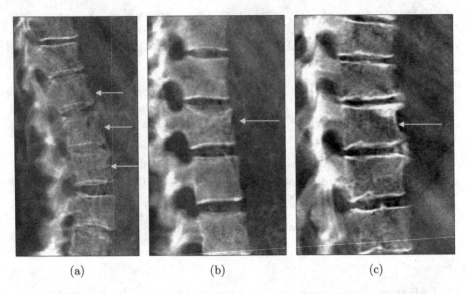

(a)   (b)   (c)

Fig. 1. Example vertebrae visualized on GE Luna iDXA images. (a) Mild scoliosis or incorrect positioning of the patient may cause tilting of the vertebrae relative to the beam direction, leading to the appearance of end-plate curvature although no fractures are present. (b) Osteoporotic vertebral fractures lead to loss of vertebral height and changes in texture due to the presence of micro-fractures; the upper end plate is not symmetrical with the lower and appears blurred. (c) Spondylosis also results in changes in vertebral shape and texture, due to the growth of osteophytes on the anterior portion of the end-plates and sclerosis, i.e. the high-intensity region within the vertebral body, below the anterior portion of the upper end-plate.

images come to clinical attention; they are frequently not reported by radiologists [2]. Many of these cases involve images acquired for other clinical indicators, so identification may be opportunistic. For example, computed tomography (CT) is arguably the ideal modality for opportunistic identification, due to the large number of procedures (4.3 million per year within the UK National Health Service [3]) and high image quality. However, a recent audit at the Manchester Royal Infirmary (MRI) revealed that only 13% of VFs visible on CT images were identified [4], similar to rates reported in the literature [2]. Proposed reasons for such low rates [2] include the difficulty of identifying vertebral height reduction on axial images. Routine coronal and/or sagittal reformatting has been proposed, and is being adopted, but reporting rates remain low [2,5]. The potential utility of computer-aided VF assessment (VFA) systems is therefore considerable.

Several authors have investigated the use of methods based on statistical shape models (SSMs) [6] to segment vertebrae in both radiographs, e.g. [7], and DXA images, e.g. [8,9]. In particular, the random-forest regression voting constrained local model (RFRV-CLM)[10] has been used for both semi- and fully automatic vertebral body segmentation in both DXA [11–13] and CT [14] images, providing superior segmentation accuracy on more severely fractured vertebrae compared to previous work using active appearance models (AAMs) [15]. However, all of these approaches share the common aim of providing a high-resolution segmentation of the vertebrae, typically as landmarks annotated on the vertebral body outline.

Several procedures for manual VFA have been described in the literature; see [16] for a recent review. Most attempt to remove the subjectivity of qualitative assessment [17] by defining fractures in terms of height reduction at the posterior, middle and anterior parts of the vertebral bodies, e.g. [18]. However, non-fracture deformities can affect vertebral shape, as shown in Fig. 1. In particular, tilting of the vertebrae can mimic the appearance of depressed end-plates. VFA therefore requires a subjective assessment of whether any apparent shape change is due to osteoporotic fracture or some other cause. The algorithm-based quantitative (ABQ) method for VFA [19] defined a heuristic for this process. The result is a complex procedure that involves consideration of multiple, interacting factors, including the apparent shape of each vertebra and the spine as a whole, which is difficult to translate into a machine vision algorithm.

Whilst machine vision based VFA methods suffer from difficulties in terms of replicating such complex, heuristic approaches, they have a potential advantage in that techniques based on SSMs can provide a precise mathematical description of the entire shape of a vertebra, and quantitatively compare this between vertebrae. We investigate the interaction of these two effects by constructing VF classifiers based on comparing the parameters of shape and appearance models of vertebrae using both k-nearest neighbours (kNNs) and random forests (RFs) [20]. These methods are compared to simple, height-based classifiers on two data sets; 320 DXA VFA images and spinal mid-line sagittal images projected from 402 CT volumes. When RFs were used to classify appearance model parameters, significant reductions in false positive rate (FPR) of $\approx$30% and $\approx$60% were achieved at 80% sensitivity for VF identification from automatic and manual landmark annotations, respectively, on both data sets.

2   Method

2.1   Data Collection and Manual Annotation

The picture archiving and communication server (PACS; Centricity Universal Viewer, GE Healthcare, Little Chalford, Buckinghamshire, UK) at the MRI was queried to produce a list of CT scans acquired during May and June 2014 and January to September 2015. Scans from non-trauma patients that included any part of the thoracic or lumbar spine and were of patients over 18 years of age, were selected. This gave a list of 868 patients' scans. The PACS was also queried for non-trauma CT scans during January to April and July to December 2014 in patients over 60 years of age that contained osteoporotic VFs, producing a second list of 132 patients. The sagittal reformatted volumes from both lists were downloaded in DICOM format. 402 volumes were selected to form a training set,

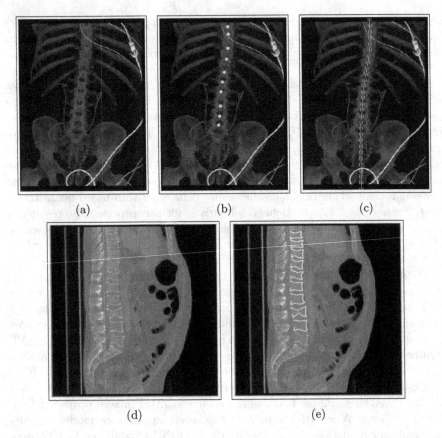

Fig. 2. (a) An example coronal maximum intensity projection of a computed tomography volume. (b) Manual annotations of the neural arch. (c) Extrapolated piecewise-linear curve and the ±5 mm range (dashed line) over which sagittal rasters were summed to produce the sagittal projection (d). (e) Manual landmark annotation.

including the 132 fracture-rich images to ensure high fracture prevalence. The remaining images were reserved for future validation purposes. The 402 image list was divided into quarters for four-fold cross validation, with the fracture-rich images distributed evenly. Each volume was up-sampled to give isotropic voxel dimensions using tri-cubic interpolation.

To avoid the difficulties of performing a high-resolution annotation of landmarks on vertebral bodies in 3D, analysis was limited to a single, two-dimensional (2D) image produced from each volume using the procedure described in [14]. The orientation of the subject within the CT scanner was highly constrained, allowing production of a maximum intensity projection showing an approximately anteroposterior view without registration. Landmarks were manually annotated on the MIP images at the distinctive, U-shaped structure on each vertebra where the laminae join to form the spinous process of the neural arch (Fig. 2(a), (b)).

A piecewise-linear curve was defined through the points and extrapolated vertically to the boundary of the volume (Fig. 2(c)). For each axial slice from the original volume, all anteroposterior raster lines (i.e. rasters of sagittal slices) that passed within D_t of this curve were averaged to give a single raster line of a sagittal image. Repeating for all axial images gave a single, thick-slice, 2D sagittal image that showed the midplane of each vertebra (Fig. 2(d)). The thickness $D_t = \pm 5$ mm was chosen by manual inspection to optimise endplate visualisation.

The images derived from CT volumes were projected onto the spinal midline, and so were unaffected by issues such as mild scoliosis. DXA images are projections through the full body, and so will show the tilting of the vertebrae encountered in this condition, making accurate diagnosis based on vertebral shape more difficult. Therefore, a second data set of 320 DXA VFA images scanned on various Hologic (Bedford, MA, USA) scanners was also used. This comprised: 44 patients from a previous study [21]; 80 female subjects in an epidemiological study of a UK cohort born in 1946; 196 females attending a local clinic for DXA BMD measurement, for whom the referring physician had requested VFA (approved by the local ethics committee).

Manual annotation of 33 landmarks on each visualized vertebra from T7 to L4, for the DXA images, and T4 to L4, for the CT midline images (Fig. 2(e)), was performed by a trained radiographer. The vertebrae were also classified by an expert radiologist into five groups: normal; deformed but not fractured; and mild (grade 1), moderate (grade 2) and severe (grade 3) fractures using the Genant definitions [18].

2.2 Height-Based Fracture Classification

A baseline for VF classification accuracy was derived by applying a simple classifier, based on six-point morphometry, as described in [13]. The anterior h_a, middle h_m and posterior h_p heights of each detected vertebra were calculated from the relevant landmarks, together with a predicted posterior height $h_{p'}$, calculated as the maximum of the posterior heights of the four closest vertebrae. The wedge $r_w = h_a/h_p$, biconcavity $r_b = h_m/h_p$, and crush $r_c = h_p/h_{p'}$ ratios were derived, and the data were whitened by subtracting the medians of each ratio and dividing by the square-root of the covariance matrix, calculated using the median standard deviation. The data contained far more normal than deformed or fractured vertebrae, so this process whitened to the distribution of the normal class. A simple fracture/non-fracture classification was performed by applying a threshold t_{class} to $r_c^2 + r_b^2 + r_w^2$; deformed vertebrae were counted correct when classified into either class.

2.3 Shape and Appearance Model Based Classifiers

SSMs provide a linear model of the distribution of a set of landmarks in an image. The training data consists of a set of images $\mathbf{I}$ with manual annotations $\mathbf{x}_l$ of a set of N points $l = 1, \ldots, N$ on each. The images are first aligned into a standardised

138   P. A. Bromiley et al.

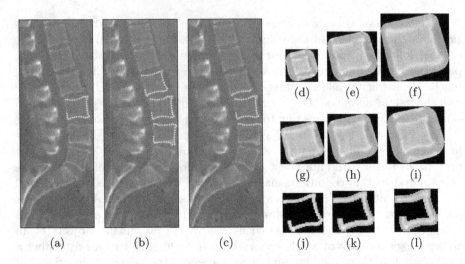

Fig. 3. Point sampling strategies, using (a) a single vertebra, (b) a triplet and (c) a vertebra plus its neighbouring end-plates (nEP). Texture sampling strategies in the single vertebra case. (d)–(f) Sampling using Delaunay triangulation with increasing w_{frame}. (g)–(i) Sampling using Delaunay triangulation with increasing w_{border}. (j)–(l) Patch-based sampling with increasing w_{patch}.

reference frame using a similarity registration, giving a transformation T with parameters θ. The concatenated, reference-frame coordinates of the points in each training image define its shape. The SSM is generated by applying principal component analysis (PCA) to the training shapes [15], generating a linear model where the position of point l is given by

$$\mathbf{x}_l = T_\theta(\bar{\mathbf{x}}_l + \mathbf{P}_{sl}\mathbf{b}_s),\tag{1}$$

where $\bar{\mathbf{x}}_l$ is the mean point position in the reference frame, $\mathbf{P}_s$ is a matrix of modes of variation, $\mathbf{P}_{sl}$ is the sub-matrix of $\mathbf{P}_s$ relevant to point l, and $\mathbf{b}_s$ encodes the shape model parameters. The matrix $\mathbf{P}_s$ is orthogonal and so

$$\mathbf{b}_s = \mathbf{P}_{sl}^T(T_\theta^{-1}(\mathbf{x}_l) - \bar{\mathbf{x}}_l).\tag{2}$$

A compact description of the shape in a query image can therefore be derived by annotating the landmarks, performing a similarity registration into the reference frame of the model, and applying (2) to generate the vector $\mathbf{b}_s$.

The SSM considers only the distribution of landmarks on a shape. However, with reference to osteoporosis and potentially confounding pathologies, information is also present in the pixel intensities. Osteoporotic VF proceeds as a cascade of micro-fractures in the vertebral end-plates [16] leading to a blurred appearance (Fig. 1). Appearance models (APMs) such as those used by AAMs [15] adopt the same PCA-based linear modelling approach as the SSM to characterize both shape and intensity information. Each training image is resampled into the reference frame by applying $\mathbf{I}_r(m, n) = \mathbf{I}(T_\theta^{-1}(m, n))$, where (m, n) specify pixel coordinates. The reference frame width w_{frame} acts as a free parameter controlling the resolution. The intensities of each pixel within an image patch covering the points are then concatenated into a vector $\mathbf{g}$, and PCA applied as before to generate a linear model based on modes of variation $\mathbf{P}_g$

$$\mathbf{g} = T_\phi(\bar{\mathbf{g}} + \mathbf{P}_g\mathbf{b}_g) \quad \text{and} \quad \mathbf{b}_g = \mathbf{P}_g^T(T_\phi^{-1}(\mathbf{g}) - \bar{\mathbf{g}}), \tag{3}$$

where T_ϕ represents an intensity normalisation. Correlations may exist between the shape $\mathbf{b}_s$ and intensity $\mathbf{b}_g$ parameters, and so the models are concatenated and a further PCA performed to extract the independent modes of variation of both shape and intensity $\mathbf{P}_c$, referred to as appearance modes

$$\mathbf{b} = \mathbf{P}_c\mathbf{c} \quad \text{where} \quad \mathbf{b} = \begin{pmatrix} \mathbf{W}_s\mathbf{b}_s \\ \mathbf{b}_g \end{pmatrix}. \tag{4}$$

The weights $\mathbf{W}_s$ scale the relative magnitude of the shape and intensity parameters, and are derived by sampling the change in $\mathbf{g}$ per unit change in $\mathbf{b}_s$ in the training images.

Two approaches for sampling the intensities contributing to $\mathbf{g}$ were tested (Fig. 3). The first used a Delaunay triangulation of the landmarks to define a region of interest, with an optional, additional border of width w_{border} to ensure the whole edge was included. However, most relevant intensity information was expected to be located close to the end-plates i.e. the site of the fractures. Therefore, an alternative strategy that involved sampling a square patch of width w_{patch} around each landmark was also implemented. Multiple approaches for defining the landmarks used were also tested (Fig. 3), including sampling from a single vertebra, a triplet of neighbouring vertebrae, and a vertebra plus the closest end-plates of its neighbours (nEP sampling). The latter were intended to aid in identification of tilted vertebra, since these are distinguished from fractures, in clinical practice, by the symmetry of adjacent end-plates (Fig. 1).

The SSM or APM extract all significant shape and intensity information from an image as a compact vector of features. A variety of classifiers could then be applied to compare the features of a query image to those of annotated and diagnosed training images. Two were studied here. First, kNN was applied, measuring Euclidean distance in the feature space of $\mathbf{b}$ or $\mathbf{b}_s$ to identify N_{kNN} neighbours. However, kNN has the drawback that all features are considered; some will not be relevant to fracture status and so will potentially act as confounding information. To determine whether this effect was significant, classification was also performed using RFs. Since each split node considers a single feature, an RF has the capability to identify only those features relevant to the target. In both cases, the problem was treated as a regression task. The gold-standard diagnosis was translated into a numerical score with $0 =$ normal, $1 =$ deformed but not fractured and 2, 3, and $4 =$ mild, moderate and severe fracture. The output of the kNN was the mean of this score across the identified neighbours, and RFs were trained as regressors to predict the score. This created a potential problem as it assumed that deformed vertebrae are intermediate in

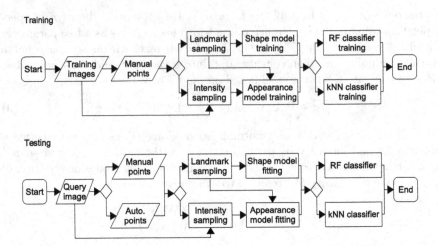

Fig. 4. Flow-chart summarising the various algorithmic choices. See main text for description.

shape between normal and fractured ones, which may not be the case. However, it more accurately represented fracture status as a position within a continuum, rather than discrete classes. The alternative, treating the problem as an explicit classification task, was investigated using a multi-class RF classifier. However, this led to significantly worse accuracy and full results are not reported here. As with the height-based classifier, a simple fracture/non-fracture classification was performed by thresholding the kNN or RF output.

Figure 4 summarises the various algorithmic choices that were evaluated. During testing, a 2D query image was input. This was either a DXA image or a thick-slice sagittal midline projection from a CT volume, produced as described in Sect. 2.1 using manual annotations of neural arch landmarks. The authors have previously described an algorithm that can automatically produce these projections [14]. This was not considered here due to lack of space. Landmark points outlining each visualised vertebral body, annotated either manually or using an automatic approach as described in Sect. 3, were then input (choice 1). The feature space (shape or appearance) and sampling procedure (single verte-bra, nEP or triplet) were then chosen as described in Sect. 2.3 (choice 2). Shape modelling required sampling only from the landmark points; appearance mod-elling required sampling from both the points and image intensities. For each visualised vertebra in the query image, the chosen model was fitted to the sam-pled data. The resultant shape or appearance features were then passed to a kNN or RF classifier (choice 3) to obtain the final classification for each verte-bra. All combinations of feature space, sampling procedure and classifier were evaluated. Model and classifier training was performed using manual annotations but otherwise followed a similar work-flow.

3   Evaluation

Throughout the evaluation, classifiers were trained and tested in a leave-1/4-out procedure using the data from all vertebral levels. During SSM and APM training, the number of modes of variation was constrained to model 98% of the variation in the data. Free parameters were empirically optimised on the CT midline images and manual annotations, such that the DXA images served as an independent evaluation set. Initially, the shape and appearance model parameters were optimised in combination with a kNN classifier. The latter had only one free parameter, N_{kNN}, greatly reducing the dimensionality of the parameter space compared to using a RF. Receiver operator characteristic (ROC) curves showing sensitivity against false positive rate (FPR) were generated by varying t_{class}, and the parameters leading to the highest value at which sensitivity equalled FPR were selected, giving $w_{frame} = 80$ pixels, $w_{border} = 30$ pixels for triangulated intensity sampling, $w_{patch} = 24$ pixels for patch-based sampling, and $N_{kNN} = 10$. This was repeated for all sampling strategies described in Sect. 2.3, and the optimae were consistent. In general, dependence on the parameters was weak for all except w_{frame}. A second round of parameter optimisation focused on the RF, using the optimised parameters for SSM/APM described above. The same ROC-curve based pattern search procedure was used to optimise the number of trees n_{tree}, the maximum depth of each tree D_{max}, and the minimum number of training samples n_{min} allowed at a split node, leading to $n_{tree} = 200$, $D_{max} = 30$ and $n_{min} = 1$.

Finally, semi-automatic annotation of the vertebrae in both the DXA and CT midline images, the latter projected using the manual neural arch annotations, was performed using a RFRV-CLM, initialised using manual annotations of vertebral centre points, following the procedure described in [12,14]. The classifiers were then applied to the automatic annotations using the optimised parameters. Classification accuracies for the optimised procedure with all combinations of features, classifier, patch and intensity sampling procedure and manual or automatic annotation were then compared.

Figures 5 and 6 show the evaluation of various sampling, feature extraction and classification procedures for the CT and DXA images, respectively, compared to baselines established by the six-point morphometry approach. A universal trend was noted across all experiments; accuracy for triplet sampling was always significantly worse than the alternatives (full results are not shown for this reason). Triplet sampling results in more modes of variation and so more features in $\mathbf{b}$ and $\mathbf{b}_s$, and adding the neighbouring vertebrae spreads the training data across the feature space depending on the fracture status of the neighbours. Both reduce data density. In contrast, whilst 6-point morphometry benefits from comparison of posterior vertebral heights between neighbours to identify crush fractures, where the height is reduced throughout a vertebral body, shape models can extract equivalent information from a single vertebra through quantification of its aspect ratio. Triplet sampling therefore adds little information, but makes it more difficult for a classifier to extract the information present.

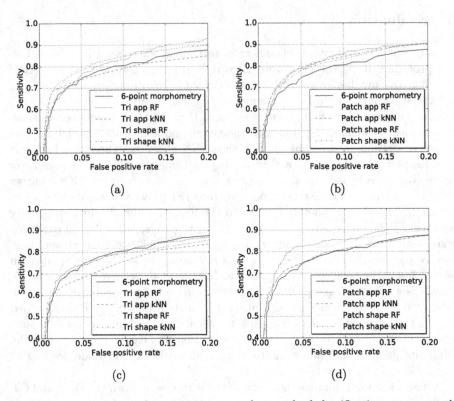

Fig. 5. Receiver operator characteristic curves for vertebral classification on computed tomography midline images. (a), (b) Point sampling from single vertebrae. (c), (d) Point sampling from vertebrae plus neighbouring end-plates. "Tri" refers to intensity sampling from Delaunay triangulated regions, "patch" to sampling from patches around each landmark point, "shape" to shape and "app" to appearance features.

Differences between the remaining sampling/modelling/classification procedures were usually small and frequently not significant, but the optimal procedure was always significantly better than 6-point morphometry. Several trends emerged from the results. On CT images (Fig. 5), there was little evidence of additional information in appearance compared to shape features. The kNN classifier showed a marked reduction in performance when triangulated intensity sampling was used, adding large numbers of uninformative appearance features (Fig. 5(a), (c)). The RF classifier also showed some evidence of this effect, with the combination of triangulated nEP sampling and appearance features resulting in performance no better than the baseline (Fig. 5c). However, the RF, in general, resulted in better accuracy than the kNN classifier and did not lose accuracy when nEP sampling was used, or when using appearance features if the number of features was controlled using patch-based sampling (Fig. 5(b), (d)).

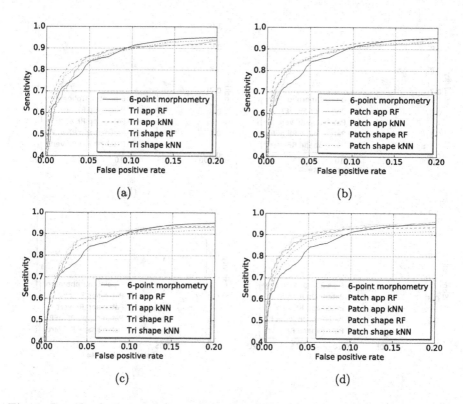

Fig. 6. Receiver operator characteristic curves for vertebral classification on dual-energy X-ray absorptiometry images. (a), (b) Point sampling from single vertebrae. (c), (d) Point sampling from vertebrae plus neighbouring end-plates. "Tri" refers to intensity sampling from Delaunay triangulated regions, "patch" to sampling from patches around each landmark point, "shape" to shape and "app" to appearance features.

DXA images (Fig. 6) represented a more challenging task since, being projections of the full vertebral body, the shape as visualised in the images was more complex, and the image quality was lower. Increased noise on individual features resulted in kNN outperforming RF when single-vertebra sampling was used (Fig. 6(a), (b)), with accuracy gains resulting from using appearance as long as the length of the feature vector was controlled by using patch-based sampling (Fig. 6(b)). However, using shape information from neighbouring vertebrae through nEP sampling, to deal with cases where the vertebrae were tilted relative to the beam direction, allowed the RF to achieve equal or better performance on shape alone (Fig. 6(d)).

Figure 7 shows results from the optimised procedure, using patch-based sampling and RF classification, for both manual and automatic annotations on both image sets. Each experiment was repeated five times, using the stochastic nature of RF training to support error estimation, and the figures show the mean and (where shown) standard deviation of the repeats. As described above, nEP

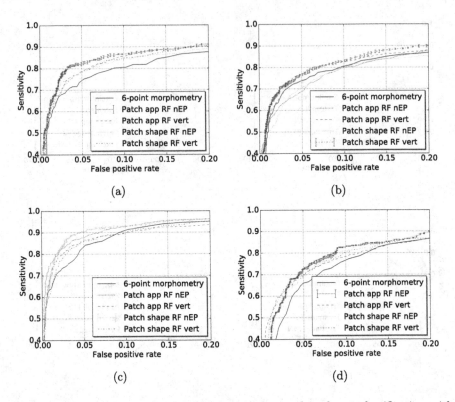

Fig. 7. Receiver operator characteristic curves for random forest classification with patch sampling in computed tomography midline (a), (b) and dual-energy X-ray absorptiometry (c), (d) images, from manual (a), (c) and RFRV-CLM (b), (d) annotations, compared to 6-point morphometry. "Shape" refers to shape and "app" to appearance features.

sampling resulted in increased accuracy for both image types when classifying from manual annotations (Fig. 7(a), (c)). However, this requires accurate annotations of all vertebrae in the triplet, increasing the risk of a fit failure being present in the automatic annotations. Single-vertebra sampling was therefore more accurate on RFRV-CLM annotations of CT images and appearance provided no additional information over shape (Fig. 7(b)). However, the difficulties of the classification task in DXA images, described above, resulted in higher accuracies when nEP sampling and appearance parameters were used, to disambiguate tilted vertebra and confounding pathologies (Fig. 7(d)). At 80% sensitivity, the optimal classifier reduced the FPR from 4.4% to 1.7% for manual and from 12.7% to 8.8% for automatic DXA annotations. For CT images, FPR was reduced from 8.9% to 3.3% for manual and 9.7% to 7.0% for automatic annotations. These equate to a significant ($p < 0.01$) reduction in FPR of ≈30% for automatic, and ≈60% for manual annotations.

4   Conclusion

We have evaluated several different methods for osteoporotic VF classification in DXA VFA and CT midline images. In this context, the 6-point morphometry approach can be viewed as the construction of a low-parameter shape model based on hand-crafted modes of variation. Since these reflect the clinical definitions used in fracture grading [18] they are guaranteed to be informative. A SSM or APM can extract all statistically significant shape and appearance information from the images as a compact feature vector, but not all of these features are guaranteed to be informative in terms of fracture classification. The way in which the subsequent classifier handles non-informative dimensions of the feature space therefore influences accuracy. Straightforward application of kNN considers all features equally, whilst a RF considers only the most informative at each split node, and so is more robust to non-informative features.

The results showed that statistically significant gains in classification accuracy can be achieved by applying kNN or RF classifiers to shape or appearance model features. The optimal procedure across both CT and DXA was to apply a RF classifier to features sampled from a vertebra and the closest end-plates of its neighbours with manual landmark annotations, but fitting errors in automatic annotations resulted in single vertebra sampling being more accurate for CT images. Evidence for improved performance when using appearance, as opposed to shape, features was generally weak and inconsistent. However, it did not result in significant reductions in classifier performance. In conclusion, the combination of appearance features and RF classification with patch-based nEP sampling, for manual annotations, and single vertebra sampling, for automatic annotations, provided optimal results. Significant accuracy gains compared to 6-point morphometry were achieved for both manual and automatic annotations on both DXA VFA and CT images using these approaches.

This work used a single model/classifier for all vertebral levels between T4 (for CT) or T7 (for DXA VFA) and L4, inclusive. Vertebral shape varies gradually across the spine, and so further improvements in accuracy might be gained through using multiple, level-specific classifiers. Roberts et al. [9] achieved higher classification accuracies on DXA VFA images using this approach, and so we intend to investigate this in future work. However, the use of level-specific classifiers requires a reasonably accurate method of level detection if combined with an automatic vertebral segmentation method, which may prove challenging given the similarity between vertebra.

Acknowledgements. This publication presents independent research supported by the Health Innovation Challenge Fund (grant no. HICF-R7-414/WT100936), a parallel funding partnership between the Department of Health and Wellcome Trust, and by the NIHR Invention for Innovation (i4i) programme (grant no. II-LB_0216-20009). The views expressed are those of the authors and not necessarily those of the NHS, NIHR, the Department of Health or Wellcome Trust. The authors acknowledge the invaluable assistance of Mrs Chrissie Alsop, Mr Stephen Capener, Mrs Imelda Hodgkinson, Mr Michael Machin, and Mrs Sue Roberts, who performed the manual annotations.

References

1. Rachner, T., Khosla, S., Hofbauer, L.: Osteoporosis: now and the future. Lancet **377**(9773), 1276–1287 (2011)
2. Adams, J.: Opportunistic identification of vertebral fractures. J. Clin. Densitom. **19**(1), 54–62 (2016)
3. Operational Information for Commissioning: Diagnostic imaging dataset statistical release. Technical report, NHS, UK (2016). http://www.england.nhs.uk/statistics/wp-content/uploads/sites/2/2015/08/Provisional-Monthly-Diagnostic-Imaging-Dataset-Statistics-2016-05-19.pdf
4. Williams, A.L., Al-Busaidi, A., Sparrow, P.J., Adams, J.E., Whitehouse, R.W.: Under-reporting of osteoporotic vertebral fractures on computed tomography. Eur. J. Radiol. **69**(1), 179–183 (2009)
5. Kariki, E., Bromiley, P., Cootes, T., Adams, J.: Opportunistic identification of vertebral fractures on computed radiography: need for improvement. Osteoporos. Int. **27**(S2), 621 (2016)
6. Cootes, T., Taylor, C., Cooper, D., Graham, J.: Active shape models - their training and application. Comput. Vis. Image Understand. **61**(1), 38–59 (1995)
7. Brett, A., Miller, C., Hayes, C., Krasnow, J., Ozanian, T., Abrams, K., Block, J., van Kuijk, C.: Development of a clinical workflow tool to enhance the detection of vertebral fractures. Spine **34**(22), 2437–2443 (2009)
8. Roberts, M., Cootes, T., Adams, J.: Vertebral morphometry: semiautomatic determination of detailed shape from dual-energy X-ray absorptiometry images using active appearance models. Invest. Radiol. **41**(12), 849–859 (2006)
9. Roberts, M.G., Cootes, T.F., Adams, J.E.: Automatic location of vertebrae on DXA images using random forest regression. In: Ayache, N., Delingette, H., Golland, P., Mori, K. (eds.) MICCAI 2012. LNCS, vol. 7512, pp. 361–368. Springer, Heidelberg (2012). https://doi.org/10.1007/978-3-642-33454-2_45
10. Lindner, C., Bromiley, P., Ionita, M., Cootes, T.: Robust and accurate shape model matching using random forest regression-voting. IEEE Trans. Pattern Anal. Mach. Intell. **37**(9), 1862–1874 (2015)
11. Bromiley, P., Adams, J., Cootes, T.: Localization of vertebrae on DXA VFA images using constrained local models with random forest regression voting. In: Proceedings of 20th International Bone Densitometry Workshop - IBDW 2014 (2014). J. Orthop. Translat., vol. 2, pp. 227–228
12. Bromiley, P., Adams, J., Cootes, T.: Localisation of vertebrae on DXA images using constrained local models with random forest regression voting. In: Yao, J., et al. (eds.) CSI 2014. LNCVB, vol. 20, pp. 159–171. Springer, Cham (2015). https://doi.org/10.1007/978-3-319-14148-0_14
13. Bromiley, P.A., Adams, J.E., Cootes, T.F.: Automatic localisation of vertebrae in DXA images using random forest regression voting. In: Vrtovec, T., Yao, J., Glocker, B., Klinder, T., Frangi, A., Zheng, G., Li, S. (eds.) CSI 2015. LNCS, vol. 9402, pp. 38–51. Springer, Cham (2016). https://doi.org/10.1007/978-3-319-41827-8_4
14. Bromiley, P.A., Kariki, E.P., Adams, J.E., Cootes, T.F.: Fully automatic localisation of vertebrae in CT images using random forest regression voting. In: Yao, J., Vrtovec, T., Zheng, G., Frangi, A., Glocker, B., Li, S. (eds.) CSI 2016. LNCS, vol. 10182, pp. 51–63. Springer, Cham (2016). https://doi.org/10.1007/978-3-319-55050-3_5

15. Cootes, T., Edwards, G., Taylor, C.: Active appearance models. IEEE Trans. Pattern Anal. Mach. Intell. **23**(6), 681–685 (2001)
16. Griffith, J.: Identifying osteoporotic vertebral fracture. Quant. Imaging Med. Surg. **5**(4), 592–602 (2015)
17. Jensen, G., McNair, P., Boesen, J., Hegedus, V.: Validity in diagnosing osteoporosis. Observer variation in interpreting spinal radiographs. Eur. J. Radiol. **4**(1), 1–3 (1984)
18. Genant, H., Wu, C., Kuijk, C., Nevitt, M.: Vertebral fracture assessment using a semi-quantitative technique. J. Bone Miner. Res. **8**(9), 1137–1148 (1993)
19. Jiang, G.: Diagnosis of vertebral fracture using an ABQ method. Osteoporos. Rev. **18**(3), 14–18 (2010)
20. Breiman, L.: Random forests. Mach. Learn. **45**(1), 5–32 (2001)
21. McCloskey, E., Selby, P., de Takats, D., Bernard, J., Davies, M., Robinson, J., Francis, R., Adams, J., Pande, K., Beneton, M., Jalava, T., Loyttyniemi, E., Kanis, J.: Effects of clodronate on vertebral fracture risk in osteoporosis: a 1-year interim analysis. Bone **28**(3), 310–315 (2001)

DSMS-FCN: A Deeply Supervised Multi-scale Fully Convolutional Network for Automatic Segmentation of Intervertebral Disc in 3D MR Images

Guodong Zeng and Guoyan Zheng[✉]

Institute for Surgical Technology and Biomechanics,
University of Bern, Bern, Switzerland
guoyan.zheng@istb.unibe.ch

Abstract. This paper addresses the challenging problem of segmentation of intervertebral discs (IVDs) in three-dimensional (3D) T2-weighted magnetic resonance (MR) images. We propose a deeply supervised multi-scale fully convolutional network for segmentation of IVDs in 3D MR images. After training, our network can directly map a whole volumetric data to its volume-wise labels. Multi-scale deep supervision is designed to alleviate the potential gradient vanishing problem during training. It is also used together with partial transfer learning to boost the training efficiency when only small set of labeled training data are available. The present method was validated on the MICCAI 2015 IVD segmentation challenge datasets. Our method achieved a mean Dice overlap coefficient of 92.0% and a mean average symmetric surface distance of 0.41 mm. The results achieved by our method are better than those achieved by the state-of-the-art methods.

Keywords: Intervertebral disc · MRI · Segmentation
Deep learning · Fully convolutional network

1 Introduction

Intervertebral disc (IVD) degeneration is a major cause for chronic back pain and function incapacity [1]. In clinical practice, spine magnetic resonance (MR) imaging (MRI) is the preferred modality in diagnosis and treatment planning of various spinal pathologies such as disc herniation, slipped vertebra and so on, not only because MRI is non-invasive and does not use ionizing radiation, but more importantly because it offers good soft tissue contrast that allows for visualization of disc's internal structure [2].

Accurate IVD segmentation from spine MR image is therefore very important for correct diagnosis and treatment planning [1,3]. Traditionally, most quantitative studies on IVD degeneration have been done by manually segmenting the data, which is tedious, time-consuming and error-prone. On the other hand, a

© Springer International Publishing AG 2018
B. Glocker et al. (Eds.): MSKI 2017, LNCS 10734, pp. 148–159, 2018.
https://doi.org/10.1007/978-3-319-74113-0_13

fully-automatic system for IVD identification will significantly reduce the time of the diagnosis. An automatic system might also help reduce errors caused by subjective factors and improve the consistency of diagnosis standards. In this way, it can immediately benefit clinical applications and spinal biomechanics research.

In the literature, different methods have been proposed of IVD segmentation [4–8]. There exist methods based on watershed algorithm [4], atlas registration [5], graph cuts with geometric priors from neighboring discs [6], template matching and statistical shape model [7], or anisotropic oriented flux detection [8]. Most of these methods work only on two-dimensional sagittal images and only a few methods [7] address the challenging three-dimensional (3D) IVD segmentation problem. See [9] for a comprehensive review of existing IVD segmentation methods.

Recently, machine learning-based methods have gained more and more interest. For example, Zhan et al. [10] presented a hierarchical strategy and local articulated model to detect vertebrae and discs 3D MR images and Kelm et al. [11] proposed to use iterated marginal space learning for spine detection in computed tomography (CT) and MR images. A unified data-driven regression and classification framework was suggested by Chen et al. [12] to tackle the problem of localization and segmentation of IVDs from T2-weighted MR data, and Wang et al. [13] proposed to address the segmentation of multiple anatomic structures in multiple anatomical planes from multiple imaging modalities via a sparse kernel machines-based regression.

The more recent development on deep neural networks, and in particular on convolutional neural networks (CNN), suggests another course of methods to solve the challenging IVD segmentation problem [14–22]. Contrary to conventional shallow learning methods where feature design is crucial, deep learning methods automatically learn hierarchies of relevant features directly from the training data [15]. More recently, 3D volume-to-volume segmentation networks were introduced, including 3D U-Net [20], 3D V-Net [21] and a 3D deeply supervised network [22].

In this paper, we propose a deeply supervised multi-scale fully convolutional network (FCN) called "DSMS-FCN" for fully automatic IVD segmentation in 3D T2-weighted MR images. After training, our network can directly map a whole volumetric data to its volume-wise label. Multi-scale deep supervision is designed to alleviate the potential gradient vanishing problem during training. It is also used together with partial transfer learning to boost the training efficiency when only small set of labeled training data are available.

The paper is organized as follows. In Sect. 2, we will describe the proposed architecture and algorithm. The application to the MICCAI 2015 IVD segmentation challenge dataset will be presented in Sect. 3, and we conclude with a discussion in Sect. 4.

2   Method

Figure 1 illustrates the architecture of our proposed neural network for the automatic IVD segmentation in 3D T2-weighted MR images. Our network employs a

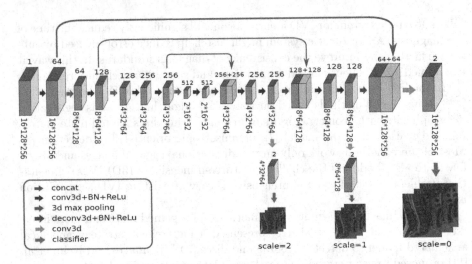

Fig. 1. A schematic illustration of our proposed network architecture. For each block, the digits above indicate the number of feature stack while the numbers below represent the data size.

deeply supervised multi-scale fully convolutional network. In this section, firstly the detailed architecture of our proposed model is elaborated, and then we will introduce the multi-scale deep supervision. Finally, partial transfer learning, which is designed to boost the training efficiency, will be described.

2.1   3D FCN with Skip Connection

Our proposed network is inspired by 3DFCN [23] but with significant differences. Similar to 3DFCN, our network is also a 3D fully convolutional network and consists of two parts, i.e., the encoder part (contracting path) and the decoder part (expansive path). The encoder part focuses on analysis and feature representation learning from the input data while the decoder part generates segmentation results, relying on the learned features from the encoder part. Our network can take arbitrary-sized volumetric data as input and outputs voxel-wise segmentation probability map in the same size as the input.

Different from 3DFCN, long and short skip connections, which help recover spatial context lost in the contracting encoder, are used in our network as shown in Fig. 1. The importance of skip connection in biomedical image segmentation has been demonstrated by previous studies [24]. Skip connections have been widely used in many different convolutional neural networks including Resi-Net [25] and 3D U-Net [20].

In 3DFCN [23], big kernel sizes (e.g. $5 \times 7 \times 7$) are utilized in the convolutional layers. However, previous studies have shown that small kernel size are more helpful for training of deep neural network [26]. For this reason, in our network, kernel size of $3 \times 3 \times 3$ and strides of 1 are utilized for all convolutional layers, and kernel size of $2 \times 2 \times 2$ is used in all max pooling layers. Batch normalization

(BN) [27] and rectified linear unit (ReLU) are adopted to speed up the training and to enhance the gradient back propagation.

2.2 Multi-scale Deep Supervision

Training a deep neural network is challenging. As the matter of gradient vanishing, final loss cannot be efficiently back propagated to shallow layers, which is more difficult for 3D cases when only a small set of annotated data is available. To address this issue, we inject two down-scaled branch classifiers into our network in addition to the classifier of the main network, which is another difference between our network and 3DFCN [23]. By doing this, segmentation is performed at multiple output layers. For the classifier at the coarse scale which is closer to the encoder part, it generates segmentation results with the coarsest resolution, while the classifiers at the middle and the fine scales generate segmentation results with the intermediate and the finest resolutions, respectively. As a result, classifiers in different scales can take advantage of multi-scale context, which has been demonstrated in previous work on segmentation of 3D liver CT and 3D heart MR images [22]. Furthermore, with the loss calculated by the prediction from classifiers from different scales, more effective gradient back propagation can be achieved by direct supervision on the hidden layers.

Specifically, let W be the weights of main network and $w = \{w^0, w^1, \dots w^{M-1}\}$ be the weights of classifiers at different scales, where M is the number of classifier branches. For the training samples $S = (X, Y)$, where X represents training sub-volume patches and Y represents the class labels while $Y \in \{0, 1\}$.

$$L_{cls}(X, Y; W, w) = \sum_{m=0}^{M-1} \sum_{(x_i, y_i) \in S^m} \alpha_m l^m(x_i, y_i | W, w^m), \qquad (1)$$

where $S = \{S^0, S^1, \dots, S^{M-1}\}$; S^0 is a sub-volume patch directly sampled from a training image while S^m contains the examples (x_i, y_i) at scale of $m > 0$, which is obtained by downsampling S^0 by a factor of 2^m along each dimension; w^m is the weights of the classifier at scale of m; α_m is the weight of l^m, which is the loss calculated by a training sample x_i, y_i at scale of m.

$$l^m(x_i, y_i | W, w^m) = -\log p(y_i = t(x_i) | x_i; W, w^m), \qquad (2)$$

where $p(y_i = t(x_i) | x_i; W, w^m)$ is the probability of predicted class label $t(x_i)$ corresponding to sample $x_i \in S^m$.

The total loss of our multi-scaled deeply supervised model will be:

$$L_{total}(X, Y; W, w) = L_{cls}(X, Y; W, w) + \lambda(\psi(W) + \sum_m \psi(w^m)), \qquad (3)$$

where $\psi()$ is the regularization term (L_2 norm in our experiment) with hyper parameter λ.

2.3 Partial Transfer Learning

It is difficult to train a deep neural network from scratch because of limited annotated data. Training deep neural network requires large amount of annotated data, which are not always available, although data augmentation can partially address the problem. Furthermore, randomly initialized parameters make it more difficult to search for an optimal solution in high dimensional space. Transfer learning from an existing network, which has been trained on a large set of data, is a common way to alleviate the difficulty. Previous studies [28] demonstrated that transferring features from another pre-trained model can boost the generalization, and that the effect of transfer learning was related to the similarity between the task of the pre-trained model and the target task. Furthermore, the same study also demonstrated that weights of shallow layers in deep neural network were generic while those of deep layers were more related to specific tasks.

To best utilize the advantage of transfer learning, we need to transfer from a model trained on a related task. In this paper, a pre-trained model in our previous work was adopted [29], which is designed for the task of segmentation of the proximal femur from 3D T1-weighted MR Images. More specifically, the weights of the main network are initialized from our previous model [29], while the weights of all branch classifiers are initialized from a Gaussian distribution $(\mu = 0, \sigma = 0.01)$.

2.4 Implementation Details

The proposed network was implemented in python using TensorFlow framework and trained on a desktop with a 3.6 GHz Intel(R) i7 CPU and a GTX 1080 Ti graphics card with 11 GB GPU memory.

3 Experiments and Results

3.1 Data Description

The training data provided by the MICCAI 2015 IVD challenge organizers consist of 15 3D T2-weighted turbo spin echo MR images and the associated ground truth segmentation [9]. These 15 3D T2-weighted MR images were acquired from fifteen patients in two different studies. Each patient was scanned with 1.5 Tesla MRI scanner of Siemens (Siemens Healthcare, Erlangen, Germany). The pixel spacings of all the images are sampled to $2 \times 1.25 \times 1.25\,\text{mm}^3$. There are 7 IVDs T11-L5 to be segmented from each image. Thus, in each image these IVD regions have been manually identified and segmented.

The MICCAI 2015 IVD challenge organizers also released two test datasets. Each test dataset consists of five 3D T2-weighted turbo spin echo MR images. Thus, in this paper, our network was trained on the fifteen 3D training data first, and are then evaluated on the ten test data.

3.2 Training Patches Preparation

In order to enlarge the training samples, data augmentation was utilized. Specifically, each training data was rotated (90, 180, 270) degrees around the y axis of the image and flipped horizontally (taking the z axis as the vertical direction). After that, we got in total 120 images for training our network.

Our network takes a fixed-sized sub-volume as input, and employs end-to-end learning and voxel-wise inference. During training, sub-volume patches with the size of $16 \times 256 \times 128$ was randomly cropped from 120 training examples whose size are about $40 \times 300 \times 300$. In each epoch of training, 120 training images were randomly shuffled and then sub-volume patches was randomly cropped with batch-size of 2 by 5 times from each volumetric training image. Before fed into the network for training, each sub-volume patch was normalized by zero mean and unit variance. In total, for each epoch of training, we trained the network using 1200 ($120 \times 5 \times 2$) sub-volume patches.

3.3 Training

We trained our network for 10,000 iterations after partial transfer learning. All weights were updated by the stochastic gradient descent (SGD) algorithm (momentum $= 0.9$, weight decay $= 0.005$). Learning rate was initialized as 1×10^{-3} and halved by every 3,000 times. In our experiment, we used three branch classifiers at three different scales. The loss weights of three classifiers α_0, α_1 and α_2 are 1.0, 0.67 and 0.33, respectively. The hyper parameter λ was chosen to be 0.005.

3.4 Testing

Our trained models can estimate labels of an arbitrary-sized volumetric image. Given a test volumetric image, we extracted overlapped sub-volume patches with the size of $16 \times 256 \times 128$, and fed them to the trained network to get prediction probability maps. For the overlapped voxels, the final probability maps would be the average of the probability maps of the overlapped patches, which were then used to derive the final segmentation results. After that, we conducted morphological operations to remove isolated small volumes and internal hole.

3.5 Valuation

The segmented results were compared with the associated ground truth segmentation. For each test image, we evaluated both the surface distance as well as the volume overlap measurements of results obtained by different segmentation.

In [9], to compute the average absolute distance (ASD) between the ground truth IVD surface and the automatically segmented surface, surface meshes from binary IVD segmentation were generated first using the Matlab toolbox Iso2mesh [30]. In contrast, in this study, we adopted the average symmetric surface distance (ASSD) as introduced in [31] to measure the surface distance. More specifically,

Table 1. Results on the Test1 dataset from the MICCAI 2015 intervertebral disc segmentation challenge.

Parameters	Mean ± STD
Dice overlap coefficients (%)	91.4 ± 0.5
Jaccard (%)	84.2 ± 1.0
Precision (%)	94.2 ± 2.5
Recall (%)	88.9 ± 2.3
ASSD (mm)	0.44 ± 0.055

STD - standard deviation
ASSD - average symmetric surface distance

ASSD is given in millimeters and based on the surface voxels (instead of surface meshes as in [9]) of two segmentation A and B. Surface voxels are defined by having at least one on-object voxel within their 26-neighborhood. For each surface voxel of A, the Euclidean distance to the closest surface voxel of B is calculated using the approximate nearest neighbor technique [32] and stored. The same process is then applied to surface voxels of B to A in order to symmetry. The ASSD is then defined as the average of all stored distances, which is zero for a perfect segmentation.

Given two binary segmentations of a test image, we compute following volume overlap measurements including Dice overlap coefficient [33], Jaccard coefficient [33], precision and recall.

3.6 Results

Table 1 shows the results of our method when evaluated on the Test1 dataset of the MICCAI 2015 IVD segmentation challenge and Table 2 shows the results of our method when evaluated on the Test2 dataset of the MICCAI 2015 IVD segmentation challenge. A mean Dice overlap coefficient of 92.0% and a mean ASSD of 0.41 mm were achieved by our method. Furthermore, slightly better results

Table 2. Results on the Test2 dataset from the MICCAI 2015 intervertebral disc segmentation challenge.

Parameters	Mean ± STD
Dice overlap coefficients (%)	92.6 ± 1.1
Jaccard (%)	86.4 ± 2.0
Precision (%)	93.8 ± 1.5
Recall (%)	91.4 ± 1.6
ASSD (mm)	0.38 ± 0.045

STD - standard deviation
ASSD - average symmetric surface distance

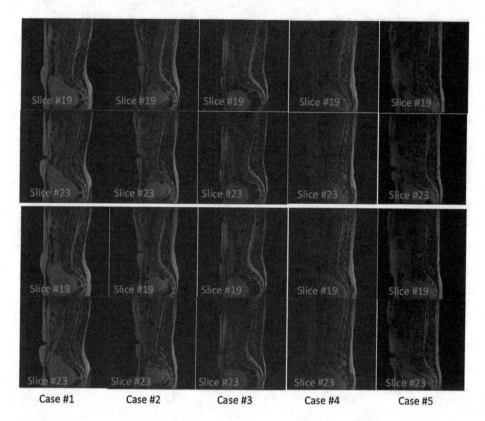

| Case #1 | Case #2 | Case #3 | Case #4 | Case #5 |

Fig. 2. Qualitative comparison of the results achieved by our method on the Test1 dataset (top two rows) and ground truth segmentation (bottom two rows). For each case, two slices are shown.

were obtained when our method was evaluated on the Test2 dataset than when our method was evaluated on Test1 dataset. Without using any time-consuming registration step or incorporating any advanced shape prior, our method achieved results that were better than those achieved by the state-of-the-art methods [9]. For example, the best segmentation method in the MICCAI 2015 IVD segmentation challenge was the on submitted by Korez et al. [34] where a mean Dice overlap coefficient of 91.8% was reported. Figure 2 shows examples of automatic segmentation achieved by our method on the Test1 dataset and Fig. 3 shows examples of segmentation achieved by our method on the Test2 dataset.

Implemented with Python using TensorFlow framework, our network took about 40 s to test one volumetric MR image with size of $40 \times 300 \times 300$.

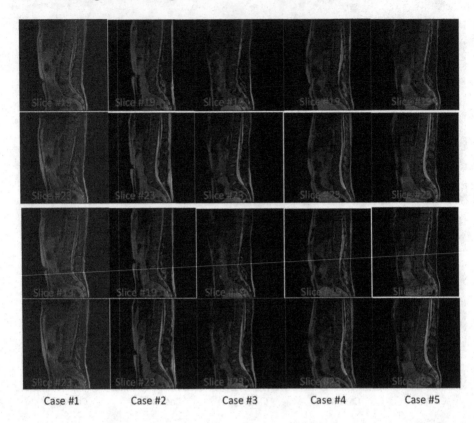

Case #1   Case #2   Case #3   Case #4   Case #5

Fig. 3. Qualitative comparison of the results achieved by our method on the Test2 dataset (top two rows) and ground truth segmentation (bottom two rows). For each case, two slices are shown.

4   Conclusion

In this paper, we proposed to use a deeply supervised multi-scale fully convolutional network to solve the challenging IVD segmentation problem. The present method was evaluated on the MICCAI 2015 IVD segmentation challenge datasets and the results achieved by the present method were better than those achieved by the state-of-the-art methods.

In comparison with 3DFCN as introduced by Chen et al. [23], where they incorporate neither skip connection nor multi-scale deep supervision, our method achieved much better segmentation results. More specifically, evaluated on the Test1 and Test2 datasets of the MICCAI 2015 IVD segmentation challenge, their method achieved a mean Dice overlap coefficient of 88.4% and 89.0%, respectively. In contrast, evaluated on the same two datasets, our method achieved a mean Dice overlap coefficient of 91.4% and 92.6%, respectively. The results demonstrated that the incorporation of skip connections and the multi-scale deep supervision, when combined with partial transfer learning, did improve the performance of a 3D FCN.

References

1. Modic, M., Ross, J.: Lumbar degenerative disk disease. Radiology **245**(1), 43–61 (2007)
2. Parizel, P., Van Goethem, J., Van den Hauwe, L., Voormolen, M.: Degenerative disc disease. In: Van Goethem, J., et al. (eds.) Spinal Imaging, pp. 127–156. Medical Radiology. Springer, Heidelberg (2007). https://doi.org/10.1007/978-3-540-68483-1_6
3. An, H., Anderson, P., Haughton, V., Iatridis, J., Kang, J., Lotz, J., Natarajan, R., Oegema, T.J., Roughley, P., Setton, L., Urban, J., Videman, T., Andersson, G., Weinstein, J.: Introduction: disc degeneration: summary. Spine **29**(23), 2677–2678 (2004)
4. Chevrefils, C., Cheriet, F., Aubin, C., Grimard, G.: Texture analysis for automatic segmentation of intervertebral disks of scoliotic spines from MR images. IEEE Trans. Inf Technol. Biomed. **13**(4), 608–620 (2009)
5. Michopoulou, S., Costaridou, L., Panagiotopoulos, E., Speller, R., Panayiotakis, G., Todd-Pokropek, A.: Atlas-based segmentation of degenerated lumbar intervertebral discs from MR images of the spine. IEEE Trans. Biomed. Eng. **56**(9), 2225–2231 (2009)
6. Ben Ayed, I., Punithakumar, K., Garvin, G., Romano, W., Li, S.: Graph cuts with invariant object-interaction priors: application to intervertebral disc segmentation. In: Székely, G., Hahn, H.K. (eds.) IPMI 2011. LNCS, vol. 6801, pp. 221–232. Springer, Heidelberg (2011). https://doi.org/10.1007/978-3-642-22092-0_19
7. Neubert, A., Fripp, J., Engstrom, C., Schwarz, R., Lauer, L., Salvado, O., Crozier, S.: Automated detection, 3D segmentation and analysis of high resolution spine MR images using statistical shape models. Phys. Med. Biol. **57**(24), 8457–8376 (2012)
8. Law, M., Tay, K., Leung, A., Garvin, G., Li, S.: Intervertebral disc segmentation in MR images using anisotropic oriented flux. Med. Image Anal. **17**(1), 43–61 (2013)
9. Zheng, G., Chu, C., Belavý, D., Ibragimov, B., Korez, R., Vrtovec, T., Hutt, H., Everson, R., Meakin, J., Andrade, I., Glocker, B., Chen, H., Dou, Q., Heng, P., Wang, C., Forsberg, D., Neubert, A., Fripp, J., Urschler, M., Stern, D., Wimmer, M., Novikov, A., Cheng, H., Armbrecht, G., Felsenberg, D., Li, S.: Evaluation and comparison of 3D intervertebral disc localization and segmentation methods for 3D T2 MR data: a grand challenge. Med. Image Anal. **35**, 327–344 (2017)
10. Zhan, Y., Maneesh, D., Harder, M., Zhou, X.S.: Robust MR spine detection using hierarchical learning and local articulated model. In: Ayache, N., Delingette, H., Golland, P., Mori, K. (eds.) MICCAI 2012. LNCS, vol. 7510, pp. 141–148. Springer, Heidelberg (2012). https://doi.org/10.1007/978-3-642-33415-3_18
11. Kelm, M., Wels, M., Zhou, S., Seifert, S., Suehling, M., Zheng, Y., Comaniciu, D.: Spine detection in CT and MR using iterated marginal space learning. Med. Image Anal. **17**(8), 1283–1292 (2013)
12. Chen, C., Belavy, D., Yu, W., Chu, C., Armbrecht, G., Bansmann, M., Felsenberg, D., Zheng, G.: Localization and segmentation of 3D intervertebral discs in MR images by data driven estimation. IEEE Trans. Med. Imaging **34**(8), 1719–1729 (2015)
13. Wang, Z., Zhen, X., Tay, K., Osman, S., Romano, W., Li, S.: Regression segmentation for M^3 spinal images. IEEE Trans. Med. Imaging **34**(8), 1640–1648 (2015)
14. Bengio, Y.: Learning deep architectures for AI. Found. Trends Mach. Learn. **2**(1), 1–127 (2009)

15. Krizhevsky, A., Sutskever, I., Hinton, G.: ImageNet classification with deep convolutional neural networks. In: Pereira, F., et al. (eds.) Proceedings of Neural Information Processing Systems – NIPS 2012, vol. 25, pp. 1097–1105. NIPS (2012)

16. Prasoon, A., Petersen, K., Igel, C., Lauze, F., Dam, E., Nielsen, M.: Deep feature learning for knee cartilage segmentation using a triplanar convolutional neural network. In: Mori, K., Sakuma, I., Sato, Y., Barillot, C., Navab, N. (eds.) MICCAI 2013. LNCS, vol. 8150, pp. 246–253. Springer, Heidelberg (2013). https://doi.org/10.1007/978-3-642-40763-5_31

17. Roth, H.R., et al.: A new 2.5D representation for lymph node detection using random sets of deep convolutional neural network observations. In: Golland, P., Hata, N., Barillot, C., Hornegger, J., Howe, R. (eds.) MICCAI 2014. LNCS, vol. 8673, pp. 520–527. Springer, Cham (2014). https://doi.org/10.1007/978-3-319-10404-1_65

18. Long, J., Shelhamer, E., Darrell, T.: Fully convolutional networks for semantic segmentation. In: Proceedings of IEEE Conference on Computer Vision and Pattern Recognition - CVPR 2015, pp. 3431–3440 (2015)

19. Roth, H., Yao, J., Lu, L., Stieger, J., Burns, J., Summers, R.: Detection of sclerotic spine metastases via random aggregation of deep convolutional neural network classifications. In: Yao, J., et al. (eds.) Proceedings of 2nd MICCAI Workshop on Computational Methods and Clinical Applications for Spine CSI 2014, LNCVB, vol. 20, pp. 3–12. Springer (2015). https://doi.org/10.1007/978-3-319-14148-0_1

20. Çiçek, Ö., Abdulkadir, A., Lienkamp, S.S., Brox, T., Ronneberger, O.: 3D U-Net: learning dense volumetric segmentation from sparse annotation. In: Ourselin, S., Joskowicz, L., Sabuncu, M.R., Unal, G., Wells, W. (eds.) MICCAI 2016. LNCS, vol. 9901, pp. 424–432. Springer, Cham (2016). https://doi.org/10.1007/978-3-319-46723-8_49

21. Milletari, F., Navab, N., Ahmadi, S.A.: V-Net: fully convolutional neural networks for volumetric medical image segmentation. In: Proceedings of 4th International Conference on 3D Vision - 3DV 2016, pp. 565–571. IEEE (2016)

22. Dou, Q., Yu, L., Chen, H., Jin, Y., Yang, X., Qin, J., Heng, P.A.: 3D deeply supervised network for automated segmentation of volumetric medical images. Med. Image Anal. **41**, 40–54 (2017)

23. Chen, H., Dou, Q., Wang, X., Qin, J., Cheng, J.C.Y., Heng, P.-A.: 3D fully convolutional networks for intervertebral disc localization and segmentation. In: Zheng, G., Liao, H., Jannin, P., Cattin, P., Lee, S.-L. (eds.) MIAR 2016. LNCS, vol. 9805, pp. 375–382. Springer, Cham (2016). https://doi.org/10.1007/978-3-319-43775-0_34

24. Drozdzal, M., Vorontsov, E., Chartrand, G., Kadoury, S., Pal, C.: The importance of skip connections in biomedical image segmentation. In: Carneiro, G., et al. (eds.) LABELS/DLMIA -2016. LNCS, vol. 10008, pp. 179–187. Springer, Cham (2016). https://doi.org/10.1007/978-3-319-46976-8_19

25. He, K., Zhang, X., Ren, S., Sun, J.: Deep residual learning for image recognition. In: Proceedings of IEEE Conference on Computer Vision and Pattern Recognition - CVPR 2016, pp. 770–778. IEEE (2016)

26. Simonyan, K., Zisserman, A.: Very deep convolutional networks for large-scale image recognition. arXiv:1409.1556 (2014)

27. Ioffe, S., Szegedy, C.: Batch normalization: accelerating deep network training by reducing. In: Proceedings of 32nd International Conference on Machine Learning - ICML 2015, vol. 37, pp. 448–456. PLMR (2015)

28. Yosinski, J., Clune, J., Bengio, Y., Lipson, H.: How transferable are features in deep neural networks? In: Ghahramani, Z., et al. (eds.) Proceedings of Advances in Neural Information Processing Systems - NIPS 2014, pp. 3320–3328. MIT Press (2014)

29. Zeng, G., Yang, X., Li, J., Yu, L., Heng, P., Zheng, G.: 3D U-Net with multi-level deep supervision:fully automatic segmentation of proximal femur in 3D MR images. In: 8th MICCAI International Workshop on Machine Learning in Medical Imaging - MLMI 2017 (2017)

30. Fang, Q., Boas, D.: Tetrahedral mesh generation from volumetric binary and gray-scale images. In: Proceedings of 6th IEEE International Symposium on Biomedical Imaging - ISBI 2009, pp. 1142–1145. IEEE (2009)

31. Heimann, T., van Ginneken, B., Styner, M., Arzhaeva, Y., Aurich, V., Bauer, C., Beck, A., Becker, C., Beichel, R., Bekes, G., Bello, F., Binnig, G., Bischof, H., Bornik, A., Cashman, P., Chi, Y., Cordova, A., Dawant, B., Fidrich, M., Furst, J., Furukawa, D., Grenacher, L., Hornegger, J., Kainmüller, D., Kitney, R., Kobatake, H., Lamecker, H., Lange, T., Lee, J., Lennon, B., Li, R., Li, S., Meinzer, H., Nemeth, G., Raicu, D., Rau, A., van Rikxoort, E., Rousson, M., Rusko, L., Saddi, K., Schmidt, G., Seghers, D., Shimizu, A., Slagmolen, P., Sorantin, E., Soza, G., Susomboon, R., Waite, J., Wimmer, A., Wolf, I.: Comparison and evaluation of methods for liver segmentation from CT datasets. IEEE Trans. Med. Imaging **28**(8), 1251–1265 (2009)

32. Arya, S., Mount, D., Netanyahu, N., Silverman, R., Wu, A.: An optimal algorithm for approximate nearest neighbor searching. J. ACM **45**(6), 891–923 (1998)

33. Karasawa, K., Oda, M., Kitasaka, T., Misawa, K., Fujiwara, M., Chu, C., Zheng, G., Rueckert, D., Mori, K.: Multi-atlas pancreas segmentation: atlas selection based on vessel structure. Med. Image Anal. **39**, 18–28 (2017)

34. Korez, R., Ibragimov, B., Likar, B., Pernuš, F., Vrtovec, T.: Deformable model-based segmentation of intervertebral discs from MR spine images by using the SSC descriptor. In: Vrtovec, T., Yao, J., Glocker, B., Klinder, T., Frangi, A., Zheng, G., Li, S. (eds.) CSI 2015. LNCS, vol. 9402, pp. 117–124. Springer, Cham (2016). https://doi.org/10.1007/978-3-319-41827-8_11

Author Index

Abramson, Richard G.   25
Adams, Judith E.   133
Al Arif, S. M. Masudur Rahman   12

Besler, Bryce A.   120
Blum, Alain   36
Boyd, Steven K.   120
Bromiley, Paul A.   133

Cameron, John   36
Cardoso, M. Jorge   72
Carr, J. Jeffrey   25
Chung, Beom Sun   85
Conway, Chris   36
Cootes, Timothy F.   133

Damopoulos, Dimitrios   59

Ebner, Michael   72
Elcock, Dave   36

Forkert, Nils D.   120
Fotiadou, Anastasia   72
Fukuda, Norio   85

Glocker, Ben   59

Hacihaliloglu, Ilker   1
Hart, Alister   72
Hartley, Katherine G.   25
Henckel, Johann   72
Hu, Peijun   25
Huo, Yuankai   25

Kadoury, Samuel   48
Kariki, Eleni P.   133
Kirschke, Jan S.   108
Knapp, Karen   12
Kong, Dexing   25
Korez, Robert   48, 95
Kukačka, Jan   108

Landman, Bennett A.   25
Likar, Boštjan   95

Menze, Bjoern H.   108
Michalski, Andrew S.   120
Miyamoto, Kohei   85
Modat, Marc   72
Murray, Andrew   36

O'Donnell, Lauren J.   85
Ollivier, Axel   85
Otake, Yoshito   85
Ourselin, Sébastien   72

Parent, Stefan   48
Park, Jin Seo   85
Pernuš, Franjo   95
Petković, Uroš   48
Plakas, Costas   36

Ranzini, Marta Bianca Maria   72
Reynolds, Steven   36

Sato, Yoshinobu   85
Sekuboyina, Anjany   108
Slabaugh, Greg   12
Stroud, Tyler   36
Sugano, Nobuhiko   85

Takao, Masaki   85
Teixeira, Pedro Augusto Gondim   36
Tobon-Gomez, Catalina   36

Valentinitsch, Alexander   108
Vercauteren, Tom   72
Vrtovec, Tomaž   48, 95

Westin, Carl-Fredrik   85
Wyeth, Daniel   36

Yokota, Futoshi   85

Zeng, Guodong   148
Zheng, Guoyan   59, 148

Printed in the United States
By Bookmasters

Printed in the United States
By Bookmasters